Employment Law

The M & E Handbook Series

Employment Law

C J Carr MA, BCL
Head of Department, School of Law, Lancashire Polytechnic

P J Kay BA, LLM
Principal Lecturer, School of Law, Lancashire Polytechnic

Fifth edition

Pitman Publishing
128 Long Acre, London WC2E 9AN
A division of Longman Group UK Limited

First published as *Labour Law* 1974
Second edition 1979
Third edition 1981
Fourth edition 1984
Fifth edition published as *Employment Law* 1990

© Macdonald & Evans Ltd 1974, 1979, 1981, 1984
© Longman Group UK Ltd 1990

British Library Cataloguing in Publication Data

Carr, C.J. (Chris J.)
Employment law. – 5th ed, C.J. Carr, P.J. Kay –
(The M & E handbook series : ISSN 0265–8828)
1. Employment. Labour. Law
I. Title II. Kay, P.J.
344.204'1

ISBN 0 7121 1197 2

Founding Editor : P.W.D. Redmond

Typeset by FDS Ltd, Penarth, South Glamorgan
Printed and bound in Great Britain

Relevant = ✓

Contents

Preface

The ever-changing nature of employment law and the enthusiasm with which Parliament continues to bolster the statutory framework regulating employment relationships does not make it any easier than hitherto to state the law on the subject in a simple and succinct manner. Nevertheless, we have sought to provide a straightforward and up-to-date picture of the present state of employment law across those areas which are of most importance to students. We hope that this *Handbook* will be of use to students studying on a range of courses, whether of a professional nature or as part of an undergraduate programme. At the time of writing the Employment Bill 1988 is still being considered by Parliament, but we have sought to indicate likely future changes in the law indicated by the Bill where this is relevant. We would like to thank Madelaine Walsh for her patient transcription of some truly awful handwriting into a pristine manuscript and Jennifer Mair of Pitman Publishing for her cheerful firmness in ensuring that we came somewhere near meeting her deadlines. Naturally we accept responsibility for any errors in the text.

C J Carr
P J Kay
Lancashire Polytechnic
September 1989

Introduction

1. Scope of employment law. Employment law is that part of English law which deals with the legal problems arising from the employment relationship. The relationship between employer and employee is based on the contract of employment and any book must necessarily concentrate on this relationship. However, with the development of trade unions, employers' organisations and, in particular, state intervention, the subject covers many aspects other than simply the contract of employment. Indeed with the passing of the Employment Act 1988, the relationship between a trade union and its members has become a subject of increased importance (*see* 15: **20–21**).

2. Sources of employment law. As with all legal subjects, employment law is based upon legislation and case law (judicial precedent). There is also the concept of custom and practice which still regulates a substantial number of employment relationships (*see* 4: **14–18**). At this stage it must be emphasised that legislation is playing an increasingly important role; indeed there is hardly a Parliamentary session which passes without a major piece of employment legislation being passed. Further, the nature of this legislation is often controversial as it has been introduced as a result of political parties seeing such legislation as a major plank of their political platforms. The economic and political changes brought about by this legislation therefore cannot be ignored.

3. Function of employment law. Traditionally it has been thought that employment law, perhaps more than any branch of law, exists largely to prevent the need for the parties to a dispute to resort to the tribunals or courts. Recent trends, such as the 'right of management to manage', have meant increased confrontation in the employment sphere and parties in such disputes seem more willing to resort to legal redress in order to test the legal merits of their actions. The law, therefore, is becoming increasingly important in such areas. The use of practice and procedures, which are based on the legal framework, are obviously still important but so is the use of the legal remedy.

NOTE: The cross references in the text consist of the relevant chapter number followed by the section number in bold type.

Table of cases

1
Administration of employment law

Introduction

Until relatively recent times, labour law was regarded merely as an aspect of the law of contract, being administered in the ordinary civil courts. However, the industrial tribunal system was established in 1964 and, since that time, various other courts and non-judicial bodies have been created, thus recognising that the problems arising from employment and industrial relations require specialised courts, tribunals etc. The procedures in these bodies are relatively informal and the 'judges' have special knowledge of employment and industrial relations. It would, however, be misleading to deal with bodies which resolve these disputes without first referring to the voluntary procedures which exist for dealing with such problems prior to their being taken to the courts and tribunals.

The voluntary procedures

1. Introduction. It is most unusual for a person with a grievance relating to his employment to have immediate resort to the legal institutions. The majority of such problems are settled informally at the work-place between the employer and employee and/or their representatives. The law encourages such procedures by recommending their creation in the Code of Practice (*see* **12**) and by requiring a reference in the written statement to a grievance procedure (*see* **2:7**).

2. Nature of voluntary procedures. Clearly the nature of such procedures varies considerably from one place of work to another and between different types of employment. In some cases these procedures will have been determined by national negotiations between employer(s) and trade union(s), whereas in others it may simply consist of the employee having an opportunity to put his/her grievance to the employer or his/her representative. In addition to such procedures there is an increasing number of 'policies' governing the employment relationship. Such policies are wide ranging in their nature and usually aimed at dealing with specific problems in the employment sphere; examples of such policies include equal opportunities and sexual harassment. Policies can also deal with current social and medical problems which employees may potentially face and these include policies on AIDS and alcohol.

Industrial tribunals

3. Creation and composition. The industrial tribunals were established by the Industrial Training Act 1964 to deal with certain disputes arising under that Act but, since that time, their jurisdiction has been considerably extended, notably in respect of claims for redundancy payments and unfair dismissal. The tribunals are organised on a regional basis and each tribunal consists of a legally qualified chairman and two lay members appointed from a panel. Normally one of the lay members would have been nominated by an employers' organisation and the other by a trade union.

4. Jurisdiction. Industrial tribunals are empowered to deal with a wide range of matters arising from a number of legislative provisions, the most important of which are as follows:

(*a*) Complaints of unfair dismissal.
(*b*) Applications for a redundancy payment.
(*c*) References regarding the written particulars of terms of employment.
(*d*) Complaints regarding guarantee payments.
(*e*) Complaints regarding suspension from work on medical grounds.
(*f*) Complaints regarding trade union membership and activities.

(g) Complaints regarding the time off work provisions.

(h) Complaints regarding the right to maternity pay and leave.

(i) Complaints under the Sex Discrimination Act 1975.

(j) Complaints under the Equal Pay Act 1970.

(k) Complaints regarding time off work for ante-natal care.

(l) Complaints regarding secret ballots on employer's premises.

(m) Complaints regarding unreasonable expulsion from trade union membership

(n) Complaints by trade unions relating to failure of consultation on redundancies.

(o) Complaints by trade unions relating to failure to inform or consult them about transfers of undertakings.

5. Procedure. Procedure in the industrial tribunals is regulated by the Industrial Tribunal (Rules of Procedure) Regulations 1985. Rule 6 provides for pre-hearing assessments of industrial tribunal cases at which the tribunal may warn either party to the proceedings that if he wishes to continue an order of costs may be made against him if he loses. The purpose of the procedure is to weed out 'unreasonable' cases. Clause 16 of the Employment Bill, before Parliament at the time of writing, allows the Secretary of State to introduce further rules governing this procedure, one of which may include the requirement to deposit up to £150 in order to continue with the application. The proceedings are intended to be relatively informal both in terms of the pre-tribunal procedure and the hearing, although it could be argued that the increasing presence of lawyers means that the amount of 'informality' is decreasing. The purpose of new rules is to speed up industrial tribunal proceedings and so, for example, tribunals no longer have to provide full reasons for their decisions in every case as Rule 9(2) merely requires tribunals to record their decision in a written document signed by the chairperson. The reasons for the decision must be recorded in a document signed by the chairperson and he/she must state in this document whether the reasons are recorded in a 'full' or 'summary' form. Full reasons, however, must be recorded in certain types of cases, for example in cases under the Equal Pay Act, Sex Discrimination Act or Race Relations Act.

Appeals on questions of law lie in respect of most of the jurisdictions of the industrial tribunals to the Employment Appeal

Tribunal: s. 136 of the Employment Protection (Consolidation) Act 1978.

6. Conciliation. In respect of most of the kinds of application which may be made to the industrial tribunals, before there is a hearing, an attempt is made to settle the matter by conciliation using the services of a conciliation officer.

Employment Appeal Tribunal (EAT)

7. Creation and composition. The EAT was established in 1975 and continued by s. 135 of the 1978 Act. It consists of judges of the High Court and Court of Appeal (and their Scottish equivalents), one of whom is appointed President, and lay members drawn from a panel of persons having special knowledge or experience of industrial relations. On each case heard, there will be a judge and, normally, two lay members sitting. The EAT is a superior court of record based in London but entitled to sit anywhere within the jurisdiction.

8. Jurisdiction. The essential function of the EAT is to hear appeals on questions of law from the industrial tribunals on most of the jurisdictions exercised by the tribunals and to hear appeals (some on questions of law only and others on questions of law or fact) from the Certification Officer (*see* **15** below). The EAT has only limited original jurisdiction under s. 5(2) of the Employment Act 1980, allowing it to determine some applications for compensation following the refusal of a trade union to admit or re-admit a person to membership of a closed shop.

9. Procedure and powers. The EAT regulates its own procedure subject to the provisions of the Employment Appeal Tribunal Rules 1980 (as amended by the Employment Appeal Tribunal (Amendment) Rules 1985). The amending regulations give effect to the changes in the industrial tribunal procedures (*see* **5** above). A party who wishes to appeal from an industrial tribunal's decision must submit a copy of the full written reasons for the decision in addition to a notice of appeal and a copy of the decision within 42 days. The EAT does, however, have a discretion to authorise the institution of the appeal before the full written reasons are sent if it considers it would lead to the 'more expeditious or economic disposal of any proceedings or would otherwise be desirable in the interests of justice'.

An appeal from the EAT on a question of law lies to the Court of Appeal and thence to the House of Lords.

Advisory Conciliation and Arbitration Service (ACAS)

10. Creation and compositon. ACAS was established in 1974 and placed on a statutory basis in 1975: Employment Protection Act 1975, s. 1. In a general sense, its forerunner was the Commission on Industrial Relations (1969–74). It is independent of Government and is managed by a Council normally consisting of a full-time chairman and nine other members including three appointed after consultation with the representatives of employers' organisations and three appointed after consultation with the representatives of workers' organisations. ACAS is based in London with offices in regional centres. To exercise its functions, ACAS has the power to appoint staff, including conciliation officers, and to request other persons to perform services, e.g. arbitration.

11. Functions. ACAS is charged with the general duty of 'promoting the improvement of industrial relations and in particular of encouraging the extension of collective bargaining and the development and, where necessary, reform of collective bargaining machinery'; *See* the Employment Protection Act 1975, s 1. Its specific functions include the following:

(a) *Conciliation in trade disputes.* The provision of assistance by conciliation or otherwise in actual or apprehended trade disputes (*see* Chapter 17) on request or otherwise: EPA 1975, s. 2(1).

(b) *Conciliation in individual cases.* The provision of conciliation facilities with a view to promoting the settlement of those disputes in which an individual has made application to an industrial tribunal: EPA 1975, s. 2(4).

(c) *Arbitration.* The provision of arbitration services either through the Central Arbitration Committee (*see* 13) or otherwise to the parties to a trade dispute, provided that all parties consent and, normally, provided that all voluntary procedures have been exhausted. Such arbitration awards may be published with the consent of the parties: EPA 1975, s. 3.

(*d*) *Advice*. The provision of specific and general advice upon a wide range of matters (e.g. negotiating machinery) to interested parties: EPA 1975, s. 4.

(*e*) *Inquiry*. The conducting of general and specific inquiries into industrial relations' questions, the results of which may be published: EPA 1975, s. 5.

(*f*) *Disclosure of information*. The investigation of disputes relating to disclosure of information: EPA 1975, ss. 17–21 (*see* 16:**5**).

(*g*) *Codes of practice*. The issuing of relevant Codes of Practice: EPA 1975, s. 6 (*see* **12** below).

ACAS is not a judicial body, but if it exceeds its jurisdiction or powers, its action may be subject to judicial review.

12. Codes of Practice. The publication and use of Codes of Practice is becoming of increasing importance in the regulation of employment and industrial relations. In this context codes issued by ACAS are under discussion but other bodies such as the Health and Safety Commission and the Equal Opportunities Commission have powers to issue codes. In addition the Secretary of State is also empowered to issue Codes of Practice, following consultation with ACAS (*see* **20**).

The status in law of such codes is that, although a failure to observe any provision of a code cannot of itself give rise to legal proceedings, in proceedings before industrial tribunals and other bodies the provisions of a code are admissible in evidence and are to be taken into account in determining the question at issue. In *Polkey* v. *A.E. Dayton Services Ltd* (1987), the House of Lords reaffirmed the importance of the appropriate Codes (*see* 12:**11**) in determining the fairness of dismissal.

ACAS has issued the following Codes:

(*a*) Disciplinary practice and procedures in employment (*see* 12:**11**);

(*b*) Disclosure of information to trade unions for collective bargaining purposes (*see* 16:**5**);

(*c*) Time off for trade union duties and activities (*see* 8:**9**).

Central Arbitration Committee (CAC)

13. Creation and composition. CAC was established in 1975, replacing the Industrial Arbitration Board (which itself had replaced the Industrial Court established in 1919). Although independent of Government and ACAS, CAC is served by ACAS staff. CAC has a chairman and members appointed by the Secretary of State for Employment.

14. Functions. The main functions of CAC are as follows:

(*a*) Determining matters relating to sex discrimination in collective agreements and pay structures.

(*b*) Making an award following an employer's failure to disclose information for collective bargaining purposes (*see* 16: 7)

The decisions of CAC are published. There is no appeal from CAC, but it is subject to judicial review if it exceeds its jurisdiction or powers: *see*, for example, *R* v. *CAC ex parte Deltaflow Ltd* (1977).

Certification Officer (CO)

15. Creation of office. The office of CO was established in 1975 (EPA 1975, s. 7) although some of its functions were previously exercised by the Chief Registrar of Friendly Societies. The office has become of increased importance due to the recent legislation (Trade Union Act 1984 and Employment Act 1988). One of the purposes of this legislation is to ensure that individual trade union members' rights are maintained and in this respect the CO has enforcement powers.

16. Functions. The main functions of the CO are as follows:

(*a*) To determine whether a trade union is entitled to a certificate of independence: EPA 1975, s. 8.

(*b*) To maintain a list of trade unions and employers' associations: Trade Union and Labour Relations Act 1974, s. 8.

(*c*) To perform certain duties under the Trade Union Act 1913 (as amended) in relation to the 'political fund' of trade unions (*see*

15:**10**). The Employment Act 1988 adds two further powers in this respect. Firstly, s. 16 creates the right to complain to the CO (or the High Court) where a trade union member claims a political fund ballot has been or will be held otherwise than in accordance with the rules drawn up by the CO. Secondly, s. 22 allows the CO to regulate his/her own procedure, including a power 'to restrict the circumstances in which the identity of an individual who has made, or is proposing to make, any such application, or complaint is disclosed to any person.' The purpose of this is to prevent a complainant from being victimised.

(*d*) To receive complaints and, if necessary, make a declaration that a trade union has failed to comply with Part I of the Trade Union Act 1984. Part I of the Act (*see* 15:**16**) deals with the duty of trade unions to hold elections for certain posts.

Appeals from decisions of the CO are heard by the Employment Appeal Tribunal.

Commissioner for the Rights of Trade Union Members

17. Introduction. The Employment Act 1988, (EA) s. 19, empowers the Secretary of State for Employment to appoint a Commissioner for the Rights of Trade Union Members.

18. Functions. Section 20 of EA 1988, states that the Commissioner is empowered to 'assist' trade union members who wish to bring enforcement proceedings in relation to the following matters:

(*a*) A failure to hold a proper ballot before industrial action: EA 1988, s. 1 (*see* 17:**15**).

(*b*) The right to inspect a union's accounting records: EA 1988.

(*c*) The recovery of union funds used to indemnify unlawful conduct; EA 1988, s. 8.

(*d*) The restraint of trustees from acting unlawfully: EA 1988.

(*e*) A failure to comply with the CO's rules for conducting a political fund ballot: EA 1988, s. 16, (*see* 15:**10**).

(*f*) A failure to comply with the provisions of the Trade Union

Act 1984 regulating election to a union's principal executive council: Trade Union Act 1984, s. 50 (*see* 15:**16**).

(*g*) The misuse of union funds for unapproved political purposes: Trade Union Act 1913, s. 3(1) (*see* 15:**11**).

(*h*) Such other matters as may be specified in an order made by the Secretary of State for Employment.

The type of assistance which the Commissioner may provide includes the costs of legal advice and representation in proceedings relating to the above matters: EA 1988, s. 20(3). The Commissioner has a discretion whether or not to provide assistance but where the application is refused reasons must be given for that decision: EA 1988, s. 20(2). However, the Commissioner is under a duty to provide assistance where the complaint concerns the ballot for political funds or elections to the principal executive council: EA 1988, s. 2(5).

Secretary of State for Employment

19. Introduction. With the increasing intervention of central government in employment and industrial relations, the Secretary of State for Employment has been given considerable powers and duties in relation to these matters.

20. Functions. The main functions of the Secretary of State are:

(*a*) Approving agreements making provision for payments to redundant persons (*see* 13:**17**).

(*b*) Approving Codes of Practice and seeking Parliamentary approval for them (*see* **12**).

(*c*) Approving dismissals procedure agreements.

(*d*) Receiving notification of proposed redundancies (*see* 13:**20**).

(*e*) Approving guarantee payments agreements (*see* 7:**15**).

(*f*) Reviewing various financial limits.

(*g*) Making regulations upon a wide range of matters.

(*h*) Issuing, after consultation with ACAS, Codes of Practice containing such practical guidance as he thinks fit for the purpose of promoting the improvement of industrial relations and keeping such codes of practice under review: Employment Act 1980, s. 3. As with

Codes issued by ACAS, a failure to observe the provisions of such a Code of Practice does not of itself render a person liable to proceedings, but in any proceedings before a court, industrial tribunal or the CAC, a Code is admissible in evidence. The present position is that either the Secretary of State or ACAS can now issue Codes superseding the original 1972 Code or their own or each other's Codes. To date the Secretary of State has issued three Codes of Practice on:

(*i*)   Picketing (1980, *see* 17:**18**).

(*ii*)   Closed Shop Agreements and Arrangements (1980). This Code has subsequently been revised to take account of the provisions on the closed shop contained in the Employment Act 1982 and the revised version came into force in 1983.

(*iii*)   Draft Code on Industrial Action Ballots (*see* 17:**16**).

As has been stated above, the Codes are admissible in evidence in both tribunals and courts. The Code on Picketing (*see* 17:**18**) was used by the High Court in *Thomas* v. *NUM* (1985) (*see* 17:**18**) in order to justify an injunction limiting the number of pickets to six. It can be argued that such codes are introducing law by back door methods in that they have not passed through a full Parliamentary procedure.

The ordinary courts

21. Introduction. Despite the creation of the industrial tribunal system, the civil and criminal courts retain a number of areas of jurisdiction in relation to employment. Obviously the system of precedent applies as in any other area of law.

22. Jurisdiction. The most important matters with which the courts are concerned are:

(*a*)   Actions by employees for damages following injury at work (*see* Chapter 14).

(*b*)   Actions in tort arising from industrial action (*see* Chapter 17).

(*c*)   Actions for breach of contract including breach of a covenant in restraint of trade (*see* 5:**21**).

(*d*)   Prosecutions under the health and safety at work legislation (*see* Chapter 14).

European Court of Justice

23. Introduction. By virtue of accession to the European Community (EC), Britain is bound by decisions of the European Court of Justice (the Court of the EC): European Communities Act 1972, s. 3. Clearly the decisions of the ECJ are only relevant when there is a conflict between British and European law.

24. Procedure. An industrial tribunal, employment appeals tribunal or any court may (by virtue of Article 177 of the Treaty of Rome) refer a case to the ECJ where there is a question of any conflict between the two sets of law. One of the major sources of references to the ECJ has been the law on equal pay (*see* Chapter 9). However, in *Pickstone* v. *Freemans PLC* (1988) the Court of Appeal felt able to apply European Law directly without reference to the ECJ (*see* 9:4). In light of this decision, it can be argued that European law is being directly incorporated into English law without having passed through any Parliamentary process.

Equal Opportunities Commission (EOC)

25. Creation and composition. The EOC was established by the Sex Discrimination Act 1975, s. 53. It consists of between eight and fifteen commissioners in addition to its full-time staff.

26. Functions. The three general duties of the EOC are:

(*a*) To work towards the elimination of discrimination in employment and elsewhere.

(*b*) To promote equality of opportunity between men and women.

(*c*) To keep under review the Equal Pay Act 1970 and the Sex Discrimination Act 1975.

The EOC produces an annual report for presentation to Parliament and is also empowered to produce Codes of Practice (*see* 12 above).

27. Powers. The main powers of the EOC in relation to employment are as follows:

(*a*) To carry out investigations during which it may require persons to produce documents or give evidence. If in the course of such an investigation the EOC is satisfied that a breach of the Sex Discrimination Act or Equal Pay Act has occurred, it may issue a non-discrimination notice against which there is a right of appeal to an industrial tribunal. The effect of such a notice, which is kept on a register, is that in the following five years the EOC may apply to a county court if it considers that a further breach of the legislation is likely: SDA 1975, ss. 67–70.

(*b*) To bring proceedings in respect of discriminatory advertisements or instruction or pressure to discriminate (*see* 9:**19**).

(c) To give assistance to aggrieved persons: SDA 1975, s. 74.

The substantive law in relation to sex discrimination and equal pay is considered in Chapter 9.

Commission for Racial Equality (CRE)

28. Creation and composition. The CRE was established by s. 43 of the Race Relations Act 1976 and replaces the former Race Relations Board and Community Relations Commission. It consists of between eight and fifteen commissioners in addition to its full-time staff.

29. Functions and powers. The function and powers of the CRE in relation to discrimination within the ambit of the Race Relations Act 1976 are similar to those exercised by the Equal Opportunities Commission in relation to discrimination dealt with by the Sex Discrimination Act 1975 (*see* **26** and **27** above). The substantive law in relation to discrimination on grounds of race etc. is considered in Chapter 9.

Health and Safety Commission (HSC)

30. Creation and composition. The HSC was established by s. 10 of the Health and Safety at Work etc. Act 1974. It has a chairman and between six and nine commissioners representing employers, trade unions and local government interests. The HSC is responsible to the Secretary of State and must adhere to directions from him.

31. Duties and powers. The HSC has a number of duties, the main ones being:

(*a*) To assist and encourage persons to further the general purposes of the 1974 Act.

(*b*) To make arrangements for research and the promotion of training and information connected with it.

(*c*) To act as an information and advisory service.

(*d*) To submit proposals for regulations.

(*e*) To approve and issue Codes of Practice (subject to the approval of the Secretary of State).

In pursuing these duties, the HSC has considerable powers, e.g. directing investigations and inquiries, appointing staff, publishing information etc.

Health and Safety Executive (HSE)

32. Creation and composition. The HSE was established by s. 10 of the Health and Safety at Work etc. Act 1974. It consists of a director and two deputies in addition to the staff whom it controls. The HSE embraces an amalgamation of bodies which had existed for some time prior to 1974 including the Factories Inspectorate, the Mines and Quarries Inspectorate and the Explosives Inspectorate. The HSE is answerable to the Health and Safety Commission except as regards the enforcement of the health and safety at work legislation.

33. Functions and powers. The function of the HSE is to enforce the health and safety at work legislation by means of inspection of premises, the issuing of improvement and prohibition notices, prosecution etc. (*see* 14:**20–22**).

Progress test 1

1. In what ways does the law encourage voluntary procedures for the settlement of disputes arising from employment?   (1)

2. What is the composition of an industrial tribunal?   (3)

3. Name the important jurisdictions of the industrial tribunals. (4)

4. What is the purpose of the pre-hearing assessment procedure before an industrial tribunal?   (5)

5. What is the jurisdiction of the Employment Appeal Tribunal? (8)

6. What are the powers of the Employment Appeal Tribunal? (9)

7. What are the functions of the Advisory, Conciliation and Arbitration Service?   (11)

8. What is the legal status of a Code of Practice?   (12, 20)

9. What are the main functions of the Certification Officer?   (16)

10. What are the functions of the Commissioner for the Rights of Trade Union Members?   (18)

11. What jurisdiction remains with the ordinary civil courts in the area of employment law?   (22)

12. What are the powers of the Equal Opportunities Commission? (27)

13. Explain the respective functions of the Health and Safety Commission and the Health and Safety Executive.   (31, 33)

2

The contract of employment (1): formation

Definition of the contract

1. General considerations. When the terms 'employee' or 'servant' are used, this assumes the existence of a contract of employment or a contract of service, as distinct from a contract for services under which a person (referred to as an 'independent contractor') performs services under contract for another person. Legally speaking, the independent contractor is self-employed and the distinction between an employee and an independent contractor is of considerable significance.

2. Reasons for the distinction. There are three main reasons for distinguishing between a contract of service (or employment) and a contract for services.

   (a) *Legislative provisions.* Many Acts of Parliament and statutory regulations demand such a distinction. For example, Part VI of the Employment Protection (Consolidation) Act 1978 (Redundancy Payments) extends only to persons who are 'employees'. This is also the case with Parts I and V of the same Act (Particulars of Terms of Employment and Unfair Dismissal). In these and other cases, persons who are not 'employees' are not covered by the statutory provisions. Furthermore, the system of taxation is different as between employed and self-employed persons. As a result of this (and other reasons), many employers, particularly in the construction industry, have deliberately chosen to engage workers on the basis that they are self-employed, thus avoiding the need to pay certain statutory levies payable in respect of employees and also eliminating a certain amount of administrative and legal responsibility: *see* 4 below.

(*b*) *Vicarious liability.* The concept of vicarious liability normally extends only to the employer/employee relationship. In other words an employer is responsible for the legal consequences of acts done by his employees during the course of their employment. This does not normally apply to the relationship between an independent contractor and the person for whom he is working. This is discussed in more detail later: *see* 10 below.

(*c*) *Implied terms.* There are certain rights, duties and obligations which are implied into every contract of employment, but they do not extend to the relationship between an independent contractor and the person for whom he is working: *see* Chapter 5.

3. Ways of distinguishing. It should be noted that many legislative provisions contain a definition of 'employee' and/or 'contract of employment' (e.g. s. 153 of the 1978 Act), but these are generally unhelpful and thus one must turn to the judicial interpretations of the terms.

It should be noted also that the question of whether the relationship of employer/employee exists is a matter for determination by the courts rather than relying solely on the description or label attached to the contract by the parties.

Young & Woods v. *West* (1980): the Court of Appeal stated that whether a person is to be regarded as self-employed or employed is a question of law, not of fact. The label which the parties attach to the relationship may be relevant to determining that relationship but it is not conclusive.

The label which the parties attach to the contract may be relevant where there has been a deliberate alteration in the basis of the employment relationship: *Massey* v. *Crown Life Insurance Co.* (1978). The fact that the worker pays his own income tax/social security contributions does not necessarily indicate that he is not an employee: *Davis* v. *New England College of Arundel* (1977).

The courts have developed several tests for distinguishing between employees and independent contractors.

(*a*) *The control test.* The first test developed by the courts was the 'control' test, i.e. did the person alleged to be the employer control the alleged employee both in respect of what work was done and as regards the manner of performance of that work? If the answer was in the affirmative the relationship of employer/employee was established. As Bramwell LJ said in *Yewens* v. *Noakes* (1880): 'A servant is a person subject to the command of his master as to the manner in which he shall do his work.'

Walker v. *Crystal Palace Football Club* (1910): the plaintiff was a professional footballer with the defendant club. The question arose as to whether the plaintiff was an employee of the club. Held: he was an employee of the club because he was subject to their overall control in respect of training, discipline and method of play.

However, it was soon recognised by the courts that this test was not satisfactory as a general method of explaining the distinction between an employee and an independent contractor in so far as certain persons with special skills (e.g. doctors, nurses, engineers etc.) were undoubtedly employed persons but they could hardly be said to be subject to the 'control' of their employers. To meet this difficulty the courts developed the 'integration' test.

(*b*) *The integration test.* This test was first stated in precise terms by Denning LJ in *Stevenson, Jordan and Harrison* v. *Macdonald and Evans* (1952):

'One feature which seems to run through the instances is that, under a contract of service, a man is employed as part of the business, and his work is done as an integral part of the business; whereas, under a contract for services, his work, although done for the business, is not integrated into it, but is only accessory to it.'

This test has been used to explain professional, artistic and entertainment relationships and the position of doctors and nurses, for whom the control test was inappropriate.

Cassidy v. *Ministry of Health* (1951): a hospital patient was deprived of the use of a hand due to the negligence of full-time medical staff. He claimed that the defendants were vicariously liable for the negligence of the staff, as the staff were employees of the Hospital Board for whom the defendants were responsible. Held: the full-time staff were employees of the Board. Denning LJ said that the staff were employees because their work was integrated into that of the organisation.

Whittaker v. *Minister of Pensions and National Insurance* (1967): the plaintiff was a trapeze artist in a circus. She spent much of her working time rehearsing and performing her act but she also assisted in doing general duties, e.g. programme selling. The question arose as to whether she was an employee. Held: although she was independent as regards her act, she was an employee of the circus because her work was integrated into that of the circus.

(c) *The economic reality test.* In recent years the courts have used a more flexible approach which incorporates both of the previous tests. This totality approach is variously referred to as the 'multiple', 'mixed' or 'economic reality' test. It means that factors such as control, integration and powers of selection etc. are simply issues which contribute to the decision which must be based on all the circumstances.

Ready Mixed Concrete (South-East) Ltd v. *Minister of Pensions and National Insurance* (1968): the worker to whom the case related was the driver of a lorry which he obtained on hire-purchase from the company. He was required to paint the lorry in the company's colours and had to obey instructions from the company's servants. On the other hand, he could use substitute drivers if he was ill or on holiday and the contract provided that he was not to be regarded as an employee (this is not conclusive in itself). In other words, certain terms of the contract tended to suggest that he was employed whilst others pointed to his being self-employed. The question arose as to whether he was an 'employee'. Held: there are three conditions which establish the existence of a contract of service:

(a) the employee agrees to provide his own work and skill;
(b) there must be some element of control exercisable by the employer; and
(c) the other terms of the contract must not be inconsistent with a contract of service.

In this case, a consideration of point (c) and particularly the question of the use of substitute drivers led to a finding that the driver was an independent contractor.

Recently the tribunals and courts have tended to ask the single fundamental question posed by Cooke J in *Market Investigations Ltd* v. *Minister of Social Security* (1969): 'Is the person who has engaged himself to perform these services performing them as a person in business on his own account?', prior to an examination of all relevant indicia.

Young & Woods v. *West* (1980): W worked for the appellants as a skilled sheet metal worker. He chose to be treated as self-employed when engaged, making himself responsible for his own income tax liabilities, national insurance contributions etc. He had no holiday or sick pay entitlement from the company. Following termination of his contract he claimed to be an employee for the purposes of pursuing a remedy for unfair dismissal. The Court of Appeal said, applying the above test, that it was impossible to regard W as in business on his own account. Apart from receiving wages without deductions and having no holiday or sick pay, W's working conditions were exactly the same as those workers who were subject to PAYE.

See also Construction Industry Training Board v. *Labour Force Ltd* (1970); *Ferguson* v. *John Dawson and Partners (Contractors) Ltd* (1976); *Thames Television* v. *Wallis* (1979); *Withers* v. *Flackwell Heath Supporters Club* (1981); *Nethermere (St Neots) Ltd* v. *Gardiner & Taverna* (1983).

4. Labour-only sub-contracting. One of the many difficult problems arising out of the distinction between an employee and an independent contractor is that, particularly in the construction industry, workers are often engaged on the basis that they are self-employed although they may appear to all intents and purposes to be employed. The reasons why this system of 'labour-only sub-contracting' has developed are many and varied but perhaps the most basic reasons are as follows.

(*a*) From the 'employer's' point of view, he is relieved of the duty to pay certain statutory levies (e.g. social security contributions) which would be payable if the worker was an 'employee'; he avoids certain administrative work (e.g. in connection with the PAYE taxation system); and the worker is not eligible to receive a redundancy payment or present a complaint of unfair dismissal.

(*b*) From the worker's point of view, he is taxed in arrears as a self-employed person and, since he is usually outside the trade union system, he can negotiate a high lump-sum payment for completion of the work without adhering to agreed terms.

However, the real disadvantage of the system lies in the fact that such workers fall outside the protection of a number of the statutory and common law rules relating to safety at work and relatively few of the State benefits are available to a worker who is injured as a result of an accident at work. In addition, it is argued that the system of labour-only sub-contracting seriously undermines the industrial relations' system in the construction industry. Furthermore, it is believed that considerable evasion of tax has occurred because of labour-only sub-contracting.

Since 1971, legislative provisions have existed whose purpose is to minimise the income tax evasion through use of a system of exempting certificates available only to genuine sub-contractors. The most recent of these provisions are those contained in the Finance Act (No 2) 1979, s. 15. By reducing the possibilities of tax evasion, it is thought that the system of labour-only sub-contracting may decline. *See Phelps* v. *Moore* (1980).

A recent judicial development in relation to labour-only sub-contracting is *Ferguson* v. *John Dawson and Partners (Contractors) Ltd* (1976): P worked for D as a labourer on a building site. He used a false name and no income tax or social security contributions were paid. The parties regarded him as self-employed for reasons which they considered to be to their mutual advantage. P was injured and brought an action for damages under the Construction (Working Places) Regulations 1966 on the basis that he was an 'employee'. D argued that P was not an 'employee'. The Court of Appeal held by a majority that D was an 'employee'. Megaw LJ cited with approval the view of the judge at first instance that 'I regard the concept of the 'lump' (i.e. labour-only sub-contracting) in the circumstances of the present case as being no more than a device which each side regarded as being capable of being put to his own advantage. . . but which in reality did not affect the relationship of the parties'. The court considered that D, through its site agent, controlled the work of P.

5. The borrowed employee. When an employee is lent or hired from one employer to another, the question arises as to which of them is to be regarded as his employer in law. The principle established in *Mersey Docks and Harbour Board* v. *Coggins and Griffith (Liverpool) Ltd* (1947) is that the first (or general) employer remains liable unless there has been an agreement to the contrary. It should be noted, however, that there can be no such transfer of an employee unless he consents to it.

Form of the contract

6. General principle. With two exceptions (merchant seamen and apprentices), there is no requirement that a contract of employment be in writing. As Mackinnon LJ said in *O'Grady* v. *Saper Ltd* (1940), a contract of employment is 'usually concluded orally by people who rarely think out, and still more rarely express, any terms'. This position undoubtedly leads to a situation where proof of the terms of the contract can be difficult. To alleviate this difficulty the Contracts of Employment Act 1963 was passed (subsequently the 1972 Act) with the basic object of ensuring that most employees were provided with some written evidence of the main terms of employment. These provisions are now contained in Part I of the Employment Protection (Consolidation) Act 1978 which applies to all employees with the following major exceptions:

(*a*) registered dock workers;

(*b*) where an employee works wholly or mainly outside Great Britain;

(*c*) part-time employees who do not have continuity of employment (*see* **16**);

(*d*) Crown employees (*see* 3: **5**).

7. The written statement. Section 1 of the 1978 Act provides that employers must provide employees to whom this part of the Act applies with a written statement containing particulars of certain terms of the contract of employment. This statement must be supplied within thirteen weeks of the commencement of employment.

The particulars which must be given are as follows.

(*a*) The names of the parties and the date of commencement of employment and the date on which the employee's period of continuous service began (taking into account any employment with a previous employer which counts towards that period) (*see* **16** below for the rules on continuity of employment).

(*b*) The scale or rate of remuneration or the method of calculating it.

(*c*) The intervals at which remuneration is paid.

(*d*) Terms and conditions relating to hours of work.

(*e*) Terms and conditions relating to entitlement to holidays (including public holidays) and holiday pay (including sufficient information so as to enable the employee's rights to accrued holiday pay to be calculated precisely on the termination of employment).

(*f*) Terms and conditions relating to incapacity for work due to sickness or injury, including any provision as to sick pay.

(*g*) Terms and conditions as to pensions and pension schemes.

(*h*) The length of notice which the employee is entitled to receive from the employer to terminate the contract (and vice versa) or, where the contract is for a fixed term, the date of expiry of the contract.

(*i*) The title of the job which the employee is employed to do. In addition, the written statement must include a note specifying the following.

(*j*) Any disciplinary rules applicable to the employee or referring him to a document which is reasonably accessible to him which specifies such rules.

(*k*) The person to whom he can apply if he is dissatisfied with any disciplinary decision relating to him.

(*l*) The person to whom he can apply if he has a grievance relating to his employment and an explanation of the further steps (if any) consequent upon such an application (or a reference to a document which is reasonably accessible to the employee which explains them).

(*m*) Whether a contracting-out certificate (under the provisions of the Social Security Pensions Act 1975) is in force in relation to that employment.

Paragraphs (*j*), (*k*) and (*l*) do not apply to disciplinary decisions, grievances or procedures relating to health or safety at work.

Any agreed changes in these particulars must be communicated to the employee in writing within one month.

Clause 9 of the Employment Bill 1988, removes the statutory requirement to include a note in the written particulars specifying disciplinary rules applicable to the employee. The above exemption only applies if the employer has less than 20 employees. The requirement to provide a note concerning the disciplinary procedure still remains.

8. Reference to another document. Instead of giving an employee individual notification of the particulars, the employer may refer the employee to a document which contains the requisite information (e.g. a collective agreement or works' rule-book). The document must be one which the employee has reasonable opportunities of reading in the course of his employment or be reasonably accessible to him in some other way. In such a case there is no need for an employer to notify the employee of changes in the particulars provided that he has indicated, in advance, that these changes will be incorporated in the reference document.

9. Significance of the written statement. It is quite clear that the written statement is not a contract but is merely evidence of certain terms of the contract of employment. As the EAT held in *System Floors (UK) Ltd* v. *Daniel* (1981): 'It seems to us, therefore, that in general the status of the statutory statement is this. It provides very strong prima facie evidence of what were the terms of the contract between the parties, but does not constitute a written contract between the parties. Nor are the statements of the terms finally conclusive: at most they place a heavy burden on the employer to show that the actual terms of the contract are different from those which he has set out in the statutory statement.' Therefore, if the written statement does not accurately reflect the terms of the contract as agreed by the parties, the agreed terms prevail over the written statement: see *Robertson & Jackson* v. *British Gas Corporation* (1983). An employee who is not given a written statement to which he is entitled, or who is given an incomplete or incorrect statement may complain to an industrial tribunal for a determination of what particulars ought to have been included. In the case of an incomplete statement or where no statement has been given the tribunal can specify what ought to have been included and in the case of an incorrect statement the tribunal can amend or replace the particulars given. However, it must be emphasised that the statute gives no power to rewrite what the parties have agreed or to make an agreement for the parties. A tribunal must simply ensure that the statutory statement records what the parties agreed: *see Mears* v. *Safecar Security* (1982). A tribunal has no power to enforce its decision (e.g. by awarding an employee back-pay). If an employee then wishes to complain of a breach of the terms of the contract of employment, he must at present use the ordinary courts, although when this jurisdiction is transferred to the industrial tribunals, the tribunal will be able to deal with both matters at the same time (*see* 1:3 *et seq*).

However, it is no doubt true to say that the fact that reference may be made to collective agreements as being the source of the terms of the contract enables the courts and tribunals to regard the collective agreement as incorporated into the individual contract of employment more easily than was formerly the case (*see* 4:9–11). As a matter of evidence, therefore, it is most important for both parties that the written statement be correct since it may be difficult to establish that the written statement does not accurately reflect the agreed contractual terms. Thus an employer might find it difficult to show that a dismissal was fair if he dismissed an employee for breach of a rule of which the employee had not been informed in the written statement: *see*, for example, *Meridan Ltd* v. *Gomersall* (1977) and *Meyer Dunmore International* v. *Rogers* (1978). As examples of the difficulties raised by inaccurate, incomplete or misleading written statements, *see Gascol Conversions Ltd* v. *Mercer* (1974) and *Burroughs Machines* v. *Timmoney* (1977).

Vicarious liability

10. General principle. The basic principle of vicarious liability is that an employer is liable in law for the torts committed by his employees whilst they are in the course of their employment. The reasoning behind this principle is two-fold.

(*a*) The tort is committed while the employee is engaged on the employer's business and therefore the employer should be liable.

(*b*) An employer is normally likely to be able to meet a damages claim (perhaps he is insured against such a risk) and therefore the injured person is in a better position to recover damages than if he could only claim against the employee.

11. In the course of employment. In order to be able to apply the concept of vicarious liability, it must be established that the employee was acting 'in the course of his employment' at the time of committing the tort. The precise meaning of this phrase is complicated but the following principles are suggested as a summary of the present law.

(*a*) An employee is regarded as being in the course of his employment if the act during which the tort is committed was expressly or implicitly authorised by the employer. For example, if a lorry driver is involved in a road accident while driving for the employer, any liability which may arise as a result of the accident falls on the driver's employer. This extends to acts which are necessarily incidental to the employment. As Lord Porter said in *Weaver* v. *Tredegar Iron and Coal Co. Ltd* (1940):

> 'The man's work does not consist solely in the task which he is employed to perform, it includes also matters incidental to that task. Times during which meals are taken, moments during which the man is proceeding towards his work from one portion of his employer's premises to another and periods of rest may all be included. Nor is his work necessarily confined to his employer's premises.'

In *Smith* v. *Stages* (1989) the House of Lords held that an employee who was paid wages by the employer to travel to and from his home, in order to carry out his job, was acting in the course of his employment.

(*b*) An employee may still be regarded as being in the course of his employment where he acts in a negligent manner or performs an act wrongly, provided that he is authorised to do that act by the employer, albeit properly. This may include several situations.

(*i*)   Where the employee behaves in an extremely foolish

manner. *Century Insurance Co.* v. *NIRTB.* (1942): a lorry driver was transferring petrol from his tanker to a store in a garage. He was smoking while he did this and a fire resulted. Held by the House of Lords: the lorry driver's employer was vicariously liable because the driver was in the course of his employment.

(*ii*) Where the employee oversteps the limits of his contractual duties, providing that he is acting for the benefit of his employer. *Kay* v. *ITW* (1968): X was employed in a warehouse to drive small vans and trucks. As he was trying to drive one of the vehicles which he was authorised to drive into the warehouse, he found a large vehicle (which he was not authorised to drive) blocking the doors. He climbed into it but due to his failure to realise that it was in reverse gear, he knocked down the plaintiff who was at the rear of the vehicle unloading it. Held: the employer was vicariously liable for the actions of X because, although he was acting outside the basic obligations of his contract of employment, he was nevertheless acting for the over-all benefit of his employer.

However, if an employee does something entirely for his own benefit, he is said to be 'on a frolic of his own' and is no longer regarded as being in the course of his employment. *Hilton* v. *Thomas Burton (Rhodes) Ltd* (1961): an employee (the plaintiff's husband) was killed while travelling in a van which was involved in an accident due to the negligence of a fellow employee. The men were returning from a public house some considerable distance away from their place of work. Held: the employer was not vicariously liable for the employee's negligence because, by going to a public house some distance away, they were 'on a frolic of their own'.

(*iii*) Where the employee disobeys an express prohibition as regards the *manner* of performing an authorised act. *Limpus* v. *London General Omnibus Co.* (1862): employees of the defendant company were forbidden to drive their vehicles in such a way as to cause an obstruction. On one occasion, an employee caused an accident by driving his vehicle in front of the plaintiff's vehicle. Held: the employer was vicariously liable because the prohibition was simply as to the *manner* of performing the authorised act of driving.

However, where there is an express prohibition as to what the employee should, or should not, do and the employee disobeys this, he is no longer regarded as being in the course of employment, despite the fact that the third party may be unaware of the prohibition: *see Twine* v. *Bean's Express Ltd* (1946); *Rose* v. *Plenty* (1975).

(*iv*) Where the employment gives rise to the opportunity to defraud. *Heasmans* v. *Clarity Cleaning Co.* (1987): Company C contracted with H to clean the offices of H. C agreed to provide all the necessary labour, insurance, cleaning materials and equipment in order to clean, in particular, the telephones. One of C's servants employed to carry out the work wrongfully used the telephones in order to make international calls. The telephone bill amounted to £1,450. Held: Purchas LJ stated 'that before the master can be held to be vicariously liable for the acts of the servant there must be established some nexus other than mere opportunity between the tortious or criminal act of the servant, and the circumstances of his employment.' Mere access to premises, in this case, was held not to be sufficient to make the employer vicariously liable.

12. Vicarious criminal liability. As a general rule an employer is not liable for the criminal offences committed by his employees in the course of employment. However, in modern times, a number of statutory exceptions have been created to the general rule, particularly as regards offences committed by the employees of corporate bodies, e.g. under the Trade Descriptions Act 1968 and the Health and Safety at Work etc. Act 1974 (*see* 14:**23**).

Selection of employees

13. Introduction. A number of statutory restrictions have been introduced upon an employer's 'right' to select employees upon whatever basis he so chooses. The main ones are the Disabled Persons (Employment) Act 1958; the Rehabilitation of Offenders Act 1974, the Sex Discrimination Act 1975 and the Race Relations Act 1976. The latter two Acts are examined in Chapter 9.

14. Disabled Persons (Employment) Act 1958. By virtue of this Act, employers employing twenty or more employees must ensure that a minimum of 3 per cent of the work-force consists of registered disabled persons unless an exempting permit has been issued to that employer. In addition, certain jobs (e.g. car park attendant) must not be filled by an able-bodied person unless no disabled person is available. It is an offence to fail to comply with the provisions of the Act.

15. Rehabilitation of Offenders Act 1974. The 1974 Act allows a person to 'live down' certain criminal convictions after a specified period. After a specified period of between six months and ten years (depending upon the sentence imposed), a conviction is deemed to be 'spent' provided no serious offence is committed during the 'rehabilitation period'. The Act provides that normally a spent conviction, or failure to disclose it, is no ground for refusing to employ or dismiss a person or discriminating against him in employment. However, it is only in respect of dismissal that a remedy is provided in that if the only reason for a dismissal was the employer's knowledge of a spent conviction, such a dismissal would, all other things being equal, almost certainly be regarded as unfair: see *Property Guards Ltd* v. *Taylor and Kershaw* (1982) (*see* Chapter 12). It should be noted that by virtue of regulations made under the 1974 Act, the Act does not apply to a number of kinds of employment including teaching, medicine, accountancy etc.

Continuous employment

16. Introduction. The concept of 'continuous employment' is most important in that nearly all of the various statutory rights of employees are dependent upon the acquisition by the employee of a minimum period of continuous employment, e.g. two years before a claim alleging unfair dismissal may be presented. In addition, if such a claim (and others) is successful, the amount of compensation awarded will be partly dependent upon the length of continuous employment of the employee.

17. Current trends The current trends in employment mean that an increasing number of people are working on a temporary and part-time basis. Employers are also increasingly using fixed term contracts (*see* 3:**16–18**) for a set length of time rather than employing a person on a permanent basis. This so called 'enterprise' culture has meant that the question of continuity is of increased importance as employees may be working for two or more years with an employer but without necessarily satisfying the basic rules.

18. Basic rules. The rules for computing the period of continuous employment are contained in Schedule 13 of the 1978 Employment Protection (Consolidation) Act.

(*a*) Employment is presumed to be continuous unless the contrary is shown.

(*b*) Any week in which an employee is employed for sixteen hours or more counts towards computing the period of employment. Hours for which a person is employed do not include hours 'on call' (*see Suffolk CC v. Secretary of State for the Environment* (1985)).

(*c*) A week counts even though an employee does not actually work for sixteen hours or more, if he/she would normally have done so but did not because of absence due to holiday, sickness, injury, pregnancy or confinement.

(*d*) Can separate concurrent contracts, with the same employer, be aggregated in order to give a person continuity of employment? (*see* 3: **16** below for fixed term contracts.) In *Lewis* v. *Surrey County Council* (1987) L had worked for S since 1969 as a photography teacher on courses in three art college departments. L had separate contracts for each college term and for each of the three courses. Each contract was confined to the particular department concerned. The contracts merely specified the total number of hours to be worked. The House of Lords held that the contracts could not be aggregated as the legislation referred only to one single contractual obligation. On the facts it was said that L worked under a series of contracts. The House of Lords did however indicate that L should have pleaded that in fact the separate contracts amounted to one single contractual obligation. There is no doubt that there will be further litigation on this point.

(*e*) Any week in which an employee is absent on account of a 'temporary cessation of work' counts in the calculation of a period of continuous employment. A wide interpretation was given to these words in *Ford* v. *Warwickshire County Council* (1983). F had been employed by the respondents as a part-time teacher between 1971 and 1979 on a series of fixed term contracts which ran from September to July each year. During the summer vacation F was not employed by the respondents. F's claim for compensation for unfair dismissal and redundancy was contested by the respondents on the basis that she did not have a long enough period of continuous employment. The House of Lords held that F was entitled to pursue her claim as the breaks between the fixed term contracts could be characterised as periods where there was absence from work 'on account of a temporary cessation of work'. Accordingly her continuity of employment, and period of continuous employment was preserved.

The courts will not take a strict mathematical approach to this issue. In *Flack* v. *Kodak Ltd* (1986) the Court of Appeal, approving the EAT, stated that all the circumstances must be taken into account and the tribunal or court should not merely limit itself to looking at the percentage that the cessation of work bore in relation to the periods of work. The relevance of the whole period of intermittent employment was shown by *Boast* v. *Willerby Caravan Ltd* (1987).

B started work as a labourer for W.C. Ltd on 10.12.84. After 14 weeks B was made redundant. Two weeks later B was re-employed for a period of 13 weeks, before being dismissed again. Following a gap of 12 weeks he was taken back into employment on 13.9.85. The employment continued unbroken until 2.6.87. B was then summarily dismissed for alleged misconduct. Held: looking at the employment history as a whole B had continuity. Any gaps did not break continuity because of the cyclical nature of the industry.

(*f*) Any week during which an employee is absent counts towards continuous employment if, by arrangement or custom, the employment is regarded as continuous.

(*g*) Any week in which an employee is on strike, or absent from work because of a lock-out, does not count in computing the period of employment but does not break continuity.

(*h*) If an employee is employed for more than sixteen hours a week and then becomes employed for less than sixteen hours but more than eight hours, he will, for a further period of twenty-six weeks, be treated as being employed for more than sixteen hours a week.

(*i*) If an employee has been employed for more than eight hours a week, but less than sixteen hours, and has been so employed for more than five years, he is regarded as having been continuously employed for that period.

19. Transfer of undertakings. There are various provisions dealing with the question of continuity of employment for the purposes of employment protection rights: see the 1978 Act, Sched. 13 para 17, and the Transfer of Undertakings (Protection of Employment) Regulations 1981. In relation to continuity there appears to be considerable overlap between the two sets of provisions; their net effect is that where any trade or business (which must be in the nature of a commercial venture for the 1981 Regulations to apply) is transferred to new owners, the continuity of employment of the employee is not broken and accordingly accrued employment protection rights are preserved.

The Regulations have caused considerable problems for the courts and tribunals. These difficulties, in the context of continuity, are illustrated by the decision in *Brook Lane Finance Co. Ltd* v. *Bradley* (1988). The purchasers assumed control of the business by a deed of assignment on 1st March and B, the vendor's company secretary, continued to work for the purchasers in order to ensure the smooth transfer of the business. The sale was not completed until 26th March. The EAT held that B was not employed by the vendor at the date of transfer and therefore did not have continuity of employment.

Progress test 2

1. What is an 'independent contractor'?   **(1)**
2. For what reasons is it necessary to distinguish between an employee and an independent contractor?   **(2)**
3. What tests have the courts adopted for distinguishing between an employee and an independent contractor?   **(3)**
4. What information must be provided in a written statement supplied under s. 1 of the 1978 Act?   **(7)**
5. Why is it important that the written statement should be accurate?   **(9)**
6. When is an employee regarded as being in the course of his employment for the purposes of vicarious liability?   **(11)**
7. Jones, an employee of Y Ltd, is instructed by his employers not to smoke while working. In contravention of this instruction, he lights

a cigarette and throws away the match. This causes a fire which damages the premises of A Ltd. Discuss. (11)

8. What is the significance of a criminal conviction being regarded as 'spent'? (15)

9. Explain the significance of the concept of 'continuous employment' and state the basic rules whereby such a period of employment is calculated. (16, 17, 18)

3

The contract of employment (2): special problems

A number of groups of employees are, for different reasons, in a special position and some of the problems relating to such special positions are considered in this chapter.

Directors and partners

1. Directors. A company director is regarded as an 'employee' for most of the statutory purposes if he has a written service contract with the company, but a non-executive director will not normally be regarded as an 'employee'. Whether such a service contract exists is a matter of law, to be determined by reference to the facts of the particular case (*see Albert J. Parsons and Sons Ltd* v. *Parsons* (1979)). Thus even a director of a 'one-man business' may be an 'employee' and, as such, be entitled to a redundancy payment from the company, as employer, if it goes into liquidation (*see Robinson* v. *George Sorbey Ltd* (1967)) and as to other such rights, *see Folami* v. *Nigerline (UK) Ltd* (1978).

However, as has been stated, it is a question of law whether or not a contract of service exists. In *Eaton* v. *Robert Eaton and Secretary of State for Employment* (1988), E was the managing director of RE Ltd. When the company ceased trading, he applied to the Tribunal for a redundancy payment. No payment was granted as there was nothing in writing to indicate that E was an 'employee' of the company and since 1981 E had not received any financial remuneration from the company because of its financial position. The EAT supported the decision of the tribunal as the facts could not rebut the presumption that E was an 'office holder' and therefore not an 'employee'.

2. Partners. A partner in a firm is self-employed. If a person is employed by partners, the relationship of employer/employee exists.

Apprentices

3. Nature of apprenticeship. A contract of apprenticeship is an agreement whereby the apprentice binds himself to the master in order to learn a trade, in return for the master's agreement to teach and instruct him. Such a contract must be in writing: Apprentices Act 1814, s. 2. The contract may only be terminated by the master if the apprentice evinces an intention not to learn (e.g. by persistent absenteeism) or for gross misconduct. Conversely, the apprentice may only terminate the contract if the master fails to provide instruction. The contract may be frustrated (*see* 10:**13–14**).

4. Unfair dismissal and redundancy. It would seem that although apprentices are entitled to claim statutory rights of unfair dismissal and/or redundancy (*see*, for example, *Finch* v. *Betabake (Anglia) Ltd* (1977)), the expiry of an apprenticeship contract is not, of itself, either an unfair dismissal or redundancy: *North East Coast Ship Repairers Ltd* v. *Secretary of State for Employment* (1978).

Public sector employees

5. Crown servants. The precise legal status of crown servants has long been the subject of controversy although, in practice, this has not given rise to many problems. The prevailing view now seems to be that the Crown and its servants enjoy a relationship analogous to a contract of employment, subject to an implied right on the part of the Crown to dismiss at pleasure, i.e. without notice: *A-G for Guyana* v. *Norbrega* (1969). It should be noted that the employees of the nationalised industries and local authorities are not Crown servants.

6. Statutory rights. Irrespective of the common law position, a number of modern employment law provisions have expressly been extended to cover Crown employees, notably the unfair dismissals' provisions: *see* s. 138 of the 1978 Act. It should be noted that unless an Act expressly so provides it does not bind the Crown: *Wood* v. *Leeds Area Health Authority (Teaching)* (1974). Note also the effect of s. 139 of the 1978 Act with regard to the staff of the House of Commons.

7. Police. The police are excluded from many of the statutory rights to which other employees are entitled, e.g. the right to present a complaint of unfair dismissal: s. 146(2) of the 1978 Act. The definition of 'police service' in the 1978 Act is wide enough to include prison officers, who also lose the relevant statutory rights: *Home Office* v. *Robinson and The Prison Officers' Association* (1981). In addition, the rights of members of the police force to be members of trade unions and to engage in industrial action are severely limited. Nevertheless, as 'office holders', police officers cannot be dismissed without a hearing and have a right to reinstatement in the event of a dismissal being found to be wrongful: *see Ridge* v. *Baldwin* (1964).

8. The armed forces. The armed forces are excluded from the various statutory rights enjoyed by employees.

9. Remedies. One of the questions which has recently been raised is whether or not a public sector employee is able to have the decision of his/her dismissal reviewed by a court through the judicial review procedure. The essence of the procedure is that if the court holds that a decision has been made in an ultra vires fashion, whether procedurally or substantively, then the decision is void. In the context of dismissal the effect will be to reinstate the employee, as it is as if the decision had never been made.

How does the law decide whether a public sector employee is able to use the judicial review procedure as opposed to claiming unfair dismissal in an industrial tribunal? In *R* v. *East Berkshire Health Authority ex p Walsh* (1985) it was held that as the employee, a nurse, had a contract of employment, any claim concerning his dismissal should be pursued in an industrial tribunal for unfair dismissal. The 'normal' route for claiming a remedy cannot be followed where the person is an 'office-holder' e.g. a police officer (*see* 7 above) or a prison officer. In this case there is no contract of employment and therefore judicial review will be the appropriate procedure to obtain a remedy as there is no alternative: *R* v. *Home Secretary ex p Benwell* (1985).

It should be noted, however, that the mere existence of a contract of employment will never preclude the courts from reviewing the decision of a public sector employer where the employment conditions of the employee are affected. In *McGoldrick* v. *London Borough of Brent* (1987), the Court of Appeal indicated that if the statutory underpinning of, in this case, a teacher, was adversely affected by the decision of a public authority then the courts would be willing to review such a decision.

Minors

10. Common law principle. The ordinary rule of the law of contract is to the effect that a minor (i.e. a person under the age of eighteen) is bound by a contract of employment if the agreement, taken as a whole, is 'substantially for his benefit'. In *Doyle* v. *White City Stadium Ltd and BBBC* (1935) an infant boxer held a British Boxing Board of Control (BBBC) licence to box. After one contest, he was disqualified and in accordance with the rules of the BBBC his 'purse' was withheld. He claimed that this could not be done because he said the contract with the BBBC was not binding on him. Held: the contract was substantially for his benefit because the other terms of the agreement were clearly beneficial to him, e.g. those which regulated the conduct of contests. Therefore the contract was binding on him and the retention of the 'purse' was not wrongful.

11. Statutory restrictions. The Children and Young Persons Act 1933 and the Employment of Children Act 1973 regulate the employment of those minors below school-leaving age (16). These Acts, and regulations made thereunder, prevent, with limited exceptions, the employment of any person under the age of 13. Between the ages of 13 and 16, a minor may be employed in part-time work subject to restrictions as to the number of hours which may be worked and as to the time of such work. In addition, there are restrictions upon employment in certain kinds of work, e.g. in factories and mines.

Between the ages of sixteen and eighteen, minors are classed as 'young persons' and in various legislative provisions (e.g. Part VI of the Factories Act 1961), restrictions are imposed upon the kind of work and the number of hours which such persons may do. It should be mentioned at this stage that the Sex Discrimination Act, 1986, s. 7 removes most of the existing statutory provisions restricting women's hours of work. It is the piecemeal nature of the legislation which causes problems in this area.

Clauses 4–7 of the Employment Bill 1988 seek to modify the differences between working conditions for women. Of more fundamental importance is Clause 8, which seeks to repeal the majority of restrictions relating to employment of 'young persons'. The aim of these repeals is to remove restrictions on hours and holidays.

Temporary employees

12. General principle. The mere fact that an employee has been engaged expressly on the basis that he is 'temporary' does not, of itself, give the employer an automatic ground for terminating the employment fairly: *Terry* v. *East Sussex County Council* (1976). Once an employee has completed the appropriate period of continuous employment (notably two years for unfair dismissal), he is eligible to claim the various statutory rights. Consequently, the fact that he is regarded as 'temporary' does not automatically make a dismissal fair although this may constitute 'some other substantial reason' for dismissing the employee and as such, provided that the employer acted reasonably (e.g possibly considered the availability of other employment), the dismissal might not be unfair (*see* Chapter 12). In *North Yorkshire County Council* v. *Fay* (1985) the Court of Appeal held that the non-renewal of a series of fixed term contracts amounted to dismissal for 'some other substantial reason'. On the facts of the case the fixed term contract was for a specific purpose, i.e. the replacement of other teachers on secondment, and as that purpose had been made known to F then any subsequent dismissal was fair.

13. Special cases. By virtue of s. 61 of the 1978 Act, an employee who is engaged expressly as a temporary employee to replace someone suspended on medical grounds or absent on maternity leave is not normally to be regarded as unfairly dismissed if the employment is terminated when the absent employee returns (*see* 7:**27**).

Probationary employees

14. General principle. An employee may be engaged subject to a probationary period, the employer thus reserving the right to terminate or confirm the employment within, or at the end of, a specified period of time. As with temporary employees (*see* **12** above), it must be stated that once the employee has achieved the necessary period of continuous employment, he is eligible to present a complaint of unfair dismissal.

15. Dismissal. As with any other dismissal which is alleged to be unfair the employer must show that he acted 'reasonably' (*see* 12:**10**). It seems that in determining whether the dismissal of a probationary employee is unfair, an industrial tribunal will normally require the employer to establish that he took reasonable steps to maintain appraisal of the probationer, that he gave appropriate guidance to the employee, that he made an honest effort to determine whether the probationer came up to the required standard and that he kept himself informed of the relevant facts (*see Post Office* v. *Mughal* (1977); *White* v. *London Transport Executive* (1981)). Many employers recognise special obligations to probationers in their terms of employment and a failure to meet these obligations may render a dismissal unfair: *ILEA* v. *Lloyd* (1981).

Employees on fixed term contracts

16. Rights of employees. Under such contracts employment rights depend on whether or not the contracts can be aggregated in order to give the employee 'continuous employment' of two or more years (see 2: **16**).

17. Of one year or more. It should be noted that the expiry of a fixed term contract without renewal is a 'dismissal' for the purposes of unfair dismissal and redundancy (*see* 12: **5**; 13: **3**). However, by virtue of s. 142 of the 1978 Act (as amended by s. 8(2) of the Employment

Act 1980), if before a fixed term contract of one year or more expires, the employee agrees in writing to exclude any claim in respect of unfair dismissal/redundancy, such an undertaking is binding. The waiver only applies to dismissal 'on the expiry of the terms' i.e. at the end of the fixed term period, therefore dismissal on grounds of discrimination during the course of the contract cannot be excluded. A further difficulty is where there is a series of fixed term contracts, of less than a year, which when aggregated are of a year or more. It has been decided, albeit at industrial tribunal level, that the relevant contract was the final contract and if this was less than a year any waiver could not apply (*McKee* v. *Tyne & Wear Passenger Transport Executive* (1987)).

18. Meaning of 'fixed term contract'. There is no statutory definition, but, following *British Broadcasting Corporation* v. *Dixon* (1979), it is now clear that a fixed term contract is not 'fixed' if it contains a clause for early termination. A fixed term contract is one which expires on a particular date, rather than on the performance of a task or the happening of an event: *Wiltshire County Council* v. *NATFHE* (1980). This view is further supported by the decision in *Brown* v. *Knowsley Borough Council* (1986) where the contract was expressed to last only so long as sufficient funds are provided by the MSC or by other firms or sponsors.

Government training schemes

19. Introduction. In recent years the number of Government Training Schemes has proliferated. The status of a person on such a scheme depends very much on its nature; e.g. the presumption is that if the scheme is essentially one of training then the person is not an employee. Further the question of continuity needs to be discussed.

20. Youth Training Scheme. By analogy with its predecessor, the Youth Opportunities Programme, the YTS is aimed primarily at training as its objects are those of work experience and learning. Therefore a person on such a scheme is not an employee: *Daley* v. *Allied Suppliers* (1983).

21. Community Programme (as replaced by the Employment

Training Scheme). The aim of the community programme was to provide temporary work for long-term unemployed adults. In *Dyson* v. *Pontefract and District Council CP Scheme* (1988), the EAT decided that participants in the community programme were employees. It will be interesting to see whether the same decision is made about participants on the employment training scheme.

22. Continuity of employment and training schemes. Clearly, if the person is an employee under the scheme then this period of training will count when aggregating length of employment (*see* 2: **18**). However, in schemes where the person is not an employee, previous training will not count towards continuity: *Kennett* v. *Syme-Rumsby* (1974). A person who is taken on after a YTS will not be able therefore to count that period of training towards his continuity of employment.

Persons over retiring age

23. Introduction. The law in this area has recently been changed because of the European Court of Justice (ECJ) decision in *Marshall* v. *Southampton and South West Hampshire Area Health Authority* (1986). The decision meant that the Equal Treatment Directive (76 1207/EEC) was directly applicable to State employees, but legislation was required to provide a remedy for private sector employees. The decision concerned men and women being required to retire at different ages which the ECJ held to be discriminatory. The response of the Government was to pass the Sex Discrimination Act 1986 which gave effect to the decision in *Marshall* but also made other amendments.

24. Unfair dismissal. Section 64 of the 1978 Act (as amended by the SDA 1986, s. 3) equalised the age at which men and women cease to be eligible to claim unfair dismissal. If the contract states the normal retirement age then there is a strong presumption that this age applies. However, this may be rebutted if evidence shows that this age is regularly departed from in practice and has been departed from in practice and has been superseded by some definite higher age.

25. Redundancy. The SDA 1986 does not amend s. 82(1) of the 1978 Act which provides that a male over the age of sixty-five, or a female over the age of sixty, is excluded from the right to a statutory redundancy payment. Therefore, a woman over 60 who is unfairly selected for redundancy has a right to claim unfair dismissal but no right to a redundancy payment.

Progress test 3

1. In what circumstances may a company director be regarded as an 'employee'?   **(1)**

2. Explain the status of Crown servants in relation to employment law.   **(5, 6)**

3. Is a minor bound by a contract of employment?   **(10)**

4. What is the significance of an employee being engaged as a 'temporary employee'?   **(12, 13)**

5. What considerations arise in deciding whether the dismissal of a probationary employee is fair?   **(15)**

6. In what circumstances may a person employed on a fixed term contract validly give up his right to present a complaint of unfair dismissal and/or redundancy?   **(17)**

7. When will a period of employment on a government sponsored training scheme contribute towards a period of continuous service for the purposes of employment rights?   **(20, 21, 22)**

8. What is the significance of the retirement age for the purposes of unfair dismissal/redundancy?   **(23, 24, 25)**

4
The contract of employment (3): terms of the contract

Introduction

1. Significance of the terms. In any dispute between an employer and employee, the terms of the contract are of considerable significance in that one party may have a right to take legal action against the other in respect of any breach of contract. Of perhaps more general importance, however, is the significance of the terms of the contract when an action for unfair dismissal is brought. In such a case, although the question of whether one or more or both parties has broken the contract is of considerable importance, other considerations arise – notably whether the employer acted reasonably in dismissing the employee (*see* 12: **16**). Prior to the introduction of the remedy of unfair dismissal, an employer could always terminate the contract (without the employee having any recourse in law) provided that he gave proper notice (*see* 10: **2**), even if the employee was merely trying to assert his contractual rights. For example, if the employee was employed in Bristol and the contract made no provision for his being moved to another place, if the employer then ordered the employee to move his place of work to London and the employee refused, at common law the employer could quite lawfully terminate the employment by giving proper notice; but such a dismissal might now be considered to be unfair: *see Little* v. *Charterhouse Magna Assurance Co. Ltd* (1980). In addition, an employee may be able to assert his contractual rights through the notion of 'constructive dismissal' (*see* 12: **6**).

2. Sources of the terms of the contract. The terms of the contract of employment may be derived from a number of sources:

- (a) minimum statutory standards;
- (b) express statements of the parties;
- (c) collective agreements;
- (d) works' rule-books;
- (e) custom;
- (f) duties of employees (*see* Chapter 5);
- (g) duties of employers (*see* Chapter 6).

3. Written statement. It should be noted that, by virtue of s. 1 of the 1978 Act, an employer is under an obligation to supply his employees with a written statement containing information as to certain terms of the contract of employment (*see* 2: **7**). It is important to appreciate that this statement is not the contract of employment — it is merely written evidence of certain parts of the contract, but may be regarded as important if no contradictory evidence is available.

Minimum statutory standards

4. General principle. In effect all those statutory rights and duties which apply to the employer/employee relationship may be said to form part of every contract of employment except those to which the statutory provisions do not apply. With very few exceptions, it is not possible for the parties to contract out of the statutory provisions. The statutory rights can only be improved upon by the contract of employment.

5. Minimum terms' orders. Certain bodies, notably Wages Councils, are empowered to make orders which take effect as part of individual contracts of employment and are enforceable as such. It should be noted that the powers of Wages Councils have been limited by the Wages Act 1986 (*see* 7: **1**).

Express statements of the parties

6. Nature of express statements. An express statement, in this context, is a statement, either oral or written, made by the employer to the employee (or vice versa) concerning the terms of the contract. Such statements may include letters of appointment, formal contracts drawn up by the employer, verbal statements as to the terms and conditions of employment upon which the person is to be employed (as to wages, hours, holidays etc.) or other statements, e.g. a memorandum from one party to the other.

7. Pre-contractual statements. If an express statement is made before the parties enter into the contract of employment, it forms part of the contract and may not be subsequently altered without the mutual consent of the parties. If one party deviates from the agreed pre-contractual terms, that party is in breach of contract unless the other consents to the deviation either expressly or by implication, e.g. by continuing to employ, or work for, the other party after becoming aware of the breach.

The whole of the question of variation will be dealt with in more detail subsequently: *see*, generally, Chapter 11.

8. Post-contractual statements. Post-contractual statements do not form part of the contract of employment unless the parties expressly or implicitly agree that such a statement does become part of the contract. If an employee is employed upon certain terms which are stated prior to the commencement of the contract and he is subsequently given a written statement (under the provisions of s. 1 of the 1978 Act) which differs from the original terms as stated, the written statement does not supersede the agreed terms because, as stated at 3 above, the written statement is not to be regarded as contractual but merely as evidence of the contract, and in such a situation the employee ought to press his employer to give him an accurate written statement. If he is unable to do this, he may seek assistance from the industrial tribunals. If he fails to obtain a correct version of his written statement the presumption may arise that he has impliedly accepted the written statement as being a mutually agreed variation of the terms of the contract of employment and he may be estopped from denying that the statement represents the actual terms of the contract.

Collective agreements

9. General principle. The term 'collective agreement' has a particular definition in s. 30(1) of the Trade Union and Labour Relations Act 1974, but in general terms it may be described as an agreement between a trade union(s) and an employer(s) or employers' association which deals, amongst other things, with the terms and conditions of employment of employees of the employer(s) who is a party to the agreement. A collective agreement must be considered at two levels.

(*a*) Its effect as between the parties to it (*see* 16: 3).

(*b*) Its effect upon the individual contracts of employment of the employees who are the object of the agreement. This second aspect is considered in this section.

It has been estimated that 75 per cent of all employees have their terms and conditions of employment determined by collective agreements and it is therefore important to know the extent to which, as a matter of law, such agreements form part of the individual contract of employment. This is sometimes referred to as the 'normative' effect of collective agreements. Several arguments have been advanced to suggest that a collective agreement must automatically be regarded as forming part of the contracts of employment of those employees to whom the agreement refers; but these arguments (e.g. that the trade union negotiates as agent of the employees) have generally been refuted by the courts: *see Edwards* v. *Skyways* (1964).

The correctness of this view has been put under pressure by the Court of Appeal decision in *Marley* v. *Forward Trust Group Ltd* (1986). M was employed as a field supervisor in F's Bristol office. His terms and conditions of employment incorporated the terms of a collective agreement with ASTMS, and included both a mobility and redundancy clause, the latter allowing a six months' trial period. However, the final clause of the agreement stated that the agreement 'is binding in honour only'. F closed their Bristol office and M worked in London, under the terms of the agreement, for a trial period. He found the job unsuitable and sought a redundancy payment. Both the IT and the EAT rejected his claim on the ground that the agreement was stated to be 'binding in honour only' and was accordingly unenforceable. The Court of Appeal rejected this and held that the terms of an unenforceable collective agreement can be incorporated into contracts of employment and are then enforceable by the individual employee. The unenforceable nature of the agreement was limited to the parties to the agreement, in this case the employer and the union.

10. Express incorporation. It is fairly well established that it is possible to incorporate a collective agreement into an individual contract of employment if the contract expressly provides that this is to be the case. In *National Coal Board* v. *Galley* (1958) it was held that a clause of a collective agreement which stated that colliery deputies would work 'such days or part days in each week as may reasonably be required by the employer' could be regarded as being part of the individual contracts of employment because the contracts of the deputies referred to that collective agreement as being the source of the terms of their contracts.

It should be noted that the written statement supplied pursuant to s. 1 of the 1978 Act permits the employer to refer an employee to a document, such as a collective agreement, as being the source of certain terms of the contract of employment. The leading case on this issue is *Robertson and Jackson* v. *British Gas Corporation* (1983). Two employees appointed as gas meter readers were told, by letter, that incentive bonus scheme conditions would apply to the work. The employees were also given a written statement of terms of employment which stated that the provisions of the collective agreement would apply to their remuneration – and that any bonuses 'will be calculated in accordance with the rules of the scheme in force at the time'. The employers gave notice terminating the scheme on the ground that it had no legal force. No new scheme was negotiated and no bonus payments were received. The employees sued for loss of wages. Held: although the collective agreement was not binding between the union and the employers, it had been incorporated into the contracts of employment. The employers could not unilaterally alter the scheme and therefore the employees were entitled to the bonus payments.

The importance of the case is that the letter of appointment was the contract and not the written statement. Therefore, all the relevant documents are pertinent in determining this issue and it is clear that a s. 1 statement is not necessarily conclusive. *See* also *Gibbons* v. *Associated British Ports* (1985); *Cadoux* v. *Central Regional Council* (1986).

A collective agreement may also expressly become part of a contract of employment by virtue of statutory provisions. There are a number of situations where this is possible:

(*a*) Under s. 65 of the 1978 Act, provision is made for application to be made to the Secretary of State for the approval of dismissals' procedures agreements. Such agreements, which replace the right to claim unfair dismissal for those employees covered, form part of the terms of employment of those employees within their ambit.

(*b*) Under s. 96 of the 1978 Act, a collective agreement may be made which substitutes for the right to claim a redundancy payment under the provisions of the 1978 Act, a right to claim under the collective agreement. If such an agreement is approved by the Secretary of State, it forms part of the terms of employment of those employees to whom it applies (*see* 13: **17**).

(*c*) Under s. 18 of the 1978 Act a collective agreement may be made which substitutes for the right to a guarantee payment under the provisions of the 1978 Act, a right to claim under the collective agreement. If approved by the Secretary of State the agreement forms part of the terms of employment (*see* 7: **10**). It should be noted that where the terms of a collective agreement are expressly incorporated and varied by consent between the union(s) and employer(s) the new terms become incorporated into the individual contracts of employment; however, unilateral variation or abrogation of the agreement by one party does not have a corresponding effect on individual employment contracts: *Robertson & Jackson* v. *British Gas Corporation* (1983).

11. Implied incorporation. On occasions, the courts have been prepared to permit the implied incorporation of collective agreements.

Sagar v. *Ridehalgh and Son Ltd* (1931). Held: employees entered employment in a Lancashire mill on whatever terms were normally observed there including the terms of relevant collective agreements. (*See also Brand* v. *London County Council* (1967).)

However, the general trend of the cases has been against the principle of implied incorporation.

Young v. *Canadian Northern Railway Co.* (1931): the plaintiff had been employed by the defendants. It was alleged by him that a collective agreement requiring that workers should be laid off in order of seniority was incorporated into his individual contract of employment. Held by the Privy Council: this agreement had not become incorporated into the contract of employment of the plaintiff despite the fact that this agreement had been normally observed as a matter of practice.

The decision is Young's case was apparently followed in *Dudfield* v. *Ministry of Works* (1964); *Faithful* v. *Admiralty* (1964).

However, it is possible that the terms of a collective agreement may be incorporated into a contract of employment by virtue of long observance (*see* Custom at **16** *below*).

Maclea v. *Essex Line Ltd* (1933): the terms of a collective agreement had been observed as a matter of practice for a number of years. Held: this agreement was incorporated into individual contracts of employment.

Works' rule-books

12. Meaning of the term. A 'works' rule-book' can take a variety of forms in so far as it may consist of an actual book given to each employee when he enters employment or at some subsequent date; alternatively it may be a book of rules which is not given to each employee but which is known to exist and which is kept in the works' office; or it may simply be a list of rules pinned on a notice-board at the place of work. The rules in such a rule-book are often laid down by the employer without consultation and normally consist of rules relating to disciplinary action, suspension, dismissal for misconduct, bad time-keeping etc. It may also contain rules as to safety procedures to be adopted at the place of work. Note that as regards disciplinary rules, these must be referred to in the written statement (*see* 2: **7**).

13. The effect of the rule-book on the contract. The question of whether a works' rule-book forms part of the individual contract of employment of the employees who work in that place depends upon the particular circumstances, but the following principles have emerged.

(*a*) If the employer gives the employee a copy of the rule-book or expressly refers the employee to it before the contract is formed and the employee agrees that it is part of the contract (e.g. by signing an acknowledgment to that effect), then it is to be regarded as part of the contract of employment.

(*b*) It may be regarded as part of the individual contract if the employee is otherwise given notice of the fact that the rule-book has contractual force, e.g. by a notice posted on the wall of the place of work which can be clearly seen. This will almost certainly be the case if the employee's attention is drawn to that fact before employment commences. If he only sees the notice after he has entered into the contract, then it is a matter of custom and practice (*see* **14** below).

In *Petrie* v. *Macfisheries Ltd* (1940) a notice was posted on the wall of the work-place stating the circumstances in which sick pay would be paid. The plaintiff claimed that the notice did not form part of his contract of employment. Held: the rule as to sick pay had been incorporated into his contract of employment by virtue of his continued working in that place This case is also illustrative of the principle that rules which are contained in the written statement will be terms of the contract. *See* also *Dal* v. *A S Orr* (1980).

(*c*) However not all works' rules will be terms of the contract of employment. This will be particularly so when there are numerous rules contained in the relevant documentation, some, for example, may have become out of date and therefore inappropriate. This principle is well illustrated by the decision in *Secretary of State for Employment* v. *ASLEF (No. 2)* (1972), a case concerning the rule book of British Rail, where Lord Denning said 'Each man signs a form saying that he will abide by the rules, but these rules are in no way terms of the contract of employment. They are only instructions to a man as to how he is to do his work'. The effect of this judgment is undoubtedly to increase the scope of managerial prerogative.

Custom

14. Different kinds of custom. Custom plays a significant part in employment law, both from the practical aspect of industrial relations where emphasis is laid upon 'custom and practice', and in the courts when they are called upon to decide what are the terms of a particular contract of employment. This topic is somewhat nebulous but it seems that there are four different categories of custom which may form part of a contract of employment.

    (*a*) Custom of a particular place of work.
    (*b*) Custom of an industry or trade.
    (*c*) Custom of a specific geographical locality.
    (*d*) Customary conduct of the parties to the contract of employment.

15. Custom of a particular place of work. When an employee has been employed in a place of work for some length of time, there may be implied into his contract of employment terms based upon the custom of that place and he may not be able to contend that he never agreed to those terms. This may be particularly true where it is shown that the employee was aware of the existence of such customs and practices. As Lord Goddard said in *Marshall* v. *English Electric Co. Ltd* (1945):

> '...an established practice at a particular factory may be incorporated into a workman's contract of service, and whether he knew it or not, it must be presumed that he accepted employment on the same terms as applied to other workers in that factory'.

The kind of customs which may arise under this head are those relating to breaks, suspension, dismissals' procedures etc.

16. Custom of an industry or trade. Many industries and trades have their own particular customs applicable in a variety of situations. If a person agrees to be bound by the customs of the industry or trade when he enters employment or he continues to be employed in that industry, it may be said that those customs have become part of his contract of employment.

In *Sagar* v. *Ridehalgh and Son Ltd* (1931) it was held that the customs of the Lancashire weaving trade were incorporated into the contract of employment of a Lancashire weaver and therefore customary deductions for faulty workmanship were lawfully deductible. As Lawrence LJ said: 'A Lancashire weaver knows and has known for very many years past precisely what his position was as regards deductions for bad work in accepting employment in a Lancashire mill'. It was also stated that the weaver's knowledge of this practice was irrelevant since he accepted employment in accordance with the usual terms.

In *Davson* v. *France* (1959) a musician was given one week's notice to terminate his engagement. He claimed that this was wrongful dismissal on the basis that it was an implied term of his contract, by virtue of a custom of the music trade, that he should receive fourteen days' notice. Held: this was wrongful dismissal because there had been a breach of an implied term.

17. Custom of specific geographical locality. Certain areas of the country have customary practices which apply to persons employed in that area or to persons employed in certain work in that area. Such customs often concern holidays, e.g. it is customary in certain parts of England for a particular day to be a holiday. If this is implied into a contract of employment, it is a breach of contract for the employer to prevent an employee from having that day as a holiday. Note that in *Sagar* v. *Ridehalgh* (*see* **16** above) there was a geographical element involved.

18. Customary conduct of the parties. The courts may be prepared to regard the conduct of the parties as an aid to the interpretation of a contract of employment. In *Mears* v. *Safecar Security Ltd* (1982) a security guard who had been absent from work for two periods totalling seven months out of an employment period of fourteen months and who had not requested nor received an sick pay during the periods of absence, applied to an industrial tribunal under s. 11(1) of the 1978 Act (complaint relating to the failure of an employer to provide an adequate written statement of the main terms of the contract; *see* **2**: **9**) for a determination of what particulars relating to sick pay ought to have been included. The Court of Appeal held that where there was no express agreement on the matter, the tribunal is entitled to consider all the facts and circumstances of the relationship between the employer and employee, including their subsequent acts and conduct under the contract. Accordingly it was held that no sick pay was payable. *See* also *O'Grady* v. *M. Saper Ltd* (1940).

NOTE: in all these cases, the longer the person has been employed in that particular work, the stronger the presumption that a custom has become part of his contract of employment.

Progress test 4

1. What is the importance of establishing the terms of a contract of employment? **(1)**

2. From what sources are the terms of a contract of employment derived? **(2)**

3. In what circumstances do post-contractual statements form part of a contract of employment? **(8)**

4. What is a collective agreement? What is meant by the 'normative' effect of a collective agreement? **(9)**

5. What is meant by saying that a collective agreement has been expressly incorporated into a contract of empoyment? **(10)**

6. On what basis may a collective agreement be implied into a contract of employment? **(11)**

7. In what circumstances may a works' rule-book be regarded as forming part of a contract of employment? **(13)**

8. To what extent may 'custom' be regarded as an effective source of the terms of a contract of employment? **(14–18)**

9. Smith is taken on by X Ltd 'on the usual terms for the industry'. These terms include a provision that overtime payment is at time and a half. A collective agreement is subsequently negotiated between X Ltd and Smith's trade union which provides for overtime payment at time and three-quarters. X Ltd refuse to make the higher payment to Smith. Discuss. **(1–18)**

5

The contract of employment (4): implied duties of employees

General considerations

1. Significance of the implied duties. Into every contract of employment are implied a number of obligations in so far as these are not inconsistent with the express terms of the individual contract of employment. These duties are based upon principles developed by the courts in the decided cases. However, the mere existence of these obligations is not, in itself, important − the important question is as to the consequences which may follow from a breach of one of the duties. The answer will vary according to which of the duties is broken and the gravity of such breach.

On occasions, the employer may be justified in dismissing the employee without notice (*see* 10: **6**), or with notice in circumstances which are not deemed to be 'unfair' within the meaning of the 1978 Act, s. 54 (*see* 12: **9**).

Alternatively, the employer may be able to obtain an injunction to prevent an employee from benefiting from a breach of one of the duties, or levy a fine on, or suspend, the employee without pay. Of course, it is also important to note that if an employer chooses to ignore a breach of one of the duties, that is the end of the matter.

2. The implied duties. The implied duties may be classified as follows:

(*a*) to be ready and willing to work;
(*b*) to use reasonable care and skill;
(*c*) to obey lawful orders;

(*d*) to take care of the employer's property;

(*e*) to act in good faith.

To be ready and willing to work

3. The basic obligation of employment. The fundamental duty which an employee owes to his employer is the duty to present himself at work, in accordance with the contract of employment, and to work at the direction of the employer in return for the implied obligation of the employer to pay wages as agreed (*see* 6: **2**)

4. Absence of employee. Therefore, if an employee is absent from work without excuse, that constitutes a breach of contract and the employer may act accordingly.

5. Taking of industrial action by an employee. An interesting recent development in this area of being ready and willing to work concerns an employee taking industrial action (*see* generally Chapter 17). What happens if the employee is only ready and willing to do a proportion of his work? Two cases need to be discussed in this context. In *Miles* v. *Wakefield Metropolitan District Council* (1987) M was a superintendent registrar of births, deaths and marriages. He normally worked 37 hours per week, three of which were on Saturday mornings. As part of industrial action M refused to carry out marriages on Saturday mornings, although he was willing to do his other work. The council made it clear that unless he was willing to perform all his duties then it would deduct his wages for that period. M did perform other work on Saturdays but the council withheld 3/37 of his wages. M sued for the lost wages. It was held by the House of Lords that where an employee refuses to perform the full range of his duties and had been told that he would not be paid if he did not, then the employers were entitled to withhold the whole of his remuneration, although he attended for work and carried out a substantial part of his duties.

The above case can be compared with the decision in *Wiluszynski* v. *London Borough of Tower Hamlets* (1989). W was employed as an estates officer. W took part in limited industrial action which took the form of refusing to answer members' inquiries. This was part of the contractual duties of W, but did not take up much of his time.

The industrial action had been taking place for a two week period before the council did anything about it and then no action was taken as W agreed to work normally. The action then continued for a five week period in total. W cleared the back-log of members' inquiries within three hours. He had satisfactorily performed all his other work during this period. The council refused to pay him any wages for this five week period. W sued for payment. Held: the council was entitled to withhold the wages as W had to perform all his contractual obligations during this period to be entitled to his contractual remuneration.

6. Withholding of pay without due cause. Employers, however, cannot unilaterally withhold or deduct pay without just cause. If the employers decide to reduce pay unilaterally, then such an action will be seen as a fundamental breach of contract giving the employee the option to repudiate the contract. However, it should be noted that such a breach does not automatically bring the contract to an end, *see Coutts* v. *Herefordshire County Council* (1984) and *Rigby* v. *Ferodo Ltd* (1988).

To use reasonable care and skill

7. Extent of the duty. The duty to use reasonable care and skill in the performance of the duties under the contract has two aspects:

(*a*) The duty not to be unduly negligent.
(*b*) The duty to be reasonably competent.

8. Not to be unduly negligent. If an employee is negligent in the performance of his work, he may be regarded as being in breach of contract. This is particularly true if there has been a pattern of negligent conduct by that employee or if the single act of negligence is especially serious. In *Lister* v. *Romford Ice and Cold Storage Co. Ltd* (1957) a lorry driver, employed by the company, carelessly reversed his lorry and injured a fellow employee, who was in fact his father. The employers paid damages to the father but claimed an indemnity from the son on the grounds that he had broken an implied term of the contract of employment, i.e. the duty not to be negligent in the performance of the work. Held: the employee would be liable because of the breach of the implied duty.

Another example of the application of the *Lister* principle is to be found in *Janata Bank* v. *Ahmed* (1981), where a bank employee, A, was successfully sued by his employers for losses caused by his negligence in authorising the overdrafts of non-creditworthy customers.

However, it is clear that if the principle of *Lister's* case is extended to its potential limits, this would seriously affect the doctrine of vicarious liability in so far as employers would be able to seek an indemnity from employees for whom they were vicariously liable. The notion of this implied duty must therefore be approached with caution. For example, in *Jones* v. *Manchester Corporation* (1952), the court held that the employers remained liable for the negligence of their employees because they had allowed inexperienced employees to perform a difficult job without proper supervision.

It should be noted that there are few cases where an employer has sued an employee for breach of the contractual duty of care. In practice an employer is much more likely simply to dismiss the employee.

9. Duty to be reasonably competent. If an employee is incompetent this in itself may constitute a breach of the contract of employment, particularly if the employee has professed his ability to do that particular work. As Willes J said in *Harmer* v. *Cornelius* (1858):

'It may be, that, if there is no general and no particular representation of ability and skill, the workman undertakes no responsibility. If a gentleman, for example, should employ a man who is known to have never done anything but sweep a crossing, to clean or mend his watch, the employer probably would be held to have incurred all risks himself'.

By implication, therefore, if an employee states that he can do a particular job and he is not, in fact, competent to do that work, the employer may regard the incompetence as a breach of contract.

Other forms of misconduct (e.g. drunkenness or fighting) may also amount to a breach of the overall obligation to use reasonable care and skill in doing his work. However, the employee must be shown to have acted unreasonably since he is not expected to be above reproach in everything he does. As to the extent to which lack of competence may be used to justify a dismissal as fair, *see* 12: **13**.

To obey lawful orders

10. Disobedience may justify summary dismissal. An employee is under a duty to obey all the lawful orders of his employer, i.e. those which are within the scope of the contract. A failure to do this is a breach of the contract of employment and may in certain circumstances, justify summary dismissal (*see* 10: **6**). However, it must be established that the order was one which is within the scope of the contract of employment. In *Price* v. *Mouat* (1862) a lace-salesman was ordered to 'card' (pack) lace but he refused and was dismissed without notice. He claimed that this was wrongful dismissal. Held: the dismissal was wrongful because the order was not one which was within the scope of the contract.

An employee is not, therefore, obliged to do any act which is deemed to fall outside the ambit of his individual contract of employment. The question of the introduction of new technology has caused problems here and must be linked to the scope of managerial prerogative in introducing new work techniques. In *Cresswell* v. *Board of Inland Revenue* (1984), the Revenue wished to introduce a computer system to assist with the PAYE system. The majority of the work associated with the system had previously been done manually. Did the employers have the ability to change the nature of the working system? Held: employees were expected to adopt the new methods and techniques in performing their contracts if the employer provided the necessary training in the new skills. It should be mentioned that the judge added the caveat that the nature should not change 'radically' as a result of the changes; clearly this is a question of degree based on the facts of individual cases.

11. Justifiable refusal to obey an order. The only circumstances in which an employee may be justified in refusing to obey an order which is apparently within the scope of his contract are:

(*a*) where such an order involves exceptional danger for which the employee is not given extra payment. In *Robson* v. *Sykes* (1938) a merchant seaman was ordered to sail on a ship which was to call at Spanish ports. He refused on the grounds that serious danger was involved on account of the Civil War. He was dismissed for his refusal but he claimed that the dismissal was wrongful. Held: his action succeeded because, while the order was prima facie within the scope of the contract, it involved unreasonable danger to the employee.

(b) where the employer orders the employee to do something which would constitute a criminal offence; see *Morrish* v. *Henleys (Folkestone) Ltd* (1973) and *Gregory* v. *Ford* (1951).

12. Disobedience and unfair dismissal. In practice, claims under the statutory procedures for unfair dismissal are much more numerous than the common law action for wrongful dismissal. Although there are circumstances where an employer may still be entitled to dismiss summarily in respect of a refusal to obey an order (e.g. where the refusal amounts to grave misconduct), the usual position will be that the employers' reasonableness in treating the refusal as a ground for dismissal will have to stand up to scrutiny before a tribunal, even though the refusal has amounted in law to breach of contract. *See* generally Chapter 12.

To take care of employer's property

13. Extent of the duty. An employee is under an obligation to take reasonable care of his employer's property. In *Superflux* v. *Plaisted* (1958) the defendant had been in charge of a team of vacuum cleaner salesmen and had negligently allowed fourteen cleaners to be stolen from his van. Held: he was in breach of his contract of employment.

14. Indemnity. In such circumstances an employee is under an obligation to indemnify his employer for the loss sustained.

To act in good faith

15. Several aspects. The implied duty of the employee to act in good faith towards his employer has several different aspects which together form the basis of what is regarded as a relationship of trust by the law.

16. Duty not to make a secret profit. An employee must not abuse his position by making a secret profit, e.g. by accepting a bribe to ensure that a person obtains a contract with the employer. This principle is clear from the case of *Reading* v. *A.G.* (1951), which concerned a member of the armed forces, in which Lord Normand said:

> '...though the relation of a member of His Majesty's forces is not accurately described as that of a servant under a contract of service...he owes to the Crown a duty as fully fiduciary as the duty of a servant to his master...and in consequence...all profits and advantages gained by the use of his military status are to be for the benefit of the Crown'.

17. Duty to disclose certain information. There appears to be no general duty on an employee to inform his employer of his misconduct or deficiencies: *Bell* v. *Lever Brothers* (1932). However, to that general principle there is one important exception, namely where the employment of that particular person is made more hazardous by virtue of an undisclosed defect on part of the employee. In *Cork* v. *Kirby Mackean Ltd* (1952) an epileptic employee was engaged by an employer but he did not disclose the fact of his epilepsy. He fell while working at some height above the ground and was killed. His widow brought an action for damages on behalf of her husband. Held: damages must be reduced because of the fact that her husband had failed to inform his employer of his condition. Singleton LJ:

> 'A man who knew himself to be in the conditions in which Mr Cork knew that he was ought to have told his employers. However anxious he was to get work, he owed a duty to himself and his fellow workmen and failure to inform the employers, followed by instructions to work at some height above the ground involved risk to the other workman as well as himself'.

There is no general duty to inform an employer of the misconduct or deficiencies of a fellow employee. However, such a duty can arise where the employee has expressly contracted to serve the best interests of the employer: *Swain* v. *West (Butchers) Ltd* (1936). The position of an employee in the hierarchy of a company may also be relevant to the existence of the duty. Thus where an employee has managerial responsibilities over a complete section of the employer's business, then a duty to report the misdeeds of subordinates may arise: *Sybron Corporation* v. *Rochem Ltd* (1983).

18. Duty not to act to detriment of employer. There is, apparently, a duty on an employee not to act in such a way as to harm the interests of the employer. For example, if an employee works in a position of financial trust, it may be a breach of his contract of employment if he is found guilty of dishonesty not connected with his employment in so far as such conduct reflects on his employer. The same may be true of gross immorality or drunkenness: *Clouston & Co.* v. *Corry* (1906).

Such conduct may justify summary dismissal, but it is probably more likely that it would be regarded as conduct which would justify dismissal that would not be regarded as 'unfair' within the meaning of s. 54 of the 1978 Act (*see* 12: **2, 9**). Of course, similar conduct occurring in connection with employment would probably constitute a breach of the duty to use reasonable care and skill (*see* **7–8** above).

19. Duty not to disclose confidential information. Persons who work under a contract of employment owe a general duty to their employers not to disclose confidential information relating to them. As Lynskey J said in *Bent's Brewery* v. *Hogan* (1945): 'In my view, it is quite clear that an employee is under an obligation to his employers not to disclose confidential information obtained by him in the course of and as a result of his employment'. This duty applies both during employment and afterwards if the employee seeks to use such information to the detriment of the employer. The remedy available to an employer for breach of this duty is to seek an injunction restraining the employee (or any other person) from using the information. The basis of this implied duty is that the information is in the nature of a property right which cannot be taken from the employer without his consent. The courts take the view that employers would not allow their employees to have access to such information unless they thought that the law would protect them against the misuse of it.

20. Meaning of 'confidential information'. It is difficult to state in general terms what may be regarded as confidential information or a trade secret, but in *Thomas Marshall (Exports) Ltd* v. *Guinle* (1978) a number of factors were identified as being relevant:

(*a*) the information must be information the release of which the owner believes would be injurious to him or advantageous to his rivals;

(*b*) the owner must believe that the information is confidential or secret, i.e. not already public knowledge;

(*c*) the owner's belief under the above two heads must be reasonable;

(*d*) the information must be judged in the light of the usage and practice of the particular industry or trade concerned.

Therefore, information which is public knowledge is not protected by this implied duty. If an employer wishes to prevent an employee from utilising non-confidential information, or information which is not personal to the employer, he can only do so by using an express covenant (*see* **21** below).

'Confidential information' relates to such matters as manufacturing processes of a secret nature, designs, customer lists, accounts etc., and *see* the *Faccenda Chicken* case below. In *Thomas Marshall (Exports) Ltd* v. *Guinle* (1978) the managing director of a company (which was in business purchasing clothing from manufacturers in the Far East and Eastern Europe for resale to large mail order and multiple stores) secretly set up a rival company. He was prevented by injunction from using or disclosing confidential information relating to such matters as names and telex addresses of manufacturers and suppliers, prices paid by his employers for goods and details of the employers' new ranges and prices paid by customers to the employer.

However, this duty does not extend to the employee's general skill and knowledge as to the method and manner of performing his work, often referred to as 'know-how'. The scope of this duty has been recently discussed by the Court of Appeal in the important case of *Faccenda Chicken Ltd* v. *Fowler* (1986) where the company sought an injunction to restrain F, and other former employees who had formed a rival company, from using 'confidential' information which they had acquired whilst working for the company. The information included purchasing requirements of customers, pricing structure and marketing strategy. There was no express term limiting the disclosure of information, therefore the question was whether a term could be implied to that effect. The Court of Appeal made a number of general observations from which it appears that while an employee remains in the employment of an employer, the duty of confidentiality forms part of a more general duty of good faith and fidelity. The duty does extend to ex-employees, but in a more limited form and it only covers trade secrets, designs, special methods of construction and other information which is of a 'sufficiently high degree of confidentiality as to amount to a secret'.

The Court of Appeal then laid down four criteria to distinguish between 'confidential' information (which is protected) and 'known how' (which is not).

(a) *The nature of the employment.* If secret information is 'habitually handled', an employee will be aware of the sensitivity of the information.

(b) *The nature of the information itself.* Such information must 'in all the circumstances be of such a highly confidential nature as to require the same protection as a trade secret'.

(c) *Confidential nature of the information emphasised by the employer.* For the application of this criterion, it is essential to establish whether the employer impressed on the employee that the information was confidential.

(d) *The 'detached' nature of the information.* For information to be classified as 'confidential', it would need to be shown whether the information could easily be isolated from other information which the employee is free to disclose.

Applying these principles, the Court of Appeal decided that neither the information about prices by itself, nor when taken together with the other sales information, had the degree of confidentiality to warrant an injunction being granted. The court took account of the following facts in making its decision.

(a) Some of the information was clearly not secret, e.g. van routes.

(b) The information about prices could not be severed from the rest.

(c) The information had been acquired in order to allow the employees to do their work and could have been memorised anyway.

(d) The information available was not restricted to senior staff.

See further application of these principles in *Roger Bullivant Ltd* v. *Ellis* (1987) and *Johnson and Bloy (Holdings) Ltd* v. *Wolstenholme Rink Plc* (1987).

In *Hivac Ltd* v. *Park Royal Scientific Instruments Ltd* (1946) five employees of the appellant company were employed to assemble hearing aids, which was a highly specialised form of work. On Sundays they did similar work for a rival company. There was no evidence to show that they had actually transmitted trade secrets. Held: because of the particular nature of the work and the possibility that information could be passed, there was justification for an order restraining the respondents from employing the five men.

Covenants in restraint of trade

21. Meaning of the term. A covenant in restraint of trade is a clause in a contract which purports to limit an employee's right to seek employment where and when he chooses upon leaving his employment. An employer may wish to insert such a covenant into a contract of employment for one of two reasons:

(a) he wishes to prevent an employee from using general information which is not covered by the implied duty of non-disclosure of confidential information (*see* **19** above); or

(b) he does not wish to rely solely on that implied duty, even in respect of matters which might be covered by it, e.g. customer lists and manufacturing processes.

22. General attitude of the courts. The general attitude of the courts to such covenants is to regard them as prima facie void as being a restraint upon the right to seek employment freely. However, if an employer can establish that such a covenant is reasonable, it may be enforceable. To prove that such a clause is reasonable, it must be shown that it is necessary to protect the employer's proprietary interests and that it is not an undue restriction upon the employee's right to seek employment elsewhere. Furthermore, the covenant must not be contrary to the public interest.

23. Factors to be considered. In determining whether a particular covenant is reasonable and therefore enforceable, the courts make reference to certain factors:

(a) *Time.* The court must be satisfied that the time for which the covenant is to run is not excessive. In general terms, it must be for no longer than is strictly necessary to prevent the employer's proprietary interests from being prejudiced. For example in *Roger Bullivant Ltd* v. *Ellis* (1987) an injunction was granted restraining an ex-employee from using a card index containing confidential information for a year after his employment ended.

(b) *Area.* The geographical area to which the covenant extends must normally be limited to the area within which the employee formerly worked. This may be countrywide if the business of the employer is a national concern (this is more likely to be a manufacturing rather than a service industry), but in certain circumstances, the limits must be very narrow. In *Mason* v. *Provident Clothing and Supply Co.* (1913) it was held that an employer could not rely on a clause which sought to obtain protection from competition from a former employee within twenty-five miles of London because the former employee's work had only brought him into contact with customers in a small area of London. In *Dewes* v. *Fitch* (1921) the contract of employment of a solicitor's clerk provided that he should not enter into employment with any other solicitor within a radius of seven miles of his former employer. Held: this was reasonable and therefore valid.

Where the clause seeks to prevent an employee from depriving his former employer of customers, the clause must normally be restricted not only to a particular geographical area but also to customers or former customers in that area: *Gledhow Autoparts* v. *Delaney* (1965); *Financial Collection Agencies (UK) Ltd* v. *Batey* (1973); *Marley Tile Co.* v. *Johnson* (1982).

(c) *Similarity of business.* The covenant must be restricted to employment in a similar kind of business as that in which the employee was formerly engaged. In *Attwood* v. *Lamont* (1920) a clause in the contract of employment of a tailor employed in a department store stated that the employee must not subsequently enter into employment with any employer whose business competed with that of the store. Held: the clause was unenforceable since it should have been limited to businesses which competed with that of the tailoring department.

(*d*) *Public interest.* The public interest in these circumstances is that society ought not to be deprived of the services of a skilled man and it seems that this virtually corresponds with the employee's interests: *Wyatt* v. *Kreglinger and Fernau* (1933); *Eastham* v. *Newcastle United FC* (1964); *Bull* v. *Pitney-Bowes Ltd* (1967).

24. Severance. If the covenant is found to be unreasonable, the contract as a whole is not necessarily to be regarded as void, unless it is impossible to distinguish the covenant from the rest of the contract. If the covenant can be severed from the rest of the contract, without altering the nature of the agreement, the unreasonable clause may be struck out: *see Commercial Plastics Ltd* v. *Vincent* (1965).

25. Effect of wrongful dismissal. If an employer breaks the contract of employment by wrongfully dismissing an employee (*see* 10: **5**), the employee may disregard any covenant in the contract which purports to limit his right to seek employment elsewhere: *General Billposting Co.* v. *Atkinson* (1909). The consequences for a restraint clause where the dismissal is unfair, as opposed to wrongful, have not been fully worked out by the courts.

26. Effect of breach of covenant. If an employee acts in breach of a covenant in restraint of trade, his former employer may seek an injunction to prevent the former employee from continuing to act in breach. However, as a matter of practice, such covenants are often inserted into contracts of employment as a deterrent rather than with any real intention of enforcing them.

Covenants in a contract which prevent an employee from working for a rival during employment will normally be upheld, although, if the effect of such a covenant is to enforce performance of the existing contract, the court may be unwilling to issue an injunction (*see* 11:7).

Patents

27. Common law position. At common law, unless the contract dealt with the matter, an employee would not normally be entitled to the benefit of any invention made by him if to allow him to do so would be a contravention of the implied duty of the employee to act in good faith.

28. Patents Act 1977. The 1977 Act (ss. 39–47) gives ownership of an invention to the employee inventor unless the invention was made in the course of the duties for which he was employed. This exception applies where either an invention should have been reasonably expected to result from carrying out his duties or, because of the nature of the employee's duties, he had a special obligation towards the employer. In addition, even if the employer is entitled to an invention made by an employee who has patented it, the employee may claim compensation from the employer if the patent has been of outstanding benefit to him. Disputes are dealt with by the Patents Court.

Progress test 5

1. What is the significance of the implied duties owed by employees?   (**1**)
2. Where an employee has taken industrial action, has he breached his contract of employment?   (**5**)
3. To what extent is a negligent employee regarded as being in breach of his contract of employment?   (**8**)
4. What orders from his employer may an employee lawfully disregard?   (**11**)
5. Jones is employed by X Ltd as a sales representative. Whilst visiting a client, he leaves his car unlocked and some samples belonging to X Ltd are stolen. discuss.   (**13, 14**)
6. Smith is a supervisor employed by Y Ltd. One of Smith's jobs is to appoint certain employees. He engages Brown on condition that Brown pays £1,000 to Smith. Discuss.   (**16**)
7. Black makes a contract with the *Daily News* to write a 'story'

exposing the fact that his former employers, Fixit Quick Ltd, do not abide by collective agreements. Fixit Quick wish to know if they can prevent publication.   (20)

8. What factors are relevant in determining the validity of a covenant in restraint of trade?   (23)

9. Where an employee has breached a restraining covenant in his contract of employment, what action may the employer take?   (26)

6

The contract of employment (5): duties of the employer

Introduction

1. Obligations. By virtue of the common law and a variety of statutory provisions, employers have a considerable number of obligations towards employees. The main examples of these duties are:

- (*a*) to pay contractually agreed remuneration;
- (*b*) to observe provisions relating to sick pay;
- (*c*) to treat employees with trust and confidence;
- (*d*) to observe provisions relating to holidays;
- (*e*) to observe provisions relating to hours of work;
- (*f*) to permit employees time off work for public duties;
- (*g*) to indemnify employees;
- (*h*) to provide references;
- (*i*) to insure employees and other duties.

NOTE: Other duties are dealt with elsewhere, e.g. in relation to safety. *See* Chapter 14.

To pay remuneration

2. General principle. The amount of remuneration to which an employee is entitled is determined by the contract, often arising as a result of collective bargaining but sometimes it is fixed by law or by machinery established by legislation, e.g. the Wages' Councils' industries (*see* 7: **6–8**).

The basic obligation of the employer arising from the contract is to pay the contractually agreed remuneration, and a failure to do so constitutes a breach of contract which, depending upon the circumstances, might be such as to constitute a constructive dismissal (see 12: 6). Traditionally it has been assumed that, subject to two well-established exceptions and one more recent exception, an employer is under no duty to provide work so long as he pays the contractually agreed remuneration. As Asquith LJ said in *Collier* v. *Sunday Referee Publishing Co. Ltd* (1940): 'Provided I pay my cook her wages regularly she cannot complain if I choose to take any or all of my meals out'. However, in addition to the three exceptions dealt with in 3 below, in recent times the general principle that an employer has no duty to provide work has been questioned, particularly in relation to skilled employees. Lord Denning said in *Langston* v. *AUEW* (1973): 'In these days an employer, when employing a skilled man, is bound to provide him with work. By which I mean that the man should be given the opportunity of doing his work when it is available and when he is ready and willing to do it.' If such a view is generally accepted by the courts, a failure on the part of an employer to provide an employee with work of the kind which he is contractually employed to do might be regarded as a constructive dismissal (*see* 12: 6): *see Breach* v. *Epsylon Industries Ltd* (1976).

3. Exceptions. Three exceptions to the general principle are well-established.

(*a*) Where the employee is employed wholly or mainly on piece-work or on a commission basis, he is entitled to receive wages which are equivalent to what he would have received had he been given work to do. This right continues for as long as the contract subsists unless there is a contrary agreement in the contract itself. In *Devonald* v. *Rosser and Sons* (1906) an employer closed his factory because of a trade recession and gave his piece-work employees one month's notice to terminate their contracts. They were given no work to do during this period and could therefore earn no wages. Held: by the Court of Appeal: there was an implied term of their contracts that they would be able to earn wages during the period of notice and they were therefore entitled to damages based upon the average of their weekly earnings during the last six weeks of their normal employment.

In practice many piece-workers are now covered by collective agreements which provide a contractual right to minimum earnings and, in addition, note the provisions of ss. 12–18 of the 1978 Act in relation to guarantee payments (*see* 7: **10**). Note also that Schedule 3 of the 1978 Act sets out the rights of the employee during a period of notice to terminate employment.

(*b*)   Where the nature of the employment is such that the actual performance of the work forms part of the consideration supplied by the employer, the employee may be entitled to compensation over and above the contractual wages. These situations are sometimes referred to as 'name in lights' clauses and if the employer fails to give the employee work to do, he may be obliged to compensate the employee for the loss sustained in not being able to enhance his reputation or advance his experience in that particular kind of work. In *Clayton* v. *Oliver* (1930) it was held that an actor who had been promised a leading role in a play, and who was not given such a part, was entitled to compensation for loss of the chance to enhance his public reputation and for the fact that his name would not be advertised as it would otherwise have been.

(*c*)   When an employee is taking part in limited industrial action (*see* 5: **5**).

Sick pay

4. General principle. An employer may have an obligation by virtue of a term in the contract of employment to pay sick pay to employees when they are unable to work because of illness. Such an obligation may arise under an express term (it has been officially calculated that at least 80 per cent of all employees are covered by occupational sick pay schemes); or an obligation may arise under an implied term. The principles governing the implication of terms relating to sick pay were discussed by the Court of Appeal in *Mears* v. *Safecar Security Ltd* (1982) where it was held that there is no general presumption of an implied right to sick pay. The job of the tribunal or court is to ascertain what was agreed expressly or impliedly and in performing this task the court '. . . should consider all the facts and circumstances of the relationship between the employer and employee concerned including the way in which they had worked the particular contract since it was made in order to imply and determine the missing term . . .'

The presumption relating to sick pay is a strictly neutral one, and an industrial tribunal should approach the matter with an open mind unprejudiced by any preconception; *see Houman & Son* v. *Blyth* (1983). The written statement ought to specify the right of the employee, if any, to payment during absence from work due to sickness (*see* 2: 7).

5. Statutory Sick Pay (SSP). Since April 1983 all employers have had a statutory obligation under the Social Security and Housing Benefits Act 1982 to pay SSP to their employees for up to eight weeks sickness absence in any single tax year, or single period of sickness spanning two tax years. SSP is payable only to an 'employee'. For these purposes an employee is defined as a person over the age of sixteen who is 'gainfully employed in Great Britain either under a contract of service or in an office (including elective office) with emoluments chargeable to income tax under Schedule E': s. 26(1). Before an employee can become entitled to SSP three conditions must be met: there must be a period of incapacity for work (PIW); the PIW must fall within a period of entitlement; the day(s) of absence must be a qualifying day(s).

(*a*) *Period of Incapacity for Work.* A PIW is any period of four or more consecutive calendar days (including days on which the employee would not be required to be available for work e.g. bank holidays, weekends). The employee must be deemed incapable of working; this will normally mean that the employee must be suffering from physical or mental illness.

(*b*) *Period of Entitlement.* A period of entitlement is the period commencing with a PIW and which ends on the occurrence of one of the following events:

(*i*)   the termination of the PIW; *or*

(*ii*)   the employee's entitlement for SSP being exhausted; *or*

(*iii*) the end of the employee's contract of employment.

(*c*) *Qualifying days.* SSP is payable only in respect of 'qualifying days' in any PIW. Qualifying days must be agreed between employer and employee and usually these agreed days will reflect the normal pattern of the working week. SSP is paid from the fourth qualifying day and onwards of any PIW.

(*d*) *Rates of SSP*. At the time of writing SSP is payable at the following rates:

Weekly Earnings	Weekly SSP
£84.00 or more	£52.10
£43.00 to £84.00	£36.25
Less than £43.00	£ Nil

Many part-time employees earn over £43.00 per week and thus qualify for SSP.

(*e*) *Employer refuses to pay SSP*. If an employer refuses to pay SSP (e.g. because he does not believe that the employee has been genuinely ill) he is obliged on receipt of a reasonable request from the employee to give him written reasons within a reasonable time. The employee is entitled to refer the matter in writing within six months to an insurance officer who will give a written decision on the reference. Either employer or employee can appeal against his decision to the local DHSS office within 28 days and the appeal will be heard by a local Appeal Tribunal, with a further appeal to a Social Security Commissioner.

(*f*) *Entitlement where employee 'directly interested' in a trade dispute*. Under Schedule 1 of the Social Security and Housing Benefits Act 1982 an employee has no entitlement to SSP where he is directly interested in a trade dispute. Such a situation can arise where in one work place an employer deals with a number of trade unions, one of which becomes involved in a trade dispute with the employer. If the consequence of that trade dispute is that groups of workers other than those in the trade union with which the employer is in dispute are laid off, those other groups of workers are 'directly interested' providing two conditions are met. First, whatever the outcome of the dispute, it must be applied to all groups of workers (and not just to those belonging to the union participating in the dispute). Second, this application of the outcome of the dispute 'across the board' should come about automatically as a result of (*i*) a legally binding collective agreement, or (*ii*) a collective agreement which is not legally binding or (*iii*) established industrial custom and practice at the place of work concerned: *see Presho* v. *DHSS* (1984).

6. Effect of sickness. The effect of sickness on the employment relationship varies with the circumstances. Sickness on the part of an employee may justify an employer in terminating the employment: *see*, for example, *East Lindsey District Council* v. *Daubney* (1977). In addition, long-term sickness may have the effect of frustrating the contract (*see* 10: **13**).

To treat employees with trust and confidence

7. General principle. In recent years the tribunals and courts have developed a wide and somewhat indefinite mutual obligation upon each party to a contract of employment to treat the other with trust and confidence. The impetus for this development has come from the evolution of legal principles surrounding the doctrine of constructive dismissal following the decision of the Court of Appeal in *Western Excavating* v. *Sharp* (1975) (*see* 12: **6**). The limits of the duty are still expanding and have been variously described as below. What is important to note is the development of this concept in modern employment law.

In *Courtaulds Northern Textiles Ltd* v. *Andrew* (1978) the EAT held: '. . .there is an implied term in a contract of employment that employers will not, without reasonable and proper cause, conduct themselves in a manner calculated or likely to destroy or seriously damage the relationship of trust and confidence between the parties'. In *Woods* v. *W.M. Car Services (Peterborough) Ltd* (1981) Lord Denning said: '... It is the duty of the employer to be good and considerate to his servants. Sometimes it is formulated as an implied term not to do anything likely to destroy the relationship of confidence between them'.

The existence of such a term has again been recently approved by the Court of Appeal in *Bliss* v. *South East Thames Regional Health Authority* (1985) and *Lewis* v. *Motorworld Garages Ltd* (1985).

Holidays

8. Contractual position. The written statement supplied to employees under s. 1 of the 1978 Act ought to state the holidays to which the employee is entitled, and whether the employee is entitled to holiday pay (and if so, how much) by virtue of his contract of employment. If an employee is not entitled to a written statement or he does not receive one from his employer, the questions of holidays and holiday pay still rest upon the contract of employment but it may be more difficult to produce evidence of these rights. This will be changed by Clause 8 of the Employment Bill 1988.

9. Statutory provisions. There are relatively few statutory enactments in relation to holidays. However, the following provisions exist.

(*a*)   Section 94 of the Factories Act 1961 provides that women and young   persons who work in factories must have a holiday on the Bank Holidays.

(*b*)   Wages Councils and the Agricultural Wages Board have the power to fix holidays and holiday pay for workers in the industries over which they have jurisdiction (*see* 7: **8**).

Hours of work

10. Contractual position. The hours which an employee is required to work are determined by reference to his individual contract of employment and it should again be noted that the written statement supplied under s. 1 of the 1978 Act ought to state the position in respect of hours of work. The number of hours that may be contractually agreed is, however, limited by certain statutory provisions (*see* **11** below).

11. Statutory limits. Section 7 of the Sex Discrimination Act 1986 removes the majority of limitations imposed concerning the hours to be worked by women. The following provisions therefore only apply to young persons and there limitations are also to be repealed in the near future. Part VI of the Factories Act 1961 limits the working day to no more than nine hours per day (ten if the factory has a five-day week) or forty-eight in a week exclusive of meal-breaks and rest intervals. There is also legislation referring to particular industries, e.g. mines, *see* the Mines and Quarries Act 1954.

There are no general limitations on persons over the age of 18, but there are a number of specific restrictions imposed in respect of particular work, e.g. coach and lorry driving. Breach of these regulations is a criminal offence punishable by fine.

Time off work

12. For public duties. Section 29 of the 1978 Act provides that an employer must permit an employee to have time off work for the purpose of carrying out duties as:

    (*a*) a Justice of the Peace;

    (*b*) a member of a local authority;

    (*c*) a member of a statutory tribunal;

    (*d*) a member of a Regional Health Authority or an Area or District Health Authority;

    (*e*) a member of the governing body of a local authority maintained educational establishment;

    (*f*) a member of a water authority.

The amount of time off (which is without pay unless the contrary is agreed) to which the employee is entitled is such as is 'reasonable in all the circumstances' having regard to certain specified factors.

A number of categories of employees are excluded from this right: ss. 144 and 146 of the 1978 Act. An employee who considers that his right has been infringed may present a complaint to an industrial tribunal normally within three months. A tribunal has the power to make a declaration and award compensation: *see Corner* v. *Bucks CC* (1978).

13. For ante-natal care. Under s. 31A of the 1978 Act (inserted by the Employment Act 1980) a pregnant employee has the right not to be unreasonably refused time off work with pay in order that she may keep appointments for receiving ante-natal care. Evidence of pregnancy and of the appointment must be produced if requested by the employer. An employee who considers that this right has been infringed may present a complaint to an industrial tribunal (normally within three months of the appointment in question). If the tribunal finds the complaint well-founded it will make a declaration to that effect and award compensation: *see Gregory* v. *Tudsbury Ltd* (1982).

To indemnify employees

14. General principle. An employer is under an obligation to indemnify his employees in respect of any expenses incurred in performing their duties under the contract of employment, e.g. travelling expenses and liability incurred as a result of wrongs committed by employees for which the employer is vicariously liable.

15. Indemnity by employee. In certain circumstances, however, an employee may be under an obligation to indemnify the employer for the loss sustained: *Lister* v. *Romford Ice and Cold Storage Co. Ltd* (1957) (*see* 5: **8**).

To provide references

16. No duty to provide one. There is no obligation on an employer to supply character references for employees although, in practice, employers normally supply them since failure to provide one speaks for itself.

17. Legal effect of references. If an employer does provide a reference it ought to be correct for three specific reasons.

(*a*) *Defamation.* If a reference is defamatory, the defamed employee may bring an action against the employer, although the defence of qualified privilege is available to the employer, i.e. the employer may show that the statements were made without malice.

(*b*) *Negligent misstatement.* A person who acts in reliance on a reference which has been issued negligently may apparently bring an action to recover any loss sustained as a consequence: *Hedley Byrne and Co.* v. *Heller and Partners* (1964). However, the person issuing the reference may avoid liability if he disclaims legal responsibility for the reference, subject, of course, to the test of 'reasonableness' contained in s. 2(2) Unfair Contract Terms Act 1977 being satisfied.

The principle of negligent misstatement has recently been extended to the relationship between a referee and his former employee to whom the reference referred. In *Lawton* v. *BOC Transhield* (1987) L had worked for BOCT Ltd for 10 years before being made redundant. He was then employed by another company on a trial basis but, before it would take L on a permanent basis, it required a reference from BOCT Ltd. The reference alluded to an incident during the period of L's employment which resulted in a formal warning being given to him. No offer of permanent employment was made. It was held that BOCT Ltd had not in fact acted negligently as there was sufficient evidence to support their opinions. However, the judge stated that an employer providing a reference owes a duty to his former employee to take reasonable care to ensure that the opinions expressed therein are based on accurate facts and that any facts disclosed are correct.

Progress test 6

1. In what circumstances is an employer required to compensate an employee if he is not given work to do?   **(2, 3)**

2. In what circumstances is an employee entitled to receive statutory sick pay? What is his remedy if an employer refuses to pay SSP?   **(5)**

3. What limitations are imposed on the hours of work which an employee may undertake?   **(10, 11)**

4. In what circumstances is an employee entitled to time off work for public duties?   **(12)**

5. Jones is seeking employment with Y Ltd and asks his present employer, ABC Ltd, to supply him with a character reference. The reference is sent direct to Y Ltd and states that Jones is a drunkard, which is untrue. As a result, Jones is refused employment with Y Ltd. The reason why ABC Ltd said that Jones was a drunkard was because they did not wish him to leave their employment. Advise Jones.   **(17)**

7
Statutory regulation of remuneration

A number of legislative provisions exist affecting the amount of remuneration and the way in which it is paid. In addition, a number of relatively recent provisions provide for an employee to be paid by his employer when, for various reasons, the employee is unable to work. These different provisions are considered in this chapter.

Wages Act 1986

1. Introduction. Part I of the Act repeals the Truck Acts 1831–1940 and other enactments imposing restrictions on the payment of wages. The Act replaces them with a new regulatory system, based on the contract of employment. Redress, under the 1986 Act, is to an industrial tribunal whereas under the previous legislation any breach of regulations was a criminal offence.

2. Who is covered by the Act? The scope of the Act is wide. Section 8(1) states that a worker means an individual who has entered or works under a contract. Section 8(2) defines contracts as ones of service, apprenticeship and those under which a person undertakes to perform any work personally for the other party. Therefore, the Act is not limited to people working under a contract of employment.

3. What is meant by wages? The Act defines wages, s. 7, in very broad terms. Wages means 'any sums payable to a worker by his employer in connection with his employment and includes any fee, bonus, commission, holiday pay or other emolument referable to his employment, whether payable under his contract or otherwise. . . .'

However a number of payments are specifically excluded and these include expenses and redundancy payments. The definition is by no means clear and the question as to whether payment in lieu of notice is included in the definition of 'wages' remains unanswered.

4. Mode of payment. One of the effects of the Wages Act 1986, was to abolish the requirement that workers be paid in the 'coin of the realm'. Therefore, we now have the concept of 'cashless' pay. It may well be that an employee has the right — predating the Act — to be paid in cash and if this were unilaterally taken away then a claim for constructive dismissal may arise (*see* 12: 6). However consensual variation of contracts has dealt with this problem.

5. Deductions. Section 1 of the Act only allows a deduction from wages if it is made either by virtue of a statutory provision (for example income tax and national insurance contributions) or by a provision of the worker's contract, or if the worker has previously indicated his agreement in writing to it. The Act makes no provision as to whether the deduction should be fair or reasonable and the only limitation in amount applies to retail workers (*see* below). It should be noted in this context that the Act does not provide for deductions in respect of industrial action; *see Miles* v. *Wakefield MDC* (1987).

Sections 2 and 3 of the 1986 Act introduce much stricter controls on retail workers who are defined as being workers who carry out retail transactions directly with members of the public or with fellow workers. The definition includes collection of money in respect of retail transactions. Under the Act any deduction in respect of cash shortages or stock deficiencies must not exceed one-tenth of the gross amount of wages payable on that day. Also, any sum demanded of such a worker in respect of these losses shall not exceed the 10% figure. The limit only applies to deductions for the two reasons above, i.e. cash shortages or stock deficiencies.

Wages Councils

6. Introduction. The Wages Act 1986, s. 12, repeals the Wages Councils Act 1979. The 1986 Act does not actually abolish wages councils but retains existing councils and severely limits their powers, and the Secretary of State no longer has power to establish new wages councils. The rationale for these changes is twofold. Firstly, job recruitment will increase and secondly there will be less of a 'burden on business'.

7. Function of the councils Existing wages councils are limited to fixing a basic minimum hourly rate, overtime entitlement and a limit on deductions from pay that an employer can make for living accommodation. (A council will issue a wages order to this effect.) Section 12(2) of the 1986 Act removes young people under the age of 21 from the scope of the regulations.

8. Composition. A wages council consists of an equal number of members from both sides of the trade or industry in question. One of the employer representatives should represent a small business unless inappropriate. Not more than five members of a council, one of whom is the chairman, should be independent, and these are nominated by the Secretary of State.

9. Effect of a wages order. A wages order has a twofold effect.

(*a*) If an employer to whom the order applies fails to observe its terms, he is liable to criminal conviction punishable by fine.

(*b*) Any worker who is paid less than the order prescribes, may sue his employer for breach of contract of employment, because a wages order is deemed to be part of the contract of employment.

Guarantee payments

For the legislation governing guarantee payments, *see* ss. 12–18 of the 1978 Act as amended by s. 14 of the Employment Act 1980 and s. 20 and Schedule 2 of the Employment Act 1982.

10. Introduction. Unless a contract of employment expressly or implicitly allows for it, an employee who is laid off (i.e. sent home because there is no work to do) is entitled to be paid during the period of such lay-off. In recent times a number of collective agreements have made provision for guaranteed minimum earnings for employees in the event of a lay-off. In 1975, provisions were introduced whereby there is a minimum entitlement to pay during the time an employee is laid off. These provisions are now contained in ss. 12–18 of the 1978 Act as subsequently amended by the 1980 and 1982 Acts.

11. Basic provision. An employee is entitled to a guarantee payment in respect of any day during which he is not provided with work (a 'workless day') due to (*a*) a diminution in the requirements of the employer's business for work of the kind which he is employed to do; or (*b*) any other occurrence affecting the normal working of the employer's business in relation to work of that kind.

12. Eligibility. To be eligible to receive such a payment, an employee must:

   (*a*) have been continuously employed for at least one month when the lay-off occurs (note that those engaged on a fixed term contract for three months or less are excluded); and

   (*b*) have been laid off for the whole of his normal working hours on a day he is normally required to work in accordance with the contract of employment: *see Mailway (Southern) Ltd* v. *Willsher* (1978); and

   (*c*) not have unreasonably refused an offer of alternative employment which was suitable in all the circumstances; and

   (*d*) have complied with any reasonable requirements imposed by the employer with a view to ensuring that his services are available; and

   (*e*) not have been laid off because of a strike, lock-out or other industrial action involving any employee of the employer or of any associated employer; and

   (*f*) have been available for employment on that day.

13. Amount of payment. An employee who is entitled to a guarantee payment is entitled to be paid at the guaranteed hourly rate (a week's pay divided by the normal weekly working hours) for the number of normal working hours for the day he is laid off subject to a maximum limit for any one day (£11.85 at the time of writing). There is a maximum entitlement of five guarantee payments in any period of three months (i.e. the maximum entitlement of an employee in one year is twenty days at £11.85 per day).

NOTE: The relationship between the statutory provisions and any provisions in a contract of employment or collective agreement must be fully considered since each must be set off against the other.

14. Enforcement. If an employer fails to pay a guarantee payment, the employee may complain to an industrial tribunal, normally within three months. If the tribunal finds the complaint well-founded, it will order the employer to pay the employee the amount due.

15. Exemption. The Secretary of State may exempt from the operation of the above provisions those employees covered by a collective agreement or wages order containing provisions as to guaranteed remuneration. At the time of writing some twenty exemption orders have been made.

Note also that by virtue of ss. 144–6 of the 1978 Act a number of categories of employees are excluded from the operation of the guarantee payments provisions.

Suspension from work on medical grounds

For the legislation governing suspension from work on medical grounds, *see* ss. 19–22 of the 1978 Act as amended by the Employment Act 1982, and *see* Protection (Medical Suspension) Order 1985.

16. Basic provision. Sections 19–23 of the 1978 Act provide that an employee who is suspended from work is entitled to be paid by his employer if that suspension is in consequence of a requirement imposed under certain statutory provisions (listed in Schedule 1 of the 1978 Act) or a recommendation made in a Code of Practice issued or approved under s. 16 of the Health and Safety at Work etc. Act 1974. For example, under Regulation 6 of the Lead Paint Regulations 1927, an inspector must give notice to an employer requiring the suspension of employees if he is satisfied that the incidence of lead poisoning among a group of employees involved in painting is excessive. An employee suspended in consequence of such a notice is entitled to be paid during the period of suspension.

17. Eligibility. To be eligible for payment during such suspension, an employee must:

(a) have been continuously employed for at least one month by that employer (note that those engaged on a fixed term contract for three months or less are excluded); and

(b) not be incapable of work due to sickness; and

(c) not have unreasonably refused suitable alternative work; and

(d) not have refused to comply with reasonable requirements imposed by his employer with a view to ensuring that his services are available.

18. Payment. An employee is entitled to be paid for up to twenty-six weeks of such suspension. Contractual payments to which the employee is entitled are set off against the statutory right to payment and vice versa. If the employer fails to pay the employee, a complaint may be presented to an industrial tribunal normally within three months. If the tribunal finds the complaint well-founded, it will order the employer to pay the employee the amount due.

19. Additional. Two additional points should be noted.

(a) If instead of being suspended, an employee is dismissed on medical grounds of the kind specified in **16** above, the qualifying period for presenting a complaint of unfair dismissal is reduced to one month from two years (*see* generally Chapter 12).

(b) If the employer wishes to engage a temporary employee to replace the suspended employee, then provided the replacement employee is informed in writing that his employment will be terminated when the suspension has ended, the dismissal of the temporary employee in order to allow the suspended employee to return to work will be regarded as for a 'substantial reason' and, providing the employer acted reasonably, the dismissal will not be unfair: s. 61 of the 1978 Act.

Note also that by virtue of ss. 144–6 of the 1978 Act, a number of categories of employees are excluded from the above provisions.

Maternity pay and leave

For the legislation governing maternity pay and leave, see ss. 33–48 of the 1978 Act as amended by ss. 11 and 12 of the Employment Act 1980.

20. Basic provisions. An employee who is absent from work due to pregnancy or confinement is entitled to receive maternity pay from her employer. In addition, there is an *independent* right to return to work following confinement and a right not to be dismissed on grounds of pregnancy (*see* 12: **18**).

It should be noted that the drafting of the statutory provisions relating to maternity is exceedingly complex. In *Lavery* v. *Plessey Telecommunications Ltd* (1983) the Court of Appeal agreed with remarks made in the EAT that the provisions are of 'inordinate complexity, exceeding the worst excesses of a taxing statute; we find that especially regrettable bearing in mind that they are regulating the everyday rights of ordinary employers and employee'.

21. Eligibility for maternity pay. To be eligible for maternity pay an employee must:

(*a*) have continued to be employed by her employer, whether or not she is at work, until the beginning of the eleventh week before the expected week of confinement, or have been fairly dismissed because of her pregnancy prior to the eleventh week before the expected week of confinement (*see* 12: **18**)

NOTE. It does not matter that the employee has actually stopped working, for whatever reason, before the eleventh week, providing that the contract of employment subsists until the eleventh week; *see Satchwell Sunvic Ltd* v. *Secretary of State for Employment* (1979) and *Secretary of State for Employment* v. *Doulton Sanitaryware Ltd* (1981)

Pregnant employees are entitled to time off work for ante natal care: (*see* 6: **13**).

(*b*) have been (or would have been in the case of an employee who has been fairly dismissed because of her pregnancy) continuously employed for at least two years at the beginning of the eleventh week before the expected week of confinement; and

(c) have notified her employer (in writing if requested) at least twenty-one days before her absence begins (or as soon as reasonably practicable thereafter) that she will be absent from work because of pregnancy; and

(d) if asked by her employer to do so, have produced a medical certificate confirming the expected week of confinement.

22. Amount of maternity pay. An employee who fulfils the conditions in **21** above is entitled to six weeks' maternity pay, payment being for the first six weeks of her absence after the eleventh week before the expected week of confinement. It should be noted that providing an employee continues to work until the eleventh week before the expected week of confinement, she is entitled to start the paid leave at any time after that: *see ILEA* v. *Nash* (1979). The amount for each week for this purpose is 90 per cent of a week's pay less the maternity allowance payable under the Social Security Act 1975 whether or not the employee actually receives such allowance. Where an employee is entitled to maternity pay from two employers, state maternity allowance must be deducted by each employer in their maternity pay evaluation, even though the allowance if paid, is paid only once: *Cullen* v. *Creasey Hotels (Limbury) Ltd* (1980). Any remuneration to which she is contractually entitled is set off against the statutory payment, and vice versa. If the employer fails to pay maternity pay to which an employee is entitled, she may present a complaint to an industrial tribunal, normally within three months. If the tribunal finds the complaint well-founded, it will order the employer to pay the amount due.

23. Maternity Pay Fund. An employer who has paid maternity pay in accordance with the above provisions may recover the full amount so paid from the Maternity Pay Fund which is financed by Class 1 social security contributions. Disputes relating to the rebate are dealt with by an industrial tribunal. If an employer pays maternity pay to an employee who is not entitled to it (e.g. because she does not satisfy the statutory requirements) then the employer is not entitled to a rebate from the Fund.

24. Eligibility for the right to return to work. To be eligible to exercise the right to return to work following pregnancy or confinement, an employee must fulfil the same conditions as for maternity pay (*see* **21** above) and, in addition, she must inform her employer in writing at least twenty-one days prior to her absence, or as soon as reasonably practicable thereafter:

(*a*) that she will be absent from work wholly or partly because of pregnancy or confinement,

(*b*) that she intends to return to work, and

(*c*) of the expected week of confinement.

In addition the employer may write to the employee not earlier than forty-nine days after the beginning of her expected week of confinement (or the date of confinement) asking her to provide written confirmation of her intention to return and informing her that failure to reply will result in the loss of her right to return. The employee must reply to the request within fourteen days or, if that is not reasonably practicable, as soon as reasonably practicable. It is thought that the inability of the employee to make up her mind as to whether or not she wishes to return to work is not a sufficient reason for failure to reply within fourteen days: *see Nu-Swift International Ltd* v. *Mallison* (1978).

25. The right to return. An employee who has been absent from work because of pregnancy or confinement is entitled to return to work in the job in which she was employed under the original contract of employment on terms and conditions no less favourable than would have been applicable had she not been absent. The right can be exercised at any time before the end of twenty-nine weeks from the *actual* week of confinement, and not the expected week of confinement previously notified to the employer: *Lavery* v. *Plessey Telecommunications Ltd* (1983). If it is not practicable for the employer to permit her to return because of redundancy she is entitled to be offered, if available, suitable alternative employment (i.e. of a kind which is suitable for her in relation to the nature and place of employment on terms and conditions not substantially less favourable than the previous employment). If the employer can show that there was no suitable vacancy for the woman whose job has disappeared because of redundancy, she will be entitled to a redundancy payment (*see* 13: **14**). If she refuses a suitable vacancy, she has no such entitlement; *see Community Task Force* v. *Rimmer* (1986).

If it is not reasonably practicable for a reason other than redundancy for the employer to permit her to return in accordance with these provisions but the employer offers her suitable alternative employment (as defined above) which she either accepts or unreasonably refuses, there is deemed to be no 'dismissal' in such circumstances and consequently no action will lie. In addition, if the number of employees employed by that employer (and associated employers) did not exceed six at the time her absence began and for any reason it is not reasonably practicable for the employer to permit her to return to work or to offer suitable alternative employment (as defined above), there is deemed to be no 'dismissal' and consequently no action for unfair dismissal or a redundancy payment will lie: s. 56A of the 1978 Act (inserted by s. 12 of the 1980 Act).

If she is not allowed to return to work in breach of her right to do so, or if she is redundant and not offered a suitable vacancy, that is treated as an unfair dismissal (*see* generally Chapter 12) unless the employer acted reasonably in so doing because of something that had happened during the employee's absence. It should be noted that if there is also a contractual right to return to work following maternity leave, the employee may exercise that right but the employee is not entitled to combine the statutory and contractual rights and take the most advantageous parts of each: *see Bovey* v. *Board of Governors of the Hospital for Sick Children* (1978).

One of the difficulties that have arisen in recent cases (see *Kelly* v. *Liverpool Maritime Terminals Ltd* (1988)) is the status of the employee's contract during her maternity leave. It now seems accepted that the contract of employment subsists during the maternity leave unless it can be shown either that the employee has resigned, or that the employer has ended the contract by dismissing the employee.

An employer may postpone an employee's return to work for up to four weeks for any specified reason, as long as he notifies her, before the day on which she had proposed to return, of the reasons and the day on which she may return.

26. Delaying the return. An employee may delay her return beyond the twenty-ninth week after the actual date of confinement in two situations:

(a) where she is ill and unable to recommence employment. The postponement of the return can be for up to four weeks and can be exercised once only: and

(b) where there is an interruption of work (because of industrial action or some other reason) which renders it unreasonable to expect the employee to return on the notified day. Her return is to be delayed until the interruption has ceased.

27. Temporary replacements. By virtue of s. 61 of the 1978 Act, if an employer engages a temporary employee to replace an employee on maternity leave, then, provided that the replacement employee is informed in writing that the employment will be terminated when the woman returns, the dismissal of the temporary employee in order to allow the woman to return will be regarded as for a 'substantial reason' and, providing that the employer acted reasonably, the dismissal will not be unfair.

28. Importance of 'continuous' employment. The right to maternity leave and the right to return, as provided for by ss. 33–48 of the 1978 Act, depend on whether or not the employee had worked for two or more years continuously. Does an employee have any such rights in the absence of such continuous employment? Any such claim would have to be in sex discrimination (*see* Chapter 9). The tribunals have stated that the test is whether a man in similar circumstances, for example having to take substantial time off for sickness, would have been treated more favourably. In *Maughan* v. *North East London Magistrates' Court Committee* (1985) M had been employed as a trainee court clerk for six weeks when she discovered she was pregnant. She proposed finishing her six months probationary period, taking four and a half months unpaid leave and then finishing her training.The employers rejected this proposal and dismissed her. There was evidence that the employers had not dismissed a man who had asked for similar unpaid leave. It was held that her dismissal was unfair on grounds of unlawful sex discrimination because a man was treated more favourably. Further the employers admitted that there was no reason why she could not have recommenced her training after the birth of the child.

Itemised pay statements

29. Basic provision. Every employee has the right to an itemised pay statement giving particulars of:

    (*a*) the gross amount of pay;

    (*b*) the amount of variable deductions and their purpose, e.g. income tax;

    (*c*) the amount of any fixed deductions, e.g. trade union contributions;

    (*d*) thenet amount of pay and, where different parts of the net pay are paid in different ways, the amount and method of each part payment.

However, the employer need not provide an itemised list of fixed deductions if he has issued the employee with a standing statement of fixed deductions containing all relevant information. In this case, provided the standing statement is kept up-to-date and reissued at least once a year, the pay statement need only include the aggregate amount of fixed deductions.

30. Complaint to industrial tribunal. If an employer fails to provide a complete and accurate pay statement, an employee may complain to an industrial tribunal, normally within three months. The tribunal, if it finds the complaint well-founded, may issue a declaration as to the particulars which ought to be included and award the employee the amount of any unnotified deductions which have been made within the thirteen weeks preceding the date of application to the tribunal: *see Milsom* v. *Leicestershire County Council* (1978) and *Scott* v. *Creager* (1979). By virtue of ss. 144 and 146 of the 1978 Act, certain categories of employees are excluded from these provisions.

Insolvency of employer

For the legislation governing the insolvency of an employer, *see* ss. 121–7 of the 1978 Act as amended by the Employment Act 1980 and the Employment Act 1982. *See* also s. 175 and Schedule 6 of the Insolvency Act 1986.

31. Basic provisions. If an employer becomes insolvent an employee acquires certain rights.

(*a*) He becomes a preferential creditor in respect of up to four months' unpaid wages or a maximum set by the Secretary of State;

(*b*) Certain other payments are also deemed to be preferential debts including guarantee payments, payment for time off for trade union activities and payment for ante-natal care.

(*c*) The employee is entitled to claim payment of certain amounts due to him from his employer from the Secretary of State who will pay them out of the Redundancy Fund. The Secretary of State needs to be satisfied that the employer is insolvent and that the employee was entitled to these debts. The classes of debt for which payment may be made include arrears of wages (up to a maximum of 8 weeks), holiday pay (up to a maximum of 6 weeks) and wages during the statutory minimum notice period.

(*d*) The employee has the right to ask the Secretary of State to make up any contributions to an occupational pension scheme which have not been paid because of the employer's insolvency.

NOTE: Depending on the circumstances of the case, any social security benefits received by an ex-employee while unemployed following the insolvency of an employer may be taken into account when determining certain classes of payment from the Redundancy Fund: *see Westwood* v. *Secretary of State for Employment* (1982).

32. Complaint to an industrial tribunal. If an employee has been refused a payment, or received less than the due sum from the Secretary of State, he may complain to an industrial tribunal, normally within three months of the communication of the decision of the Secretary of State. Where the tribunal finds that the Secretary of State ought to have made a payment, it will issue a declaration to that effect stating the amount of any payment which it finds ought to have been made. By virtue of ss. 144–6 of the 1978 Act, certain categories of employees are excluded from these provisions.

Progress test 7

1. What deductions may be lawfully made from the wages of an employee covered by the Wages Act 1986 and in what circumstances may such deductions be made? **(1–5)**

2. Smith is offered a job as a labourer by X Ltd but he is told that he must agree to be paid by cheque since the payment system of the firm is computerised. Is this lawful? **(4)**

3. What powers and functions do the Wages Councils possess? **(6, 7)**

4. How is a wages order enforced? **(9)**

5. In what circumstances is an employee eligible to receive a guarantee payment? **(12)**

6. What conditions must be satisfied before an employee is entitled to receive maternity pay? **(21)**

7. Explain the rules relating to exercising the right to return to work following pregnancy or confinement. **(25)**

8. What information must be contained in an itemised pay statement? **(29)**

9. What rights does an employee acquire on the insolvency of his employer? **(31)**

8

Rights of employees regarding trade unions

In this chapter references are to the Employment Protection (Consolidation) Act 1978 ('the 1978 Act') as amended by the Employment Acts 1980 and 1982 ('the 1980 Act and the 1982 Act'). It should be noted in particular that s. 23 of the 1978 Act has been substantially amended by the Acts of 1980 and 1982, and s. 58 of the 1978 Act was substituted by s. 3 of the 1982 Act. The Employment Act 1988 has further altered the law in this area. Changes have been made regarding closed shop dismissals (see below) and s. 3 of the 1988 Act restricts trade unions taking disciplinary action against members who have not taken part in industrial action (*see* 15: **20** below). It should also be noted that further government legislation will be forthcoming in this area.

Introduction

1. General. The 1978 Act contains a number of rights as regards trade union membership and activities. These may be classified as follows:

(*a*) The right to be a member of an independent trade union.

(*b*) The right not to be a member of a trade union, whether independent or not.

(*c*) The right to participate in the activities of an independent trade union.

(*d*) The right to time off work for trade union duties.

(*e*) The right to time off work for trade union activities.

2. Independent trade union. The rights dealt with in this chapter largely depend upon whether the trade union in question is 'independent' and in certain cases as to whether the trade union is 'recognised'. These terms are considered at 15: **6** and 16: **5** respectively.

Right to be a member

3. Basic principle. The dismissal of an employee will be regarded as unfair if the reason for the dismissal is that he is or proposes to become a member of an independent trade union: s. 58 of the 1978 Act (*see* 12: **19**). In addition, every employee has the right not to have action short of dismissal taken against him by his employer for the purpose of 'preventing or deterring him from being or seeking to become a member of an independent trade union, or penalising him for doing so': s. 23(1)(a) of the 1978 Act. Thus in *Carlson* v. *The Post Office* (1981) it was held that the refusal of an employer to issue a parking permit to a member of an independent, but unrecognised, trade union was enough to 'penalise' the employee.

4. Complaint to industrial tribunal. A complaint may be presented to an industrial tribunal normally within three months by an employee alleging that his employer has infringed the right under s. 23. If the tribunal finds the complaint well-founded (no account being taken of any pressure exerted on the employer), the tribunal may issue a declaration and award such compensation as is 'just and equitable' having regard to certain specified factors: *see Brassington* v. *Cauldon Wholesale Ltd.* (1978) and *Cheall* v. *Vauxhall Motors Ltd* (1979). There is no qualifying period of continuous employment necessary to support a complaint under these provisions.

Right not to be a member

5. Basic principle. If an employee is dismissed because he is not a member of a trade union (whether independent or not), or because he refuses to become a member, such dismissal is unfair: s. 58(1)(c) of the 1978 Act (*see* 12: **19**). Similarly he has the right not to have action short of dismissal taken against him for the purpose of compelling him to become a member of a trade union (whether independent or not): s. 23(1) of the 1978 Act. Where a union membership agreement as defined by the legislation (*see* 12: **20**) is in existence, the above rights are modified. Section 11 of the Employment Act 1988, repeals the previous legislation contained in the 1978 Act, and makes it automatically unfair to take action short of dismissal against a person because of their refusal to join a union in accordance with a union membership agreement. The remedy is by way of complaint to an industrial tribunal.

6. Union membership agreements and the right not to join. Section 11 of the Employment Act 1988 repeals the previous legislation on this subject and s. 11(a) makes it automatically unfair to dismiss an employee for a reason relating to non-membership of a union, irrespective of whether the closed shop is supported by a ballot (*see* 12: **20**).

Right to take part in trade union activities

7. Basic principle. The dismissal of an employee will be regarded as unfair if the reason for the dismissal is that he wishes to take part in the activities of an independent trade union at an appropriate time: s. 58 of the 1978 Act (*see* 12: **19**). In addition every employee has the right not to have action short of dismissal taken against him by his employer for the purpose of 'preventing or deterring him from taking part in the activities of an independent trade union at any appropriate time, or penalising him for doing so': s. 23(1)(b) of the 1978 Act. Although 'activities' are not defined in the statute, such activities as voting in union elections and attending union meetings are clearly included. There is an important distinction between the individual activities of an employee as a trade unionist and the activities of a trade union which affect individual employees. In *Therm A Stor Ltd* v. *Atkins* (1983) the Court of Appeal held that employees who were dismissed in retaliation for attempts by a trade union to be recognised for collective bargaining purposes were not protected by s. 58. That provision is concerned solely with the dismissal of an employee for his activities, not with the dismissal of an employee for the activities of the union itself.

The Court of Appeal has recently interpreted the meaning of s. 23 in *Ridgway and Fairbrother* v. *National Coal Board* (1987). In this case the two applicants complained that they did not receive a pay increase because of their membership of the National Union of Mineworkers, when members of the Union of Democratic Mineworkers had received increased pay. The Court of Appeal held that (*i*) the action had affected the two members as individuals as they had been directly affected, i.e. they had lost pay; (*ii*) s. 23 outlaws not only action to deter trade union membership in general but also membership of a particular union.

The term 'appropriate time' in s. 58 of the 1978 Act refers to time which is outside working hours or inside working hours if, by arrangement agreed or consent given, it is permissible for the employee to take part in the activities at that time: see *Robb* v. *Leon Motor Services Ltd* (1978) and *Dixon* v. *West Ella Developments Ltd* (1978).

NOTE: Although in a proper case consent may be implied, an employer's consent is not to be deduced from mere silence: *Marley Tile Co. Ltd* v. *Shaw* (1980).

As regards use of the employer's facilities for participating in activities, if there is a 'union membership agreement' in force (*see* 12: **20**), the employees covered by it only have the right to take part in trade union activities on the employer's premises if the trade union in question is a party to, or specified in, the agreement. However, an employer should allow trade union members to hold a meeting on his premises unless this would cause undue inconvenience: *Carter* v. *Wiltshire County Council* (1979).

8. Complaint to industrial tribunal. In the event of an employee alleging that the employer has infringed his right to participate in trade union activities, a complaint may be made to an industrial tribunal in respect of action short of dismissal and dealt with as in 4 above.

Time off work for trade union duties and activities

9. Trade union duties. An employer must permit an employee who is an official, i.e. a person 'elected or appointed in accordance with the rules of the union to be a representative of its members', of an independent trade union recognised by him for collective bargaining purposes, to have 'reasonable' time off work with pay during working hours to enable the employee to carry out duties which are concerned with industrial relations between the employer and employees, and to undergo training relevant to those duties (the training having been approved by the Trades Union Congress or by the trade union of which he is an official): s. 27 of the 1978 Act. The Advisory, Conciliation and Arbitration Service has prepared a Code of Practice (Number 3 — 'Time off for trade union duties and activities') dealing with the amount of time off which should be permitted and related matters (*see* 1: **12**).

The tribunals and courts have given a wide interpretation to those duties concerned with industrial relations which are covered by the right to time off work. In *Beal* v. *Beecham Group Ltd* (1982) it was held that the duties of a union official extended beyond actual collective bargaining activity with an employer and were capable of embracing work done in preparation for such negotiations. Accordingly, attendance of a union official at a conference held for the purpose of determining national bargaining policies was held to be a trade union duty for the purposes of the provisions.

However, the nature of the activities must be of direct relevance to industrial relations between the employer and employee. This principle was illustrated by the decision in *British Bakeries (Northern) Ltd* v. *Adlington* (1989). A and another person attended a meeting, organised by their trade union, concerning a proposed repeal of the Baking Industry (Hours of Work) Act 1954. The Act is an integral part of the collective agreement governing the industry. A claimed that the meeting was 'concerned with industrial relations'. The Court of Appeal held that there was sufficient proximity to industrial relations as any repeal would affect the relationship between employer and employee. Further, an employee, in order to qualify for paid time off, must give his employer adequate notice and information: *Poole* v. *Plessey Nottingham* (1988).

Clause 10 of the Employment Bill limits the right to paid time off to matters for which the union is recognised by the employer. One of these matters is terms and conditions of employment.

10. Trade union activities. An employer must permit an employee who is a member of a recognised independent trade union (i.e. recognised for collective bargaining purposes) to have 'reasonable' time off, not necessarily with pay, during working hours for the purpose of taking part in the activities of that trade union, e.g. attendance at meetings, regard being had to the ACAS Code of Practice (*see* 9 above). This provision expressly excludes time off for taking industrial action: s. 28 of the 1978 Act.

11. Complaint to an industrial tribunal. Failure to permit an employee time off under ss. 27 or 28 gives rise to a right to complain to an industrial tribunal, normally within three months. If the tribunal finds the complaint well-founded, it may make a declaration and award compensation.

Progress test 8

1. What rights does an employee have as regards being a member of a trade union?   (3)

2. What powers does an industrial tribunal have if it finds a complaint under s. 23 of the 1978 Act well-founded?   (4)

3. What is the extent of the right not to be a member of a trade union?   (5)

4. In what circumstances is an employee entitled to exercise his right to take part in trade union activities on the employer's premises?   (7)

5. In what circumstnces is an employee entitled to time off work to carry out trade union duties?   (9)

6. Explain when an employee is entitled to time off work to participate in trade union activities.   (10)

9
Discrimination in employment

Introduction

1. Scope of the chapter. In this chapter a number of Acts of Parliament are considered, together with associated regulations. The earlier enactments have been subject to considerable amendment by subsequent legislation and it is important to refer to the amended, rather than the original, legislation.

The enactments which will be considered are the Equal Pay Act 1970 (as amended by the Sex Discrimination Act 1975 and the Equal Pay (Amendment) Regulations 1983), the Sex Discrimination Act 1975 (as amended by the Sex Discrimination Act 1986) and the Race Relations Act 1976. It should be noted that although these Acts are concerned with eliminating discrimination on certain grounds in a number of areas, this chapter is concerned with their impact in the context of employment.

2. 1970 and 1975 Acts. In broad terms, the Equal Pay Act 1970 is concerned with less favourable treatment of a person of one sex as compared to the other in respect of matters (pay and other terms and conditions) governed by the contract under which a person is employed whereas the Sex Discrimination Act 1975 deals with less favourable treatment in matters not governed by the contract (e.g. selection, training, promotion, dismissal, etc.) on grounds of sex and/or marital status. Thus the two Acts are designed to be mutually exclusive but complementary.

Some appreciation of the policies underpinning the above enactments is of assistance in appreciating how they operate. In the case of equal pay the growing number of women in the nation's workforce and the fact that historically women's earnings are, on average, considerably lower than those of men, have provided the twin pressures leading to our equal pay legislation (although it must be remembered that the Act applies to men and women). In the case of discrimination on grounds of sex, traditional stereotyping has always worked to the disadvantage of women in employment. Undoubtedly some progress has been made as a result of the Equal Pay Act 1970 and the Sex Discrimination Act 1975. It is also true that such progress has been much more limited than many would have hoped for and that a number of difficulties remain.

3. 1976 Act. In broad terms, the Race Relations Act 1976 is concerned with discrimination on grounds of 'colour, race, nationality or ethnic or national origin' in the same areas of employment covered by the Sex Discrimination Act. The Act follows closely many of the provisions relating to sex discrimination in the 1975 Act.

Equal pay

4. The Equal Pay Act 1970 and the Treaty of Rome. The influence of the Treaty of Rome and the effect of certain European Community Directives have been considerable in this area and have significant practical consequences for any applicant contemplating bringing an action alleging breach of the 1970 Act.

Article 119 of the Treaty of Rome provides that: 'Each Member State shall ... maintain the application of the principle that men and women should receive equal pay for equal work. For the purpose of this Article, pay means the ordinary basic or minimum wage or salary and any other consideration, whether in cash or kind, which the worker receives, directly or indirectly, in respect of his employment from his employer.'

The Article is directly enforceable by individuals in the courts of member states of the EEC: *see Defrenne* v. *Société Anonyme Belge de Navigation Aérienne (SABENA)* (1976). Accordingly, if the domestic legislation of a member state in relation to equal pay falls short of the standards required by Article 119, an individual may be able to plead the Article: *see,* for example, *Macarthys Ltd* v. *Smith*

(1980). However, it is important to realise that the relationship between Article 119 and our own domestic law is complex, and a detailed survey of the problematic issues is beyond the scope of this book.

The prevailing uncertainty in this area is perhaps best demonstrated by the different reasoning adopted in achieving the same result in the Court of Appeal and House of Lords in *Pickstone* v. *Freemans Plc* (1988). The Court of Appeal in that case ruled that, because of the detailed drafting of the amended 1970 Act, the applicant was not entitled to succeed under the Act, but *was* entitled to succeed in her claim under Article 119. One effect of this ruling was that is seemed that s. 1(2)(c) of the Act failed to meet the UK's obligations under Article 119. The House of Lords, however, interpreted s. 1(2)(c) in such a way as to allow the applicant to succeed, thus ensuring that the UK's treaty obligations were met. In other words, the relationship between the two systems of law still contains some uncertainty in this area. However, it suffices to say that in any case where the interpretation of the Equal Pay Act (or, in some circumstances, the Sex Discrimination Act 1975) falls to be decided, the courts and tribunals will endeavour to interpret the domestic statutes so as to give effect to Article 119: *see Garland* v. *British Rail Engineering* (1982) and *Pickstone* v. *Freemans Plc* (1988).

The application of Article 119 in conjunction with an EC Directive of 1975 (the Equal Pay Directive), which clarified the obligations under Article 119, in *Commission of European Communities* v. *The United Kingdom* (1982) led directly to parliamentary approval of the Equal Pay (Amendment) Regulations 1983 which amended the Equal Pay Act to bring UK law into line with its European obligations.

5. Scope of the Act. Despite its short title, the 1970 Act is designed to secure equal treatment as between men and women not only as regards pay but also as regards other terms and conditions e.g. sick pay, mortgage schemes: (*Sun Alliance and London Insurance Ltd* v. *Dudman* (1978)).

Certain terms are, however, excluded from the operation of the Act.

(*a*) Terms 'affected by compliance with the laws regulating the employment of women': s. 6(1)(a). It should be noted, however, that the effect of s. 7 of the Sex Discrimination Act 1986 is to repeal parts of the Hours of Employment (Conventions) Act 1936, the Mines and Quarries Act 1954 and the Baking Industry (Hours of Work) Act 1954 which contained discriminatory provisions in relation to women. The consequence is that s. 6(1)(a) of the 1970 Act is unlikely to be used significantly in the future.

(b) Terms 'affording special treatment to women in connection with pregnancy or childbirth': s. 6(1)(b): *Coyne* v. *Exports Credits Guarantee Department* (1981). Thus, for example, a man cannot claim paternity leave if a woman's contract allows for maternity leave.

(c) Terms 'related to death or retirement, or to provision made in connection with death or retirement': s. 6(1A)(b). It should be noted, however, that under s. 6(1A)(a) it is provided that an equality clause 'shall operate in relation to terms relating to membership of an occupational pensions scheme'.

Some tension has arisen over the relationship between Article 119 of the Treaty of Rome and s. 6(1A). Article 119 requires that: 'Each Member State shall . . . maintain the application of the principle that men and women should receive equal pay for equal work.' In *Worringham* v. *Lloyds Bank* (1982) male and female staff were required to join occupational pension schemes; once over the age of 25 the treatment of men and women was the same, but below that age men, but not women, were required to contribute five per cent of their salary to the pension scheme. To compensate for this difference men under the age of 25 received a five per cent addition to their gross pay; this had the consequence that men under 25 had a higher gross salary for the purpose of calculating certain benefits, such as redundancy payments and mortgage facilities. Also, if a male employee left Lloyds Bank his contributions were returned, whereas if a woman left under the age of 25 there was no refund. Following a reference by the Court of Appeal the European Court of Justice held that a contribution to a retirement benefits scheme which is paid by the employer in the name of the employees by means of an addition to the gross salary and which helps to determine the amount of that salary is 'pay' under Article 119. The Court of Appeal subsequently gave effect to the judgment of the European Court of Justice in the instant case, by declaring that on terminating their employment with the Bank female employees were entitled to be paid a sum equal to the refund of pension contributions they would have received had they been male employees (although differential retirement ages for men and women are not unlawful).

Note that the operation of the Act includes employees, the self-employed and those in Crown employment but not the armed forces. While the Act is expressed in the female, it applies equally to men: s. 1(3). It covers persons of all ages: s. 11(2).

6. How the Act works. The Act uses the device of the 'equality clause': 'if the terms of a contract under which a woman is employed at an establishment in Great Britain do not include (directly or by reference to a collective agreement or otherwise) an equality clause they shall be deemed to include one': s. 1(1).

The effect of the equality clause is to give a woman the right to equal pay with a man when:

(a) the woman is employed on 'like work' with a man in the same employment: s. 1(2)(a); or

(b) the work she is doing is 'work rated as equivalent' with that of a man following a job evaluation study: s. 1(2)(b); s. 1(5). However, there is no requirement that a job evaluation study be carried out where an employer did not consent;

(c) the work the woman is doing is of 'equal value', in terms of the demands made upon her, to that of a man in the same employment: s. 1(2)(c).

Inclusion of the deemed equality clause based on 'like' work and 'work rated as equivalent' has been in the Equal Pay Act 1970 from its inception, but a clause based on work of 'equal value' is more recent in origin and has an interesting history. In 1975 the Council of the EC issued a Directive on equal pay which had the effect of clarifying the obligations owed by member states under Article 119 of the Treaty of Rome. Article 1 of the Directive states: 'The principle of equal pay for men and women outlined in Article 119 of the Treaty . . . means, for the same work or for work to which equal value is attributed, the elimination of all discrimination on grounds of sex with regard to all aspects and conditions of remuneration.' The effect of the Directive was to require all member states to introduce suitable legislation to give effect to the requirements of the Directive.

In *Commission of European Communities* v. *The United Kingdom* (1982) enforcement proceedings were brought before the European Court of Justice alleging that the UK had failed to fulfil its obligations under the Directive. The Commission argued that the Directive required that a woman receive equal pay for work which, although different from that of a man, is of equal value, even where no job evaluation study had been carried out. The Court held that the UK had failed in its obligations in that no compulsory procedures existed to ensure equal pay where work of equal value was being done. Accordingly, in the Equal Pay (Amendment) Regulations 1983 the third strand to the equality clause, based on work of equal value, was introduced. This is considered further at 9 below.

7. Like work. Under s. 1(2)(*a*) a woman is entitled to equal pay as a man 'where the woman is employed on like work with a man in the same employment'. Section 1(4) defines 'like work' in the following terms. 'A woman is to be regarded as employed in like work with men if, but only if, her work and theirs is of the same or a broadly similar nature and the differences (if any) between the things she does and the things they do are not of practical importance in relation to terms and conditions of employment: and accordingly in comparing her work and theirs regard shall be had to the frequency or otherwise with which any such differences occur in practice as well as to the nature and extent of the differences.'

The wording of s. 1(4) is intended to prevent irrelevant or insignificant differences being used to justify not paying equal pay. Alleged 'additional responsibilities' which are said to justify different pay rates must be real. In interpreting s. 1(4) the courts and tribunals have adopted a fairly broad approach.

Capper Pass Ltd v. *Lawton* (1977): L was a cook in the kitchen from which the directors of the company were served. She worked a forty-hour week cooking lunches for a small number of people. She sought equal pay with an assistant chef who worked a forty-five hour week in the company's canteen preparing different meals on a large scale. Held: she was entitled to an equal hourly rate of pay because the differences were 'peripheral'. The Employment Appeal Tribunal said that the correct approach to s. 1(4) was to ask the following:

(a) is the work of the same or a broadly similar nature? This must be answered by a general consideration of the two kinds of work;

(b) are any differences which do exist of 'practical importance'? If the answer to this is 'no', it is 'like work'.

Phillips J said that the industrial tribunals should disregard 'trivial differences' and should not undertake too minute an examination or be constrained to find that work is not like merely because of 'insubstantial differences'.

Dugdale v. *Kraft Foods Ltd* (1976). Held: the time at which work is performed should be disregarded when considering whether there is 'like work' and thus a woman's claim for equal pay with a male quality control inspector succeeded even though the men were required to work shifts. The fact that the men worked shifts could be dealt with by paying a shift premium when shifts were actually worked.

Coombes (Holdings) v. *Shields* (1978): a female counter-hand employed in a betting shop claimed equal pay with a man doing the same work. The employer said that the man was paid more because he was required to deal with any trouble which arose. Held: on the facts, this did not justify a finding that the man and the woman were not doing 'like work' and hence the woman was entitled to equal pay. *See also Eaton* v. *Nuttall* (1977).

The following general points should also be noted:

(a) A woman may compare herself with any man employed by the employer at that establishment if she is doing 'like work' (or 'work rated as equivalent') and not merely the man with whom the employer says she should compare herself: *Ainsworth* v. *Glass Tubes and Components Ltd* (1977). It is clearly sensible for the woman to choose a reasonably typical comparator. If the chosen comparator is untypical the employer may be able to rely on the 'genuine material difference' defence: *see* 10 below; but it must be emphasised that the chosen comparator has to be representative of a number of other workers: *see Thomas* v. *National Coal Board* (1987).

(b) Comparison may be made with an ex-employee whom the

woman has replaced provided the interval between the employments was short: *Macarthys Ltd* v. *Smith (No. 1)* (1978). But note that a change in the volume of work which leads to the dismissal of a male predecessor may provide the employer with a defence: *Albion Shipping Agency* v. *Arnold* (1981).

(c) The doctrine of *res judicata* applies to equal pay applications, i.e. unless it can be shown that there has been some appreciable change in the facts, a woman cannot bring a second application for equal pay if an industrial tribunal has decided against it: *McLoughlin* v. *Gordons (Stockport) Ltd* (1978).

8. 'Work rated as equivalent.' There is no obligation upon an employer to carry out a job evaluation or work rating exercise but if he does do so within the definition of s. 1(5), he is obliged to pay equal pay etc. if a woman's work is rated as equivalent with that of a man employed at the same establishment. Section 1(5) states that: 'A woman is to be regarded as employed on work rated as equivalent with that of any men if, but only if, her job and their job have been given an equal value, in terms of the demand made on a worker under various headings (for instance effort, skill, decision) . . . or would have been given an equal value but for the evaluation being made on a system setting different values for men and women on the same demand under any heading.'

Where such a claim is made by a woman, she must establish that it satisfies the requirements of s. 1(5): *England* v. *Bromley London Borough Council* (1978). The industrial tribunal must then apply it unless it is shown that there was a fundamental error or a plain mistake on the face of the record: *Green* v. *Broxstowe District Council* (1977).

Once a job evaluation study has been carried out it will be regarded as binding on the employer for the purposes of the Equal Pay Act, even though he has not implemented it: *O'Brien* v. *Sim Chem Ltd* (1980). But *see also Arnold* v. *Beecham Group Ltd* (1982).

9. 'Work . . . of equal value to that of a man in the same employment.' Under s. 1(2)(c) of the 1970 Act (added by the Equal Pay (Amendment) Regulations 1983: *see* 6 above) an equality clause is to be implied into a contract of employment: 'Where a woman is employed on work which . . . is, in terms of the demands made on her (for instance under such leadings as effort, skill and decision), of equal value to that of a man in the same employment . . .' This clause applies only where the provisions relating to 'like work' and 'work rated as equivalent' do not apply.

The procedure which an industrial tribunal must follow where a reference has been made under s. 1(2)(c) is governed by s. 2A of the 1970 Act (added by the 1983 Regulations). The tribunal must not determine any dispute as to whether any work is of equal value unless either:

(a) there are no reasonable grounds for determining that the work is of equal value (in which case the complaint will simply be dismissed); or

(b) it has required a member of a panel of independent experts to prepare a report in relation to the question of whether the work is of equal value and the report has been received (in which case the tribunal will consider the report and decide whether the woman is entitled to equal pay).

NOTE: The panel of independent experts is designated by ACAS. Members of the panel must not be officers or employees of ACAS.

In determining whether there are no reasonable grounds for assessing whether the work of a woman is of equal value to that of a man there shall be taken to be no reasonable grounds where the work of the woman and the man in question have been given different values in a job evaluation study, unless the evaluation discriminated on grounds of sex.

The leading authority on work of equal value, and a most instructive case, is *Hayward* v. *Cammell Laird Shipbuilders Ltd* (1988). The applicant was employed as a cook in a shipyard canteen. She claimed, under s. 1(2)(c) of the Act, that she was doing work of equal value to male shipyard workers who were being paid at a higher rate. An evaluation by an independent expert was followed by a finding by an industrial tribunal that she was doing work of equal value to the male comparators. However, at a subsequent hearing, the industrial tribunal found that *all* her terms and conditions of employment should be compared with the male employees and not just the terms relating to basic pay and overtime. Accordingly, her claim for equal pay was dismissed. On appeal, ultimately to the House of Lords, it was held, overturning the decision of the industrial tribunal, that on its true construction s. 1(2) of the Act referred to the specific term or terms of the contract (i.e. those relating to pay in this case) about which complaint had been made. This meant that even though the contract of employment taken as a whole was not less favourable than those of the male comparators, the specific term on pay was to be compared with those of the male employees. Accordingly, the case was remitted to the industrial tribunal for a decision on the applicant's specific pay entitlement. *See also Leverton* v. *Clwyd County Council* (1989).

10. Defences available to the employer. Under s. 1(3) of the 1970 Act (as substituted by the 1983 Regulations) it is provided that an equality clause shall not operate where the employer proves that the variation is genuinely due to a material factor which is not the difference of sex and that factor:

(*a*) (in the case of an equality clause implied through 'like work' and 'work rated as equivalent') must be a material difference between the woman's case and the man's; and

(*b*) (in the case of an equality clause implied through work of 'equal value') may be such a material difference.

There is some uncertainty over the precise scope and meaning of this rather complex provision, but it is important to distinguish the ways in which 'like work' and 'work rated as equivalent' on the one hand, and 'work of equal value' on the other, are treated. In the case of like work and work rated as equivalent, an employer will not be obliged to pay equal pay if there is a genuine material factor which differentiates between the woman's case and the man's, as long as that factor is a material difference between the two cases. Under the legislative predecessor of the present s. 1(3) the employer's defence in these circumstances was worded in slightly different terms, but such factors as length of service, academic qualifications and the place of employment (e.g. London, as opposed to Blackburn) have been held, in appropriate circumstances, to constitute genuine material differences: *see*, for example, *Snoxell* v. *Vauxhall Motors* (1977).

It used to be thought that the genuine material difference defence relating to 'like work' and 'work rated as equivalent' rested on factors personal to the employees concerned, but in *Rainey* v. *Greater Glasgow Health Board* (1987) the House of Lords took a broader approach and stated that the employer's defence is not limited to personal differences, but can apply where the employer can show economic factors affecting the efficient carrying on of the business, as long as those factors are not based on intentional sex discrimination. Accordingly, the employer in this case, who was paying newly-recruited prosthetists higher rates of pay than existing employees in order to attract recruits from the private sector, was not obliged to raise the pay of the female applicant to the rate being paid to the new recruits.

In the case of 'work of equal value', the employer's defence is slightly different. Here the employer must show that the variation is genuinely due to a material factor which *may* be a material difference — in other words it is not mandatory that it *is* a material difference. The purpose of this different approach seems to be to allow the employer to plead economic arguments as justifying differential rates of pay more readily than was thought to be the case, at least before the decision in *Rainey*, in relation to like work and work rated as equivalent.

11. Individual enforcement of the Act. A woman (or man) may enforce an equality clause by presenting a complaint to an industrial tribunal. Such a complaint may be referred to a tribunal by an individual, an employer or, in certain circumstances, by the Secretary of State for Employment. If the tribunal finds that an individual is entitled to equal pay, it may make a declaration to the effect and award up to two years' back pay. The burden of proving that s. 1(2) is satisfied lies upon the complainant. It the employer wishes to rely on the genuine material factor defence, he must establish it. It should be noted that the tribunal must follow a special procedure where a claim is based on work of equal value.

Sex Discrimination Act 1975

In this section, references are to the Sex Discrimination Act 1975 (as amended by the Sex Discrimination Act 1986).

12. Scope of the 1975 Act. In relation to employment, the Sex Discrimination Act is intended to render discrimination on grounds of sex and/or the fact that a person is married (irrespective of age) unlawful as regards those areas of employment not dealt with by the terms of the contract (which are the province of the Equal Pay Act: *see* above). The Act applies to the Crown: s. 85.

The Act renders discrimination on the above grounds unlawful except in the following cases.

(*a*) Discrimination by way of 'special treatment afforded to women in connection with pregnancy or childbirth': s. 2(2).

(*b*) Where in the previous year there were no or few members of one sex doing a particular job, certain discrimination in favour of members of that sex is allowed: s. 48.

(*c*) Discrimination in the selection, promotion or training of a person is permissible where being a man or a woman is a 'genuine occupational qualification':

(*d*) There are special rules relating to the police, prison officers and ministers of religion: ss. 17–20.

(*e*) There are special rules relating to death or retirement: s. 6(4). The position here has been much influenced by Community Law, which in turn led to the amendment of the 1975 Act by the Sex Discrimination Act 1986. Under Community Law it is quite clear that the domestic legislation of a member state may fix discriminatory retirement ages: *Burton* v. *British Railways Board* (1982). However, the position with regard to discrimination which *flowed from* differential retirement ages has been more problematic. In *Garland* v. *British Rail Engineering* (1982), all employees enjoyed concessionary rail travel during their employment and this concession extended to their immediate families. After retirement, however, the families of retired women (but not of retired men) lost these concessions. Following a reference by the House of Lords the European Court of Justice ruled that the different concessionary arrangements were discriminatory under Article 119 on the basis that 'pay' included indirect benefits. In the light of the European Court of Justice ruling the House of Lords held that the provision of different travel facilities for retired male and female employees was unlawful discrimination; this involved interpreting the exception to the general principle contained in s. 6(4) of the Act as originally drafted narrowly.

The difficulty with such an approach is that it would not always be possible to construe the statute in such a way: *Duke* v. *Reliance Systems Ltd* (1988). Additionally, in *Marshall* v. *Southampton and South West Hampshire Area Health Authority (Teaching)* (1986), the European Court of Justice held that the exclusion of the right of a woman to bring an unfair dismissal claim after she reached the age of 60 (whereas the age is 65 for men) was contrary to the Equal Treatment Directive.

Subsequently, and also in the light of the decision of the European Court in *Commission of the European Communities* v. *UK* (1984), the 1986 Act was passed in order to bring the 1975 Act into line with Treaty obligations.

The present position is that under s. 6(4) provisions in relation to death or retirement are excluded from the operation of the Act, and except insofar as they apply to provisions relating to retirement, it remains unlawful to discriminate in relation to promotion, transfer, training, demotion or dismissal. What this means in practice is that if there is a fixed retirement age for men with a particular employer, a woman cannot be compelled to retire at a lower age. However, it should be noted that although the Act applies, in this context, *to retirement*, it does not directly affect matters relating to differential *pension* ages. Accordingly, there are still some problematic issues to be resolved in this area.

13. Areas of employment covered. Section 6 provides that the following areas of employment are within the scope of the Act.

(*a*) (Section 6(1)(*a*).) Arrangements for selecting employees and the making of offers of employment, e.g. discriminatory arrangements for holding interviews, refusing to employ members of one sex for certain kinds of jobs etc. *See Saunders* v. *Richmond-upon-Thames Borough Council* (1977) for case dealing with allegedly discriminatory interviewing of candidates.

(*b*) (Section 6(1)(*b*)). The terms upon which employment is offered but not the terms themselves when employment has been obtained, this latter matter being within the scope of the Equal Pay Act (*see* above). *See Greig* v. *Community Industry and Ahern* (1979).

Following the decision of the EAT in *Clymo* v. *Wandsworth London Borough Council* (1989), it is clear that the provisions of s. 6(1) deal only with situations which arise before a contract of employment is entered into. Alleged discriminatory acts which occur once the employment has commenced fall under s. 6(2).

(*c*) (Section 6(2)(*a*)). Access to promotion, training, transfer or any other benefit, facilities or services. *See Peake* v. *Automative Products* (1977) for a case which examined the general objectives of the Act.

(*d*) (Section 6(2)(*b*)). Dismissal or the subjecting of a person to any other detriment, e.g. suspension from work.

There are a number of examples in the cases of situations where a 'detriment' has been said to apply to an employee, but a particularly significant and important issue in this context is that of sexual harassment. In *Strathclyde Regional Council* v. *Porcelli* (1986), the applicant, one of three laboratory technicians in a school, alleged that she had been subjected to a campaign of harassment by the two male technicians, which included sexual harassment. She alleged that this was designed to make her leave her place of employment. The Court of Session held that since the treatment meted out to her was only meted out to her because she was a woman, she had been subjected to a detriment under s. 6(2)(*b*). It was irrelevant that there was no sexual motive behind the harassment.

14. Advertisements. It is unlawful to publish or cause to be published an advertisement which indicates, or might reasonably be taken to indicate, an intention to do an act which is contrary to the Act: s. 38(1). Use of terms such as 'salesgirl' or 'waiter' in job advertisements are thus precluded: s. 38(3). The term 'advertisement' is defined as including 'every form of advertisement whether to the public or not': s. 82. The publisher, as opposed to the person causing it to be published, has a defence if he can prove that he acted reasonably in reliance upon a statement by the person causing the advertisement to be published to the effect that the publication would not be unlawful: s. 38(4).

The provisions relating to advertisements are enforceable only by the Equal Opportunities Commission (*see* 1:**25**) seeking a declaration and/or a County court injunction to restrain publication. *See Equal Opportunities Commission v. Robertson* (1980).

15. The meaning of discrimination. The Act embodies three kinds of discrimination.

(*a*) *Direct discrimination*: s. 1(1)(*a*) and s. 3(1)(*a*) – this is 'less favourable' treatment on grounds of sex/being married, e.g. operating a rule that female employees' contracts of employment automatically terminate on marriage: *North East Midlands Co-operative Society v. Allen* (1977). *See also Hurley v. Mustoe* (1981)

Statistical evidence relating to the employer's business may be used as rebuttable evidence of discrimination, e.g. the fact that no woman is employed by an employer may suggest that there is a policy of discrimination and vice versa, but this is not automatically so: *see Johnson v. Timber Tailors (Midlands) Ltd* (1978).

Note that there can only be direct discrimination if there can be a direct comparison between men and women. Thus in *Schmidt v. Austicks Bookshops Ltd* (1977) it was held that it was not direct discrimination for an employer to impose rules relating to the way his employees dressed even though the precise content of those rules differed as between the sexes.

(*b*) *Indirect discrimination*: s. 1(1)(*b*) and s. 3(1)(*b*) – this is where the complainant must show that:

(*i*)   the employer applies a 'requirement or condition' which he applies or would apply to members of the other sex/single persons; and

(*ii*)   the proportion of the complainant's sex/married persons who 'can comply with it is considerably smaller than the proportion of' the other sex/single persons who can comply with it; and

(*iii*)   the employer cannot show the requirement or condition

(*iv*) that it is to the complainant's detriment because he/she cannot comply with it.

It should be noted that if it is proved that, despite indirect discrimination, the respondent did not *intend* to treat the complainant less favourably, no compensation can be awarded: s. 66(3).

An example of the operation of this provision would be where an employer requires all his employees to be over six feet tall. Point (*i*) would be satisfied; point (*ii*) could be established by reference to established statistics; point (*iii*) would require the employer to establish that the nature of the job demanded employees of that height and point (*iv*)would mean that a complaint could only be presented if the complainant was less that six feet tall.

Price v. *Civil Service Commission* (1978). Held: a Civil Service condition that candidates for certain posts should be no more than 28 years of age was indirect discrimination because women in their late twenties were frequently occupied in having and bringing up children. The word 'can' in s. 1(1)(*b*) should not be so strictly construed as to mean that any woman could comply because women were not bound to have children. It is necessary to consider not merely the 'theoretically possible' but also whether a person can do something 'in practice'.

Clarke v. *Eley (IMI) Kynoch Ltd* (1982): Held that the redundancy procedure of the employers which provided that part-time workers would be selected before full-time workers applied a requirement or condition within the meaning of s. 1(1)(*b*) in that in order to qualify for selection on the basis of 'last in first out' (the second stage of the employer's procedure) an employee had to be employed full-time. The proportion of women who can satisfy the requirement of working full-time is considerably smaller than the proportion of men. Accordingly such a procedure was found to be indirectly discriminatory.

Turner v. *The Labour Party and the Labour Party Superannuation Society* (1987). Held: that an alleged discriminatory condition, whereby the applicant argued that an occupational pension provision discriminated against her as a single parent (who are mostly women) in the arrangements for the pension entitlements of her dependants on her death, was not to her detriment. The reason for the decision was that the conditions for benefit from a pension fund have to be satisfied in the future, and not at the date when a contribution was made. Accordingly, the alleged discriminatory condition could not be held to be to her 'detriment' because she 'cannot comply with it' (s. 1(1)(b)(iii)). It cannot be said of a single woman that she 'cannot' marry.

16. Justifiability. Direct discrimination is unlawful *per se*. Indirect discrimination is not unlawful if it can be shown to be justifiable under s. 1(b)(ii). In *Clarke* v. *Eley (IMI) Kynock Ltd (supra)* the EAT considered whether the discriminatory requirement was 'justifiable'. In the years immediately following the passing of the SDA the test for justifiability was stringent: an employer had virtually to establish that the requirement or condition imposed was 'necessary' rather than merely 'convenient': see *Steel* v. *Union of Post Office Workers* (1978). However, this test has been eroded and the matter is now much more open to the application of the discretion of an industrial tribunal applying the open-ended test adopted in the Clarke case of 'was it right and proper in the circumstances to adopt the requirement?' Nevertheless, in applying this test the EAT found that the industrial tribunal had not misdirected itself in finding that the requirement was not justifiable.

On the question of justifiability, *see also Panesar* v. *The Nestle Co. Ltd* (1980) and *Ojutiku* v. *Manpower Services Commission* (1982).

17. Discrimination by victimisation: s. 4. This is discrimination against a person who has brought proceedings, given evidence or information, alleged a contravention etc. under the Sex Discrimination Act or Equal Pay Act. Such a person must not be treated 'less favourably' by the alleged discriminator than another person in those circumstances is or would be treated.

18. Genuine occupational qualifications. In relation to discrimination on grounds of sex (as opposed to discrimination against married persons), s. 7 provides that certain kinds of employment are excluded from the operation of the Act, namely where being a member of one sex is a 'genuine occupational qualification' for the job. Two general points should be noted.

(*i*) These provisions do not apply to the terms upon which employment is offered, dismissal or subjecting a person to any other detriment.

(*ii*)   With the exception of (*h*) below, these provisions do not apply to the filling of a vacancy where the employer already has male (or female) employees capable of filling it and whom it would be reasonable to employ on those duties and whose numbers are sufficient to meet the employer's likely requirements without undue inconvenience.

Being a man (or woman) is a genuine occupational qualification for a job where:

(*a*)   the essential nature of the job calls for a man for reasons of physiology or authenticity, e.g. actors, models (s. 7(2)(*a*));

(*b*)(*i*)   for reasons specified by s. 7, the job needs to be held by a man to preserve decency or privacy: *see Wylie* v. *Dee and Co.* (1978) and *Timex Corporation* v. *Hodgson* (1981) (s. 7(2)(*b*));

(*ii*)   the job is likely to involve the holder of the job doing his work, or living, in a private home and needs to be held by a man (or woman) because objection might be taken to allowing a woman (or man) the degree of physical or social contact with a person living in the home (s. 7(2)(*b*)).

(*c*)   the nature or location of the establishment effectively requires the employee to 'live in' and, in the absence of separate sleeping accommodation and sanitary facilities, it is not reasonable to expect the employer to provide such things (it should be noted, however, that the absence of sanitary facilities is not generally a lawful reason for refusing to employ members of one sex) (s. 7(2)(*c*);

(*d*)   the nature of the establishment where the work is done, i.e. a hospital, prison or special care establishment virtually exclusively for men, requires that the job be held by a man (s. 7(2)(*d*));

(*e*)   the holder of the job provides personal services relating to welfare, education or similar and those services can most effectively be provided by a man (s. 7(2)(*e*));

(*f*)   the job needs to be held by a man because of restrictions imposed by the laws regulating the employment of women (s. 7(2)(*f*)). Amendments made by the Sex Discrimination Act 1986 now mean that this exception is of much less significance than hitherto, because of the repeal of several major industrial safety provisions regulating the employment of women by the 1986 Act;

(g) the job needs to be held by a man because it is likely to involve the performance of duties outside the United Kingdom in a country whose laws or customs are such that the duties could not, or could not effectively, be performed by a woman;

(h) the job is one of two held by a married couple.

19. Enforcement of the Act. It should be remembered that the Equal Opportunities Commission has important functions in connection with the enforcement of the Sex Discrimination Act.

As regards individual enforcement of the Act, an individual may complain to an industrial tribunal: s. 63. A complaint must normally be presented within three months of the alleged discrimination (s. 76) although it would seem that the tribunals have a wide discretion to hear cases out of time: *see Hutchison* v. *Westward Television Ltd* (1977) and, for a particularly interesting example of the width of this discretion, the decision of the EAT in *Foster* v. *South Glamorgan Health Authority* (1988).

The burden of proof is on the complainant but normally the tribunal would hear what the respondent has to say: *see Moberly* v. *Commonwealth Hall (University of London)* (1977) and *Humphreys* v. *Board of Managers of St. George's Church of England (Aided) Primary School* (1978). There is a special pre-tribunal procedure facilitating the obtaining of information and effective presentation of a complaint: s. 74 and Sex Discrimination (Questions and Replies) Order 1975 *but see Science Research Council* v. *Nasse* (1979) as to the issue of whether a complainant is entitled to see confidential reports, references, etc.

If the tribunal finds the complaint well-founded it can make a declaration and recommend that the respondent take a certain course of action (but note *Irvine* v. *Prestcord* (1981): a tribunal cannot recommend the increase in pay of the complainant under s. 65(1)(c) and/or award compensation: s. 65(1)(b). The maximum compensation at the time of writing is £8,925. It should be noted that compensation awarded under s. 65 can include a sum for injury to feelings: *see Coleman* v. *Skyrail Oceanic Ltd* (1981). Note also that in the case of indirect discrimination no compensation will be awarded unless the respondent intended to discriminate on grounds of sex or marital status: s. 66(3).

20. Miscellaneous provisions. The following points should be noted.

(a) By virtue of s. 39, it is unlawful for any person (e.g. an employer) who has authority over another person (e.g. an employee) to instruct him to discriminate. Enforcement of this provision is by the Equal Opportunities Commission: s. 72.

(b) Section 40 provides that pressure (by providing a benefit or subjecting to a detriment) to discriminate is unlawful. Enforcement of this provision is by the Equal Opportunities Commission: s. 72.

(c) Section 41 provides that where an employee does an act of discrimination in the course of his employment, it is deemed to have been done by his employer: see, for example, *Strathclyde Regional Council* v. *Porcelli* (1986). It is a defence for the employer to show 'that he took such steps as were reasonably practicable to prevent the employee from doing . . . in the course of his employment acts of that description'. Thus, in *Balgobin & Francis* v. *London Borough of Tower Hamlets* (1987), an employer which did not know of the unlawful discrimination but had taken adequate steps to supervise staff and publicise its equal opportunities policy was able to rely on this defence.

(d) Section 42 provides that any person who knowingly aids another person to discriminate is treated as though he had discriminated himself. It is a defence to show that he acted reasonably in reliance upon a statement made to him by the other person that the act would not be unlawful.

Race Relations Act 1976

References in this section are to the Race Relations Act 1976.

21. Scope of the Act. The 1976 Act is concerned with discrimination on grounds of 'colour, race, nationality or ethnic or national origin': s. 3(1). Some difficulty has been experienced over the question of the meaning of 'ethnic . . . origin' and in particular its relationship with 'race'. However in *Mandla* v. *Lee* (1983) the House of Lords resolved the matter. The question was whether Sikhs are a group of persons defined by ethnic origin so as to fall within the protection of s. 3(1). It was held that Sikhs did constitute an ethnic group; 'ethnic' was used in the Act in a sense much wider than that of 'race', and an ethnic group can be identified by some or all of such essential factors as a long history, cultural tradition, common geographical origin, common language and a common religion (different from neighbouring groups).

It should be noted that a racial group cannot be defined by the factor of language alone: accordingly, a requirement that applicants for a post as an assistant in a local authority residential home be Welsh speakers did not constitute a breach of the Act: *Gwynedd County Council* v. *Jones* (1986). The EAT in that case held that even if the language requirement had been discriminatory under the Act, it was nevertheless justifiable.

The 1976 Act is concerned not only with employment but covers also such things as the provision of services, housing etc. Otherwise, *mutatis mutandis*, the 1976 Act is based on similar principles to the Sex Discrimination Act 1975 and, as such, it is not intended to discuss in detail the areas of employment covered, advertisements, the meaning of discrimination and the enforcement of the Act.

22. Exceptions. As with the Sex Discrimination Act 1975, there are a number of exceptions to the 1976 Act including where being of a certain race etc. is deemed to be a 'genuine occupational qualification'. These are somewhat narrower than those in the 1975 Act but include, in addition, employment involving 'working in a place where food and drink is . . . provided to and consumed by members of the public or a section of the public in a special ambience for which, in that job, a person of that racial group is required for reasons of authenticity': s. 5(2), e.g. a Chinese waiter for a Chinese restaurant.

23. Enforcement of the Act. The Act may be enforced by individuals, but the Commission for Racial Equality also has wide powers of investigation.

An individual may complain to an industrial tribunal within three months of the act of discrimination. If the tribunal finds that the complaint is justified it may make a declaration of the rights of the individual (and the respondent), it may order compensation, and it may recommend action to be taken by the respondent to obviate or reduce the effect of the discrimination on the complainant.

As far as compensation is concerned, this may include

compensation for injury to feelings. Useful guidance on the assessment of compensation was provided by the Court of Appeal in *Alexander* v. *Home Office* (1988):

(*a*) the object of an award for unlawful racial discrimination is restitution;

(*b*) where the discrimination has caused actual pecuniary loss (e.g. the refusal of a job) then damages can be calculated relatively easily;

(*c*) the calculation of loss occasioned by injury to feelings 'depends on the experience and good sense of the judge and his assessors' (*per* May LJ). Awards should not be minimal, because that would trivialise the policy of the Act, but they should be restrained. Excessive awards also damage the policy of the Act;

(*d*) the measure of damages may be affected by the conduct of the applicant as well as by the conduct of the respondent.

The Commission for Racial Equality may conduct formal investigations (by virtue of s. 48) and may serve a non-discrimination notice on an employer where it discovers unlawful discriminatory acts in the course of an investigation. This notice may require the employer not to commit such discriminatory acts and to inform the Commission of steps taken to remedy the situation. Where the non-discrimination notice is not being complied with at any time within five years of the issue of the notice, the Commission can seek an injunction in the county court restraining the employer from continuing to commit discriminatory acts.

24. Codes of Practice. The Commission for Racial Equality is empowered to issue codes of practice on certain matters: s. 47(1). A Code of Practice for the elimination of racial discrimination and the promotion of equality in employment came into force in April 1984 and it provides practical guidance to employers (and trade unions) on how to achieve the broad aims of the 1976 Act. Employers are recommended to adopt an equal opportunity policy to ensure that no unlawful discrimination occurs and that equal opportunity is genuinely available. Such a policy should be regularly monitored. It should be noted that the Code is not legally binding and that a failure to comply with the Code does not necessarily amount to discrimination. However, it is likely that a failure to comply with the Code will have a persuasive influence before a tribunal.

Progress test 9

1. What is the relationship between the Equal Pay Act 1970 and the Sex Discrimination Act 1975? **(2)**

2. What has been the impact of membership of the EC on tribunal decisions and legislation on equal pay? **(4, 5, 6)**

3. With what areas of employment is the Equal Pay Act 1970 concerned? **(5)**

4. How is it decided if a woman is doing 'like work' to a man? **(7)**

5. What is meant by 'work rated as equivalent'? **(8)**

6. What procedure must a tribunal follow when a complainant alleges that she is doing work of 'equal value' to a man? **(9)**

7. What defences are available to an employer when a complainant alleges that she is doing (*a*) like work, or (*b*) work rated as equivalent or (*c*) work of equal value to a man? **(10)**

8. What areas of employment are covered by the Sex Discrimination Act 1975? **(13)**

9. Who is entitled to bring proceedings in respect of an allegedly discriminatory job advertisement and against whom? **(14)**

10. What is meant by 'indirect discrimination'? **(15)**

11. In what circumstances is being a man a 'genuine occupational qualification' and what is the significance of this? **(18)**

12. What powers does an industrial tribunal have if it finds a complaint of sex discrimination well-founded? **(19)**

13. What is the scope of the Race Relations Act 1976? **(21)**

10
Termination of employment (1): methods

There are a number of ways in which a contract of employment may come to an end and these are examined in this chapter. The consequences of a termination of employment vary with the circumstances and are considered in the following three chapters.

Dismissal with notice

1. Effect of notice. At common law, a contract of employment could be validly terminated by an employer giving notice to an employee in accordance with the terms of the contract (express or implied) or, in the absence of such a term, by giving reasonable notice. If sufficient notice was given, the employee had no further rights and this meant that dismissal could be entirely arbitrary. However, in recent times provisions have been introduced whereby an employee may be entitled to compensation for loss of his job despite the fact that he was given notice (*see* Chapters 12 and 13). It should be noted that once notice has been given, it can only be effectively withdrawn with the consent of the other party: *see Brennan* v. *Lindley and Co.* (1974).

2. Amount of notice: employer to employee. The length of notice which must be given by an employer to an employee is determined by reference to the following criteria to be applied in the following order.

(*a*) *Express terms of the contract.* If the contract of employment expressly provides for a period of notice, this must be observed unless that period is less than the statutory minimum to which that particular employee is entitled under (*d*) below.

It should be noted that the written statement supplied to employees under the 1978 Act ought to state the length of notice to be given by both parties to the contract (these periods may differ).

(*b*) *Implied term of the contract.* In the absence of an express term it may be possible to imply a term into the contract, e.g. from custom. Again, such a period may not be less than the statutory minimum. In *Davson* v. *France* (1959) a musician was given one week's notice to terminate his engagement. He claimed that this was wrongful dismissal in so far as it was an implied term of his contract (by virtue of a custom of the music trade) that he should receive at least fourteen days' notice. Held: such a term would be implied and the dismissal was therefore wrongful.

(*c*) *Reasonable period.* If there is no express or implied term of the contract, the courts may rely on a 'reasonable' period. What is 'reasonable' depends upon such factors as the status of the employee, salary, length of employment with that employer, age etc. The 'reasonable' period cannot be less than the statutory minimum.

Thomas v. *Gatti* (1906): chorus-girl — two weeks.

Adams v. *Union Cinemas* (1939): manager of 120 cinemas — six months.

Mulholland v. *Bexwell Estates Co. Ltd* (1950): manager of estate agencies — three months.

Phillips v. *Alkem* (1969): a senior female clerk who had been employed for eighteen years — four weeks. (Note that this was merely her statutory minimum at that time).

Hill v. *C.A. Parsons and Co. Ltd* (1972): a senior professional engineer who had been employed for thirty-five years — at least six months (*see* 11: 8).

(*d*) *Statutory minima.* In the absence of any of the above criteria, or where they produce a period less than the following, the statutory minima in s. 49 of the 1978 Act must be applied in respect of those employees covered by that section. Section 49 provides that for an employee continously employed for between one month and two years, the notice period is one week; for an employee employed for more than two years, he is entitled to one week for each year of continuous employment subject to a maximum of twelve weeks' notice after twelve years of employment.

It should be noted that these rights of minimum notice do not apply to a contract for the performance of a specific task which is not expected to last for more than three months, unless the employee has been continuously employed for a period of more than three months.

3. Date of termination of the contract. For the purposes of the legislation on unfair dismissal and redundancy the date of termination of the contract is referred to as the 'effective date of termination' (s. 55(4) of the 1978 Act) and the 'relevant date' (s. 90(1) of the 1978 Act) respectively. It is often important to identify these dates precisely, e.g. for the purposes of determining whether an employee has sufficient qualifying service to pursue an unfair dismissal or redundancy claim, or for calculating his period of continuous service. The basic rules for determining these dates are:

(a) Where notice is given, the date on which it expires.

(b) Where a contract is terminated without notice, the date when the termination takes effect.

(c) Where a fixed term contract expires without being renewed, the date of expiry.

One problem which has exercised the courts and tribunals is that of identifying the date of termination where, as is common, the employee is dismissed with salary in lieu of notice. Although the matter is not without difficulty, it is submitted that the date of termination is the date of dismissal, not the expiry of the period in respect of which salary in lieu is paid: *see Dedman* v. *British Building and Engineering Appliances* (1974); *Robert Cort* v. *Charman* (1981).

However, in certain situations the effective date of termination will be deemed to be the date when the statutory minimum notice would have expired. In *Lanton Leisure Ltd* v. *White* (1987) the EAT ruled that employers cannot deprive an employee of the benefit of this provision by simply labelling the reason for dismissal as 'gross misconduct' and invoking their right to dismiss without notice for good cause. The existence of an internal appeal does not rebut the general principle that a person is dismissed when the notice is given. In *Batchelor* v. *British Railways Board* (1987) the Court of Appeal held that a notice containing words 'you are dismissed with immediate effect' terminated the employee's employment immediately, despite the existence of an internal appeal.

It should be noted that, under s. 55(5) (as substituted by the Employment Act 1982), if the statutory period of notice would have expired later than the effective date of termination, then for certain purposes only the later date is deemed to be the effective date of termination. These purposes are:

(*a*) ascertaining the qualifying period for the right to a written statement of reasons for dismissal (*see* 11: **11**);

(*b*) ascertaining the qualifying period for the right not to be unfairly dismissed (*see* 12: **3**);

(*c*) calculation of the basic award for unfair dismissal (*see* 12: **30**);

(*d*) ascertaining the period of continuous employment for the purposes of redundancy payments (*see* 13: **14**).

4. Rights during notice. An employee's rights during the period of notice are the same as during the continuance of the contract and are protected by Schedule 3 of the 1978 Act.

Summary dismissal

5. Meaning of summary dismissal. Summary dismissal is where an employer dismisses an employee without giving the employee the amount of notice (*see* **2** above) to which that employee is entitled by virtue of the contract of employment. If there is no justification for the summary dismissal, such dismissal is wrongful. An action for wrongful dismissal may be brought by an employee who has been summarily dismissed without justification (or if the amount of the notice is insufficient: *see* **2** above).

The remedy for wrongful dismissal is damages representing the loss of wages during the period of notice that ought to have been given (*see* 11: **1**). However, wrongful dismissal may also be 'unfair dismissal' within the meaning of the 1978 Act (*see* 12: **9**), although both actions could not be taken by the aggrieved employee. Nevertheless, in certain circumstances a dismissal which is wrongful will not be deemed to be unfair (e.g. where a person is dismissed for misconduct without notice which makes it not 'unfair' but the misconduct is not such as to justify dismissal without notice); and conversely, a dismissal may be unfair but not wrongful, i.e. because the correct notice has been given.

It may sometimes be difficult to decide whether there has actually been a 'dismissal' or whether the employer has been merely angry or abusive towards the employee, e.g. where the employer tells the employee in no uncertain terms, to go away. It would seem that the test is: 'How would a reasonable employee in all the circumstances have understood what the employer intended by what he said and did?': *Tanner* v. *Kean Ltd* (1978) and *Chesham Shipping Ltd* v. *Rowe* (1977).

6. Circumstances which justify summary dismissal. The question of what justifies summary dismissal is not one that can be answered with a simple rule since each case must be decided according to the particular circumstances. However, a general principle has emerged that summary dismissal is justified if the conduct of the employee is such that it prevents 'further satisfactory continuance of the relationship': *Sinclair* v. *Neighbour* (1967). The attitude of the courts towards the issue of conduct justifying summary dismissal has tended to alter with changing social attitudes: compare *Turner* v. *Mason* (1845) with *Laws* v. *London Chronicle Ltd* (1959) below.

The status of the employee in question is a relevant consideration as is the fact that the employee has a history of misconduct as opposed to an isolated incident.

In *Turner* v. *Mason* (1845) a domestic servant sought permission from her employer to visit her mother whom she said was dying. The employer refused permission but the servant disobeyed the prohibition and was summarily dismissed. Held: the dismissal was not wrongful.

In *Laws* v. *London Chronicle Ltd* (1959) the plaintiff had been employed for only three weeks as secretary to an advertising manager. The manager 'walked out of ' an editorial conference following an argument and the plaintiff followed him despite an order from the managing director for her to remain. The plaintiff was summarily dismissed. Held: the dismissal was wrongful.

In *Jupiter General Insurance Co. Ltd* v. *Shroff* (1937) an insurance company had refused a proposal for insurance but shortly afterwards an employee of the company, who knew of the previous refusal, granted a policy on the same proposal. He was summarily dismissed. Held: the dismissal was not wrongful.

'It must be remembered that the test to be applied must vary with the nature of the business and the position held by the employee . . . and . . . it can be in exceptional circumstances only that an employer is acting properly in dismissing an employee on his committing a single act of negligence' (Lord Maugham).

In *Sinclair* v. *Neighbour* (1967) the manager of a betting shop borrowed money from the till, without attempting to hide the fact and with every intention of returning it, although he was aware that this practice was forbidden. He was summarily dismissed. Held: the dismissal was justified.

In *Pepper* v. *Webb* (1969) a gardener who had been 'acting in a very unsatisfactory way' for some time, refused an order which was within the scope of his contract of employment and was abusive in this refusal. He was summarily dismissed. Held: the dismissal was justified and the fact that there was a history of misconduct was a relevant consideration. (*See also* 5: **8**).

At common law there was no need for an employer to state the reason for summary dismissal provided that one existed which was sufficient to justify his action: *see Boston Deep-Sea Fishing and Ice Co.* v. *Ansell* (1888). However, under s. 53 of the 1978 Act, an employee with six months continuous service is entitled to be provided by his employer, on request, with a written statement of the reasons for dismissal (*see* 11: **11**).

7. Dismissals' procedures. The following two principles apply to dismissals' procedures which form part of the contract of employment of an employee who is dismissed with or without notice.

(*a*) If the contract states that dismissal is to be according to an established pattern (e.g. that there will be two warnings before dismissal occurs), it is a breach of contract if the procedure is not observed: *Tomlinson* v. *L.M.S. Rly.* (1944).

(*b*) If the contract states that the dismissal may only occur for certain specified reasons, a dismissal is wrongful (and probably unfair also) if the reason for the dismissal is other than specified in the contract.

8. Waiver of rights. If an employer wishes to allege that an employee's conduct justified a summary dismissal, the right must have been exercised within a reasonable time of the conduct which allegedly justified the action since delay may amount to a waiver of the breach of contract.

Employee leaving

9. With notice. An employee is entitled to terminate employment at any time by giving the amount of notice required by the contract. In determining the amount of notice to be given, the criteria are the same as in **2** above except that the statutory minimum for employee to employer is simply that where the employee has been continuously employed for at least one month, he must give at least one week's notice: s. 49(2). If the employee is deemed to have been entitled to terminate employment by reason of the employer's conduct, that may constitute a 'constructive dismissal' and the fact that he gave notice makes no difference (*see* 12: 6).

10. Without notice. An employee is entitled to terminate his employment without notice if the conduct of the employer justifies it. Such a circumstance may well constitute a 'constructive dismissal' and the employee may act accordingly (*see* 12: 6).

Termination by agreement

11. General principle. The parties to a contract of employment as with any other contract, may terminate their relationship by agreement at any time upon such terms as they may agree, e.g. payment of money as a 'golden handshake'. It should be noted that a termination by agreement is not a 'dismissal' for the purposes of the redundancy and unfair dismissals' provisions of the 1978 Act (*see* Chapters 12 and 13). However, the tribunals are concerned to ensure that any alleged agreement to terminate a contract of employment is real and not merely the result of pressure imposed on an employee who is unaware of the significance of agreeing to terminate the contract and who faces dismissal as an alternative to so agreeing: *see Lees* v. *Arthur Greaves (Lees) Ltd* (1973). It should be noted that s. 140 of the 1978 Act places restrictions on the rights of parties to contract out of the provisions of the Act. This provision is plainly designed to protect employees, and the tribunals will endeavour to give effect to this policy: *see Tracey* v. *Zest Equipment* (1982).

12. Variation of the contract. Any variation of the contract of employment must be mutually agreed since a unilateral variation of the contract is a breach of its terms.

Termination by frustration

13. Meaning of the term. 'Frustration occurs whenever the law recognises that without default of either party a contractual obligation has become incapable of being performed because the circumstance in which performance is called for would render it a thing different from that which was undertaken by the contract'. Lord Radcliffe in *Davis Contractors* v. *Fareham UDC* (1956).

In the context of a contract of employment, the term 'frustration' means that circumstances have arisen, without the fault of either party, that make it impossible for the contract to be performed in the way that may be reasonably expected and the contract thereby automatically terminates without the need for notice to be given. Frustration of the contract is not deemed to be a 'dismissal' for legislative purposes.

14. Circumstances which may frustrate. The question of whether a contract of employment is frustrated depends upon the circumstances of each case but the following may be frustrating circumstances.

(*a*) *Sickness.* It is suggested that the question of whether a contract of employment is frustrated by the employee's sickness may be determined by reference to Phillips J's judgment in *Egg Stores (Stamford Hill) Ltd* v. *Leibovici* (1977):

'there will have been frustration of the contract, even though at the time of the event the outcome was uncertain, if the time arrives when looking back one can say that at some point (even if it is not possible to say precisely when) matters had gone on so long, and the prospects for the future were so poor, that it was no longer practical to regard the contract as still subsisting. Among the matters to be taken into account in such a case in reaching a decision are these:

(1)   the length of the previous employment;

(2)   how long it had been expected that the employment would continue;

(3)   the nature of the job;

(4)   the nature, length and effect of the illness or disabling event;

(5)   the need of the employer for the work to be done, and the need for a replacement to do it;

(6)   the risk to the employer of acquiring obligations in respect of redundancy payments or compensation for unfair dismissal to the replacement employee;

(7)   whether wages have continued to be paid;

(8)   the acts and statements of the employer in relation to the employment including the dismissal of, or failure to dismiss, the employee; and

(9)   whether in all the circumstances a reasonable employer could be expected to wait any longer'.

The courts, as a general rule, have been reluctant to hold that a contract has been frustrated because of sickness (and indeed generally), because a wide acceptance of the doctrine would undermine the aims of the employment protection legislation: *see Harman* v. *Flexible Lamps Ltd* (1980).

A slight change can be seen though in the Court of Appeal decision in *Notcutt* v. *Universal Equipment Co.* (1986). A worker, with 27 years service, who was two years from retirement suffered a permanently incapacitating heart attack. The court decided that this rendered performance of the contract impossible and therefore the contract was frustrated as he was unable to perform his obligation to work. The employee was therefore not entitled to sick pay during his statutory period of notice.

(b) *Imprisonment.* The question as to whether imprisonment frustrates a contract of employment has also caused problems. The same guidelines as for sickness have been used in cases; *see Hare* v. *Murphy Brothers Ltd* (1974). Again the courts and tribunals have been reluctant to apply the doctrine in cases relating to imprisonment because of the loss of employment rights: *Norris* v. *Southampton City Council* (1982).

Recently, however, the Court of Appeal has allowed a four year apprenticeship contract to be frustrated by a six month borstal sentence: *FC Shepherd & Co. Ltd* v. *Jerrom* (1986). In this case court held that such a period of imprisonment made the performance of the contract impossible.

Progress test 10

1. How does one decide the amount of notice which an employee is entitled to receive from his employer to terminate the contract of employment?   (2)

2. What is the 'effective date of termination' of a contract of employment?   (3)

3. What is meant by 'summary dismissal'?   (5)

4. What is the relationship between wrongful dismissal and unfair dismissal?   (5)

5. In what circumstances may summary dismissal be justified?   (6)

6. What is the significance of an employee terminating his employment because of the employer's conduct?   (9, 10)

7. In what circumstances may a contract be regarded as frustrated because of an employee's ill health?   (14)

11
Termination of employment (2): consequences

The consequences of a termination of employment inevitably vary with the circumstances but the two most significant are undoubtedly a complaint of unfair dismissal (*see* Chapter 12) and a claim for a redundancy payment (*see* Chapter 13) There are, however, a number of other possible actions which are examined in this chapter.

Action for wrongful dismissal

1. **General principle.** An employee who has been wrongfully dismissed (i.e. unjustifiably with no notice or with insufficient notice) may bring an action for damages against his former employer representing the amount of wages owed to him in respect of work already done and in respect of wages that the employee would have earned had he been given the amount of notice to which he was entitled (*see* 10: **2**). The amount of wages that may be recovered is assessed in accordance with the ordinary principles of the law of contract, i.e. the loss which arises from the breach of contract in the 'ordinary course of things' and any loss of which the employer ought to have been aware. Hence, the wages lost includes money which was normally earned and any additional benefits, such as 'tips', which are lost as a result of the breach.

In *Manubens* v. *Leon* (1919) a hairdresser was wrongfully dismissed and claimed damages. Held: he was entitled to damages representing lost wages and also a sum representing 'tips' since the employer must be taken to be aware that such a loss would be sustained.

Damages for wrongful dismissal cannot normally include compensation for injured feelings or pride or the fact that future earnings are affected: *Addis* v. *Gramophone Co.* (1909), but *see Cox* v. *Phillips Industries Ltd* (1976) and *Bliss* v. *SE Thames RHA* (1985). In certain circumstances damages for wrongful dismissal may include compensation for loss of opportunity to enhance reputation (*see* 6: 3)

It should be noted that where an employee is dismissed without receiving the period of notice to which he is contractually entitled, this may have the effect of preventing his acquiring the necessary qualifying period to bring an unfair dismissal claim. In such a case, the loss of his statutory right may be a quantifiable head of loss for the purpose of damages for wrongful dismissal: *Stapp* v. *Shaftesbury Society* (1982).

2. Deductions from damages. The object of damages is to compensate the innocent party for what he actually lost, not to punish the party in breach of contract, and therefore the courts have developed principles to ensure that the employee who has been wrongfully dismissed receives compensation only for his actual loss. Consequently, a number of deductions are made from the sum which represents the loss of wages during the period of notice that ought to have been given.

(*a*) *Other earnings.* Earnings from other employment which the employee obtains during the time representing the notice period that he ought to have received must be deducted, or a sum representing the amount that the court considers he would have earned had he made reasonable efforts to find employment. This is part of the duty of the innocent party to mitigate his loss. However, the employee is only obliged to take reasonable steps and is therefore entitled to expect to find similar employment: *Yetton* v. *Eastwoods Froy* (1967).

It has been argued that such a deduction ought not to be made, since, if the employer had paid wages in lieu of notice, the employee would be under no obligation to return any part of the wages already paid by the former employer. This argument seems to have considerable merit: *Norton Tool Co. Ltd* v. *Tewson* (1972).

(*b*) *Tax.* When damages are awarded for wrongful dismissal, the total amount of the damages must be reduced by the amount of tax that would have been payable on the damages if it had been received as wages. Since the Income and Corporation Taxes Act 1970 ss 187–8 this rule applies in respect of the first £25,000 of damages, whereas as regards any amount in excess of that figure, the damages are payable without deduction but the Inland Revenue taxes the excess: *see Parsons* v. *BNM Laboratories* (1964).

(*c*) *National Insurance contributions.* While an employee is un-employed, his National Insurance contributions are normally credited by the State on his behalf. Since these contributions would have been paid by the employer, a sum representing those contributions during the notice period is deducted: *Cooper* v. *Firth Brown Ltd* (1963).

(*d*) *Unemployment benefit.* Any sum received under the state un-employment benefit scheme is normally deducted in accordance with the general rule of compensation rather than punishment. It has been argued that this ought not to be deducted since it is simply in the nature of an insurance scheme to which the employee has contributed: *Parry* v. *Cleaver* (1970).

Money received under private insurance schemes or by way of income support is not deducted.

Damages against employee

3. General principle. Where an employee fails to give sufficient notice to his employer, the employer may sue the employee for damages representing the loss which follows from the breach of contract.

4. Quantification of loss. In practice, such actions are infrequent because the loss is often minimal; but it may be possible to quantify the loss, e.g. the difference (if any), in rates of payment between the employee in breach and the replacement and the cost of advertising, or, in the case of an employee involved in a manufacturing process, the loss of production (if any) resulting from the failure to give correct notice.

Specific performance

5. Meaning of the term. Specific performance is an order from the court directing that the parties to a contract perform their contractual obligations.

6. Non-availability. It is a fundamental principle of labour law that specific performance is never granted to compel performance of a contract of employment and this principle is now embodied in s. 16 of the Trade Union and Labour Relations Act 1974. However, it should be noted that industrial tribunals have the power to order the reinstatement or re-engagement of an employee who has been unfairly dismissed (*see* 12: **27**) and may reinforce such an order by awarding additional compensation if it is not complied with.

Injunction

7. Meaning. An injunction is an order from a court forbidding certain conduct, e.g. the breaking of a term of the contract of employment. Hence it may be used to prevent a breach of a covenant restraining an employee from taking employment with a rival of his former employer (*see* 5: **21**).

8. Effect. In certain circumstances, the granting of an injunction may be tantamount to ordering specific performance of the contract. In general, the courts have been aware of this and have refused to grant an injunction if the effect would be to compel performance: cf. *Warner Bros. Pictures Inc.* v. *Nelson* (1937) and *Page One Records* v. *Britton* (1967). By virtue of s. 16 of the Trade Union and Labour Relations Act 1974, no court may issue an injunction if the effect of such an order would be to compel an employee to do any work or to attend at any place for work.

However, where the injunction compelling performance is to the benefit of the employee, the court may be prepared to grant such an order.

In *Hill* v. *C.A. Parsons and Co. Ltd* (1972) the defendant employers wished to enter into an agreement with an organisation of workers whereby it was agreed that all employers in certain sections, including the plaintiff, would be obliged to join that organisation.

This arrangement was legal at the time but under the Industrial Relations Act 1971 (which was not then in force although it had been passed) it would have been invalid. The plaintiff did not wish to join the organisation and he was dismissed with four weeks' notice. He claimed that this was wrongful dismissal. Held by the Court of Appeal: the plaintiff had been wrongfully dismissed since he was entitled to at least six months' notice, and furthermore an injunction was awarded which prevented the employee from being dismissed until that time elapsed by which time he would have a remedy under the 1971 Act.

The decision in *Hill* (*above*) is arguably a case limited to its own particular facts as it was the trade union applying the pressure and therefore trust and confidence remained between the employer and employee. It should also be noted from the case that damages were seen as an inadequate remedy and therefore the injunction was granted.

Recent decisions, which although not many in number are significant enough to mention, have increasingly allowed the employee to elect which remedy to take; i.e. damages or injunction. In *Powell* v. *London Borough of Brent* (1987) the Court of Appeal granted an interlocutory injunction requiring employers who had selected an employee at an interview to retain her for that job, despite their wish to re-advertise the post. The crucial factor in the decision was that the court found that the employers had sufficient confidence in her ability and therefore trust and confidence remained. Similar reasoning was adopted in *Hughes* v. *London Borough of Southwark* (1988). The case did not concern dismissal but an injunction was granted restraining an employer from requiring its employees to perform services beyond the scope of their contractual duties. The point to note is that the injunction was granted because mutual trust and confidence existed between the employer and employee; indeed the very reason why the extra work was demanded by the employer was because of the competence of the employees.

Declaration

9. General principle. A declaration is an order from a court which simply determines the rights of the parties in the case. It has no binding force in itself and is not available to all employees being restricted to those persons whose employment is derived from statute: *Vine* v. *National Dock Labour Board* (1957).

In *McClelland* v. *NIGHSB* (1957) it was held by the House of Lords that a declaration could be granted to determine the rights of an employee of the Board (the defendants) who had been dismissed in contravention of the terms of her apppointment.

10. Order of industrial tribunal. In exercising the various jurisdictions which they have, the industrial tribunals have the power to declare the rights of the parties (see 1: 4).

Written statement of reasons for dismissal

11. Claim by employee. An employee who has been continuously employed for at least six months (2: 16) and who has been dismissed is entitled to receive, upon request, a written statement of the reasons for his dismissal. Clause 11 of the Employment Bill 1988 will extend the period of continuous employment to two years before this entitlement arises. This statement, which must be provided within fourteen days of the request being made, is admissible in any proceedings, e.g. before an industrial tribunal hearing a complaint of unfair dismissal.

12. Remedy for infringement. A claim may be presented to an industrial tribunal by an employee that his employer has 'unreasonably refused' to provide a written statement of the reasons for dismissal or that it is 'inadequate or untrue': s. 53(4). *See Lang and Sons Ltd* v. *Aubrey* (1977); *Horsley Smith and Sherry Ltd* v. *Dutton* (1977), and *Daynecourt Insurance Brokers Ltd* v. *Iles* (1978). The right to a written statement only arises where the employee has been dismissed by his employer; occasionally the situation arises where the employee maintains that he has been dismissed but the employer maintains that he has resigned. In *Broomsgrove* v. *Eagle Alexander Ltd* (1981) the EAT held that the test to be applied in this situation is an objective one. 'Where the employer reasonably believes that there was no dismissal, it may well be difficult to say that he unreasonably refused to give the reasons for a dismissal which he genuinely believed never occurred.' If the tribunal finds the complaint well-founded, it may make a declaration as to what the

reasons for the dismissal were and make an a\
to the complainant.

Suspension

13. On full pay. In accordance with the general p
employer fulfils his contractual obligation by pa͟ ͟ ͟ ͟ es in
accordance with the contract of employment, he maͅ suspend an
employee on full pay without being in breach of contract (*see* 6: **2**).

14. Without pay. An employer may only suspend an employee
without pay if the contract expressly or impliedly provides for this:
Marshall v. *English Electric Co. Ltd* (1945). If the contract does not
so provide, it is a breach of contract for an employer to suspend an
employee without notice: *Hanley* v. *Pease* (1915). Therefore, an
employee who is suspended without contractual authority may treat
himself as dismissed and claim accordingly.

Progress test 11

1. Upon what principles are damages for wrongful dismissal
assessed? (**1**)

2, What deductions are made from damages for wrongful
dismissal? (**2**)

3. What is an injunction and when may it be awarded in relation
to a contract of employment? (**7, 8**)

4. In what circumstances is an employee entitled to a written
statement of the reasons for his dismissal? (**11**)

5. What remedy may be awarded by an industrial tribunal which
finds a complaint relating to a written statement of reasons for
dismissal well-founded? (**12**)

6. In what circumstances may an employee be lawfully suspended
without pay? (**14**)

Unfair dismissal

Introduction

References in this chapter are to the Employment Protection (Consolidated) Act 1978 (as amended by the Employment Acts of 1980, 1982, and 1988).

1. Significance. The significance of the concept of unfair dismissal is that it represents a further, and most important, step towards recognising the property right which an employee has in his job. Additionally, it is no longer possible for an employer to end a contract by simply giving notice and thereby totally discharging his responsibilities. The threat of dismissal is no longer quite so important since the employee has a remedy if the threat is implemented.

2. Basic principle. Section 54 of the 1978 Act provides that, subject to certain specified exceptions, every employee has the right not to be unfairly dismissed. It should be noted that a complaint of unfair dismissal does not depend upon the employer having acted in breach of contract but simply that the employer has terminated the contract in circumstances which are unfair.

3. Excluded categories of employees. Certain categories of employees are excluded from the right to present a complaint of unfair dismissal:

(*a*) Employees who, at the effective date of termination of the contract (*see* 10: **3**), have been continuously employed for less than two years: s. 64 (*see* 2: **16**). There is no distinction drawn by the law relating to the number of people employed.

(*b*) Persons over retiring age (*see* 3: **24**).

NOTE: Employees in (*a*) and (*b*) are not excluded from the right to present a complaint of unfair dismissal when the reason for the dismissal is related to the membership (or non-membership) or activities of a trade union.

(*c*) Persons employed in the police service; (*see* 3: **7**).

(*d*) Share fishermen.

(*e*) Employees who ordinarily work outside Great Britain.

(*f*) Employees employed on certain fixed term contracts; (*see* 3: **16**).

(*g*) Persons covered by a designated dismissals' procedure agreement (*see* below).

Dismissal

4. Burden of proof. If an action for unfair dismissal is to succeed, the employee must first establish that he was 'dismissed' within the meaning of s. 55. In most cases the fact of dismissal is conceded but in cases of alleged 'constructive dismissal' (*see* **6** below), the employee must establish it.

5. Definition. Section 55(2) provides that:

'an employee shall be treated as dismissed by his employer if, but only if – (*a*) the contract under which he is employed by the employer is terminated by the employer whether it is so terminated by notice or without notice, or (*b*) where under that contract he is employed for a fixed term, that term expires without being renewed under the same contract, or (*c*) the employee terminates that contract, with or without notice, in circumstances such that he is entitled to terminate it without notice by reason of the employer's conduct'.

As regards (*a*) *see* 10, **1** and **5**; as regards (*b*) *see* 3: **16**.

6. Constructive dismissal. Section 55(2)(c) refers to the concept of so-called 'constructive dismissal'. If an employee leaves employment entirely voluntarily, there is no 'dismissal' but if the employee is deemed to be 'entitled to terminate it without notice by reason of the employer's conduct', it is a 'dismissal' irrespective of whether the employee gave notice or not.

The courts and tribunals have been concerned to define the circumstances in which an employee is entitled to regard himself as constructively dismissed. Before *Western Excavating (ECC) Ltd* v. *Sharp* (1978), the tribunals found that sufficiently 'unreasonable' behaviour on the part of an employer entitled an employee to leave his job and claim constructive dismissal. However, in *Western Excavating*, the Court of Appeal rejected the 'unreasonableness' test and established that the correct test is one based on strict contractual principles. Accordingly an employee is only able successfully to argue constructive dismissal where the employer has breached the contract in such a way as to justify the employee in treating himself as discharged from further performance. The action of an employer may involve breach of an express or implied term.

(a) *Express term*. In *Hill Ltd* v. *Mooney* (1981) the EAT held: 'The obligation on an employer to pay remuneration is one of the fundamental terms of a contract. In our view, if an employer seeks to alter that contractual obligation in a fundamental way ... such attempt is a breach going to the very root of the contract and is necessarily a repudiation.' *See also Industrial Rubber Products* v. *Gillon* (1977); *Gillies* v. *Richard Daniels & Co. Ltd* (1979).

In *Coleman* v. *S. & W. Baldwin* (1977) it was held that by taking away an important part of an employee's responsibilities and leaving him with residual duties of a humdrum nature, the employer had repudiated the contract of employment. *See also Woods* v. *W. M. Car Services (Peterborough) Ltd* (1982); *Wadham Stringer Commercials (London) Ltd* v. *Brown* (1983).

In *Derby City Council* v. *Marshall* (1979) it was held that by instructing an employee (who worked as a warden of an old people's home) that she was to be on call during the whole of a five-day duty period, the employer had expressed an intention not to be bound by the contract so that the employee was entitled to treat it as at an end. But note, where the employer has the contractual right to alter working hours, changing the hours without the consent of the employee is not a breach of contract: *Dal* v. *Orr* (1980).

(b) *Implied term*. Following *Western Excavating (ECC) Ltd* v. *Sharp* (1978) some uneasiness was felt in the tribunals and EAT about the relative narrowness of the strict contract test compared with the earlier, and wider, 'unreasonableness' test. The crux of the problem is that, before 1978, a series of minor intrusions by the employer upon the contractual relationship might well have amounted to unreasonable behaviour on his part, justifying the employee in resigning, even though no single incident amounted to a repudiation of the contract. Following *Western Excavating* the problem has been that a strict application of the contract test would allow the employer more latitude than hitherto. Since 1978 the matter has been resolved; tribunals and courts have been prepared to imply and interpret the terms of the contract in such a way as to bring the present position close to the position before *Western Excavating*. In particular, the development of doctrine surrounding the implied duty of trust and confidence owed by employers has been important: *see* 6: **7**. Thus in *Woods* v. *W. M. Car Services* (1981), the EAT said:

'Experience in this Appeal Tribunal has shown that one of the consequences of the decision in the Western Excavating case has been that employers who wish to get rid of an employee or alter the terms of his employment without becoming liable either to pay compensation for unfair dismissal or redundancy payment have had to resort to methods of 'squeezing out' an employee. Stopping short of any major breach of the contract, such an employer attempts to make the employee's life so uncomfortable that he resigns or accepts the revised terms. Such an employer, having behaved in a totally unreasonable manner, then claims that he has not repudiated the contract and therefore that the employee has no statutory right to claim either a redundancy payment or compensation for unfair dismissal. It is for this reason that we regard the implied term we have referred to as being of such importance. In our view, an employer who persistently attempts to vary an employee's conditions of services (whether contractual or not) with a view to getting rid of an employee or varying the employee's terms of service, does act in a manner calculated or likely to destroy the relationship of confidence and trust between employer and employee. Such an employer has therefore breached an implied term.'

See also The Post Office v. *Roberts* (1980), *Courtaulds Northern Textiles Ltd* v. *Andrew* (1978), *British Aircraft Corporation* v. *Austin* (1978).

NOTE: If the employer commits a repudiatory breach of the contract of employment, the employee can if he chooses continue to work, or he can accept the repudiation, in which case the contract is at an end and he has been constructively dismissed. The employee does not have to elect to affirm the contract or accept the repudiation within any reasonable or other time, and mere delay does not constitute affirmation of the contract. However, prolonged delay on the part of the employee may constitute implied affirmation: *W. E. Cox Toner* v. *Crook* (1981).

The implication of terms into a contract of employment is not necessarily always in favour of the employee as the recent decision of the Court of Appeal in *Courtaulds Northern Spinning Ltd* v. *Gibson* (1988) shows. Here an employee, a heavy goods vehicle driver, claimed constructive dismissal when he was moved from one depot to a depot one mile away. The contract of employment made no express reference as to mobility. A term was implied to the effect that the employee could be transferred anywhere within reasonable commuting distance of his home. The transfer, in this case, did not breach the contract and the complaint of unfair dismissal therefore failed.

7. Early termination by employee. Section 55(3) provides that where an employee has been given notice by his employer, he may give counter-notice to terminate the contract before it was due to expire and he is nevertheless to be regarded as 'dismissed' for the reason for which the employer gave notice originally.

8. Repudiation by the employee. From time to time it has been suggested that an employee who, by his conduct, repudiated the contract, thereby terminated his contract so that in law there was no dismissal. However, the better view today is that termination of the contract does not occur until the repudiation of the contract is accepted by the employer. Accordingly in law a dismissal takes place: *London Transport Executive* v. *Clarke* (1981).

When is dismissal unfair?

9. General considerations. The following general observations may be made.

(*a*) 'The expression "unfair dismissal" is in no sense a common-sense expression capable of being understood by the man in the street, which at first sight one would think it is': Phillips J in *Devis and Sons Ltd* v. *Atkins* (1977).

(*b*) Whether a dismissal is unfair is affected, but not conclusively determined, by whether one or both parties has broken the terms of the contract of employment.

(*c*) The employer cannot, in seeking to show that a dismissal was not unfair, rely on alleged misconduct not known to him at the time of the dismissal: *Devis and Sons Ltd* v. *Atkins* (1977). This may, however, affect the amount of compensation awarded (*see* **29–32** below).

(*d*) An otherwise fair dismissal is not automatically rendered unfair by a failure to give proper notice: *Treganowan* v. *Robert Knee and Co. Ltd* (1975).

10. Reasonableness. It is for the employer to establish the reason for the dismissal (from within those permitted—*see* **12** below). The tribunal must then satisfy itself as to whether 'in the circumstances (including the size and administrative resources of the employer's undertaking) the employer acted reasonably or unreasonably in treating it as a sufficient reason for dismissing the employee; and that question shall be determined in accordance with equity and the substantial merits of the case': s. 57(3) of the 1978 Act as amended by s. 6 of the Employment Act 1980. This provision is of considerable significance and means that the tribunal must be satisfied that, in dismissing the employee, the employer acted reasonably both in terms of the substantive decision to dismiss and the procedure which led up to the dismissal.

In judging whether the employer has acted reasonably in taking the decision to dismiss it is clear that the tribunal must not substitute its own view of whether the decision was reasonable for that of the employer. The EAT laid down the following general principles in *Iceland Frozen Foods Ltd* v. *Jones* (1982):

(a) In applying s. 57(3), a tribunal must consider the reasonableness of the employer's conduct and not simply whether they (the members of the tribunal) consider the dismissal fair.

(b) In judging the reasonableness of the employer's conduct a tribunal must not substitute its own decision as to what was the right course to adopt for that of the employer.

(c) In many cases there is a band of reasonable responses to the employee's conduct within which one employer might take one view and another quite reasonably take another.

(d) The function of a tribunal is to determine whether in the particular circumstances of the case the decision to dismiss fell within the band of reasonable responses which a reasonable employer might have adopted. If the dismissal falls within the band it is fair; if it falls outside the band it is unfair. *See also British Leyland (UK) Ltd v. Swift* (1981).

The amendments introduced into s. 57(3) had the effect of removing the burden of proof of proving reasonableness from the employer and requiring industrial tribunals to take into account the size and administrative resources of the employer's undertaking in assessing the reasonableness of his action.

To date these amendments have made little significant difference to the pre-existing position: *see Abbots & Standley* v. *Wesson-Glynwed Steels Ltd* (1982) (burden of proof); *Henderson* v. *Granville Tours Ltd* (1982) and *Brandon & Goold* v. *Murphy Bros* (1983) (size of undertaking).

11. Code of Practice. In deciding whether an employer acted reasonably, the industrial tribunal is required to have regard to the provisions of the ACAS Code of Practice 'Disciplinary practice and procedures in employment' (*see* 1: 12). In broad terms this provides that the disciplinary rules (and the likely consequences of breach thereof) and procedures ought to be made known to each employee and that a disciplinary procedure ought to contain certain essential features, e.g. provide for an individual to be given an opportunity to state his case before disciplinary decisions are reached and to be allowed to be accompanied by a trade union representative or similar. In addition, the Code suggests that no employee should be dismissed for a first breach of discipline except in cases of serious misconduct and that there ought to be a right of appeal against disciplinary decisions. In operating the procedure, a system of warnings ought to be used so that employees are given an opportunity to improve their conduct. Records of such warnings etc. should be kept but disregarded after a specified period of satisfactory conduct.

The provisions of the Code of Practice are not to be regarded as a rigid set of rules which, if not observed, will inevitably result in a finding of unfair dismissal, but rather as an important set of guidelines which, if not observed, will make it difficult though not impossible for the employer to establish that he acted reasonably and hence that the dismissal was fair: *Retarded Children's Aid Society* v. *Day* (1977); *Wood* v. *Kettering Co-operative Chemists Ltd* (1979).

The importance of the above procedural requirements received a severe set-back by the formulation of the so called 'no difference' principle. The principle was formulated by the EAT in *British Labour Pump Co. Ltd* v. *Byrne* (1979). The effect of the principle was that procedural unfairness may be allowed if the employer could show, on the balance of probabilities, that even if a proper procedure had been followed the employer would still have dismissed the employee and that dismissal would have been fair. In other words, the unreasonableness of the procedure made 'no difference' to the decision. The Court of Appeal approved the principle in *W. & J. Wass Ltd* v. *Binns* (1982).

The 'no difference' principle has, however, been overruled by the House of Lords in *Polkey* v. *A. E. Dayton* (1987). The effect of the decision is to restore the importance of procedural requirements in determining the reasonableness of the dismissal. It should be noted that the effect of *Polkey* is to prevent an employer introducing retrospective claims that the procedure would have made 'no difference'. However, if at the time of the dismissal the employer felt that any consultation or warning 'would be utterly useless he might well have acted reasonably even if he did not observe the provisions of the code', *per* Lord Mackay in *Polkey*.

Reasons for dismissal

12. Introduction. There are five categories of reasons which, if one is established by the employer, may make the dismissal fair provided that the tribunal is satisfied that the employer acted reasonably (*see* 10 above). These may be summarised under the following heads.

(*a*) Capability or qualifications.
(*b*) Conduct.
(*c*) Redundancy.
(*d*) Illegality of continued employment.
(*e*) Some other substantial reason.

These are dealt with in the next five paragraphs.

13. Capability or qualifications. The employer may show a reason which 'related to the capability or qualifications of the employee for performing work of the kind which he was employed by the employer to do': s. 57(2)(*a*).

(*a*) 'Capability' is defined as 'assessed by reference to skill, aptitude, health or any other physical or mental quality': s. 57(4)(*a*).

Thus an employer may seek to show that the employee was incompetent, but it must be remembered that the employer must also show that he acted reasonably in dismissing for that reason. Consequently the tribunal may wish to be satisfied that, for example, there had been a proper appraisal of the employee's performance, that he had been given adequate training and supervision, an opportunity to improve his performance and the necessary facilities to enable him to be competent: *see Winterhalter Gastronom Ltd* v. *Webb* (1973); *Littlewoods Organisation Ltd* v. *Egenti* (1976); *Cook* v. *Linnell and Sons Ltd* (1977). The need for appraisal, supervision and guidance is particularly important in the case of probationary employees: *Post Office* v. *Mughal* (1977); *ILEA* v. *Lloyd* (1981). (*See* 3: **14**). In exceptional circumstances, one serious error of judgment might justify dismissal on grounds of capability: *Taylor* v. *Alidair Ltd* (1978). Similarly, where it is alleged that an employee's ill health justified his dismissal, the tribunal will wish to be satisfied that the employer only dismissed the employee after having gathered sufficient information upon which to base such a decision: *East Lindsey District Council* v. *Daubney* (1977); *Spencer* v. *Paragon Wallpapers* (1977). The employer may also be required to consider offering the employee suitable alternative employment in such circumstances, but there is no obligation on him to create a special job for an employee in poor health: *Merseyside and North Wales Electricity Board* v. *Taylor* (1975).

(*b*) 'Qualifications' means 'any degree, diploma or other academic, technical or professional qualification relevant to the position which the employee held': s. 57(4)(*b*). It was recently stated that qualifications can also relate to aptitude or ability: *Blue Star Ship Management Ltd* v. *Williams* (1979). In *Blackman* v. *Post Office* (1974) a telegraph officer was required to pass an aptitude test. He failed it three times which was the maximum number of attempts permitted. Held: dismissal was fair.

14. Conduct. This term is not defined in the 1978 Act but the cases establish that a wide range of different kinds of misconduct may be used to justify a dismissal. However, probably the most important consideration in deciding whether a dismissal for misconduct is reasonable (and hence fair) is whether the provisions of the Code of Practice (*see* 11 above) have been complied with in respect of the dismissal, having regard to such matters as only 'serious misconduct' being sufficient to justify a dismissal for first breach of discipline and an employee being provided with an opportunity to state his case prior to a decision to dismiss being taken. Thus in *Budgen and Co.* v. *Thomas* (1976) a dismissal was held to be unfair as the employee had not been given an opportunity to explain herself despite the fact that on the face of it she had been dishonest. On the other hand, provided a proper investigation is carried out, a dismissal for alleged misconduct may be fair even though it subsequently transpires that the employee had not committed the 'offence': *Ferodo Ltd* v. *Barnes* (1976). It is impossible to list all the kinds of misconduct which may justify dismissal but the following categories are perhaps the most commonly used.

(*a*) Refusal to obey reasonable instructions from the employer: *Farnborough* v. *Governors of Edinburgh College of Art* (1974); *Boychuk* v. *H. J. Symons Holdings Ltd* (1977).

(b) Dishonesty towards the employer: *Trust House Forte Hotels Ltd* v. *Murphy* (1977); *British Home Stores Ltd* v. *Burchell* (1978); *British Leyland UK Ltd* v. *Swift* (1981) and *Sillifant* v. *Powell Duffryn Timber Ltd* (1983).

(c) Criminal conduct outside employment but affecting it: *Singh* v. *London Country Bus Services Ltd* (1976); *Moore* v. *C. & A. Modes* (1981).

(d) Sexual misconduct: *Whitlow* v. *Alkanet Construction Ltd* (1975); *Wiseman* v. *Salford City Council* (1981).

(e) Drunkenness: *Connely* v. *Liverpool Corporation* (1974).

(f) Fighting: *Parsons* v. *McLoughlin* (1978).

(g) Absenteeism: *Williams* v. *Lloyds Retailers Ltd* (1973); *Hutchinson* v. *Enfield Rolling Mills Ltd* (1981).

(h) Interference with 'clocking-in' machine: *Dalton* v. *Burton's Gold Medal Biscuit Co.* (1974); *Elliot Bros.* (*London*) *Ltd* v. *Colverd* (1979).

One of the difficulties with the concept of conduct relates to the question of group misconduct where, despite all reasonable investigations, the employer is unable to identify the culprit. Previously, it has been decided that it was fair to dismiss two people in such a situation (*Monie* v. *Coral Racing Ltd* (1981)). The law has now considered the situation where there are three employees under suspicion in *Whitbread & Co.* v. *Thomas and others* (1988). In this case, despite repeated attempts by the employer, it was not possible to identify which one employee out of the three concerned was responsible for numerous stock losses over a period of years. The EAT laid down three criteria to be adopted when making a decision in such a case: (a) the act complained of would have justified dismissal if the culprits could have been identified, (b) that act had clearly been committed by a member or members of the group in question, and (c) all reasonable steps had been taken, including a full investigation, to ascertain the real culprits. On the facts the EAT held that as all three criteria were satisfied the decision to dismiss the three employees was fair.

15. Redundancy. The employer may show that the dismissal was because the employee was redundant: s. 57(2)(c). In such a case, the employer must establish that the employee was redundant and not simply rely on the presumption of redundancy which arises by virtue of s. 91(2) of the 1978 Act: *Midland Foot Comfort Centre Ltd* v. *Moppett* (1973).

However, section 59 provides:

'Where the reason or principal reason for the dismissal of an employee was that he was redundant, but it is shown that the circumstances constituting the redundancy applied equally to one or more other employees in the same undertaking who held positions similar to that held by him and who have not been dismissed by the employer, and either (*a*) that the reason (or if more than one, the principal reason) for which he was selected for dismissal was one of those specified in s. 58(1) (*see* **19** below); or (*b*) that he was selected for dismissal in contravention of a customary arrangement or agreed procedure relating to redundancy and there were no special reasons justifying a departure from that arrangement or procedure in his case then . . . the dismissal shall be regarded as unfair'.

As regards (*b*), in the absence of a 'customary arrangement or agreed procedure', the above provision can have no application. In this context an 'agreed procedure' can include an agreement concluded before the question of redundancies arises or one agreed once they have arisen: *Evans and Morgan* v. *A. B. Electronic Components Ltd* (1981). On the other hand a 'customary arrangement' is 'something which is so well known, so certain and so clear as to amount in effect to an implied agreed procedure'; *see Bessenden Properties Ltd* v. *Corness* (1974). If an employee wishes to allege that he was selected contrary to a customary arrangement or agreed procedure he must establish it. In *Suflex Ltd* v. *Thomas* (1987) the EAT found that 'last in first out ('LIFO') subject to . . . the needs of the company' was not too uncertain to constitute a 'customary arrangement' within the meaning of s. 59. The EAT found that as the company had relegated LIFO to the lowest place on the scale of factors taken into account, the selection was unfair. However, this must be compared with another EAT decision in *Rogers* v. *Vosper Thorneycroft* (1988). Here it was held that an arrangement that in the event of redundancy volunteers should be sought first, did not constitute an agreed procedure for selection.

In addition to s. 59, the cases establish that s. 57(3) also applies to dismissals for redundancy (i.e. the employer must show that he acted reasonably in dismissing for that reason) although it is clear that an industrial tribunal must not make a finding of unfair dismissal simply as a means of 'topping up' what it regards as an inadequate redundancy payment or out of sympathy for a redundant employee: *Lifeguard Assurance Ltd* v. *Zadrozny* (1977).

Tribunals have been cautious not to come to the conclusion too readily that a dismissal on grounds of redundancy is unfair, but *Williams* v. *Compair Maxam Ltd* (1982) the EAT set out the following standards of behaviour by which tribunals should be guided, particularly when dealing with unionised employees.

(*a*) As much warning as possible of impending redundancy should be given to employees (and trade unions: *see* 13: **20**).

(*b*) Trade unions should be consulted so as to decide the best means by which the desired management objectives can be achieved fairly and with as little hardship as possible. Employers and unions should seek to agree the criteria for selection for redundancy.

(*c*) Criteria for selection should not depend solely upon the opinion of the person making the selection; criteria should be capable of objective certification, e.g. attendance record, efficiency at the job, experience, length of service.

(*d*) The employer should ensure that the selection is made fairly in accordance with these criteria.

(*e*) The employer should investigate whether it is possible to offer an employee alternative employment rather than dismiss him.

The EAT emphasised that the above guidelines are not principles of law, failure to comply with which will result in a dismissal for redundancy being unfair. It should be noted that the guidelines are more appropriate to cases of substantial redundancies where there is a recognised trade union than to the case of redundancies in a small business where there is no union. *See A. Simpson & Son (Motors)* v. *Reid and Findlater* (1983).

16. Illegality of continued employment. The employer may show 'that the employee could not continue to work in the position which he held without contravention (either on his part or that of his employer) of a duty or restriction imposed by or under an enactment': s. 57(2)(*d*). This provision might therefore include an employee whose contract requires him to hold a driving licence losing that licence: *see Fearn* v. *Tayford Motor Co.* (1975). Nevertheless, the employer must still act reasonably and should therefore consider giving the employee an opportunity, if he so wishes, of making satisfactory alternative arrangements to cover the period of his disqualification: *Mathieson* v. *Noble and Sons Ltd* (1972).

It should be noted that, for an employer to rely on s. 57(2)(*d*) as a ground for dismissal, the continued employment of the employee must in fact breach a statutory enactment; it is not enough if the employer merely genuinely though mistakenly believes that an enactment is being breached: *Bouchaala* v. *Trust House Forte Hotels Ltd* (1980).

17. Some other substantial reason. The employer may show 'some other substantial reason of a kind such as to justify the dismissal of an employee holding the position which the employee held': s. 57(1) (*b*). Thus reasons other than those discussed above may be used to justify a dismissal.

It is impossible to compile an exhaustive list but the following are among those which have been used under this category in the particular circumstances of the case.

(*a*) Unreasonable refusal to agree to the inclusion in the employee's contract of a restrictive covenant relating to soliciting business from the employer's clients: *R. S. Components* v. *Irwin* (1973).

(*b*) Irreconcilable conflict of personalities principally caused by the dismissed employee: *Treganowan* v. *Robert Knee and Co.* (1975). Where such a conflict exists every step short of dismissal should be taken to try and improve the situation: *Turner* v. *Vestric Ltd* (1981).

(*c*) Unreasonable refusal to agree to an alteration in working hours and arrangements: *Ellis* v. *Brighton Co-operative Society Ltd* (1976); *Hollister* v. *National Farmers' Union* (1978); but *see also Evans* v. *Elmeta Holdings Ltd* (1982).

(*d*) An ultimatum from a key customer requiring a particular employee's dismissal: *Scott Packing and Warehousing Co.* v. *Patterson* (1978); but *see also Dobie* v. *Burns International Security Services (UK) Ltd* (1983).

(*e*)   The temporary nature of employment: *Dean* v. *Polytechnic of North London* (1973). It should be noted, however, that this is not automatically so: *Terry* v. *East Sussex County Council* (1976).

(*f*)   Under the Transfer of Undertakings (Protection of Employment) Regulations 1981 it is provided that dismissal of an employee before or after a relevant transfer shall be regarded as unfair if the reason for the dismissal is the transfer or a connected reason. However, if the dismissal is for an 'economic, technical or organisational' reason, that is regarded as a 'substantial reason' for a dismissal: reg. (8)(2)(*b*). The employer is still required to act reasonably under s. 57(3): *see Meikle* v. *McPhail (Charleston Arms)* (1983). The wording 'economic, technical or organisational' has been interpreted in a number of recent decisions. The English EAT in *Wheeler* v. *J. Golding Group of Companies* (1987) held that a reason for dismissal can only come within the definition if it relates to the conduct of the business. Therefore outside pressure from the purchaser to dismiss would not be sufficient, unless it came within the definition. A similar approach was taken by the Scottish EAT in *Gateway Hotels Ltd* v. *Stewart* (1988). However, doubt has been put on this narrow interpretation by the Scottish Court of Session (equivalent to the English Court of Appeal) in *Forth Estuary Engineering Ltd* v. *Litster* (1988). The House of Lords in *Litster* v. *Forth Dry Dock & Engineering Co. Ltd* (1989) held that an employee who is dismissed solely because of an impending transfer is automatically transferred to the transferee. However, if the dismissal of the employee is for 'economic, technical or organisational' reasons then the liability will not pass to the transferee, unless the employees concerned are employed until the moment of transfer. In addition, s. 61 of the 1978 Act provides two circumstances in which the dismissal of a temporary employee is to be regarded as being for a substantial reason (*see* 7: **19** and **27**).

In all the above cases, the employer must nevertheless establish that he acted reasonably. Thus in (*c*), for example, it would be unreasonable if the employer did not give the employee adequate opportunity to comply with the request to change his working hours.

18. Dismissal on grounds of pregnancy. It is automatically unfair to dismiss an employee because she is pregnant or for any other reason connected with her pregnancy, unless the employer can establish that at the effective date of termination, because of her pregnancy, she:

(a) is or will have become incapable of adequately doing the work she is employed to do; or

(b) cannot or will not be able to do the work she is employed to do without a contravention (either by her or her employer) of a duty of restriction imposed by law: s. 60.

In *Brown* v. *Stockton-on-Tees Borough Council* (1988) the House of Lords held that if a woman was selected for redundancy because she is pregnant, such a dismissal is automatically unfair under s. 60. Indeed Lord Griffiths stated that 'it surely cannot have been intended that an employer should be entitled to take advantage of a redundancy situation to weed out his pregnant employees'.

However, even where the circumstances of (a) or (b) (above) apply, the dismissal is still unfair if the employer has a suitable vacancy, i.e. appropriate for a pregnant woman to do and not substantially less favourable than her existing employment in relation to the nature, terms and place of employment, which he fails to offer her. If there was no suitable alternative employment available or the employee refused such an offer, the dismissal of a pregnant employee for the reasons specified in (a) or (b) is fair. It should be noted that the pregnant employee must satisfy the formal qualifying period before she acquires the right not to be unfairly dismissed because of her pregnancy: *Singer* v. *Millwood Ladsky & Co.* (1979).

Dismissal for trade union reasons

References in this section are to s. 58 of the 1978 Act. This section was substituted by s. 3 of the Employment Act 1982.

19. Trade union membership or activities. Except in exceptional cases (*see* **20** below) a dismissal is automatically unfair if the employee can establish that the principal reason for it was:

(a) that the employee was, or proposed to become, a member of an independent trade union (*see* 15: **6**); or

(b) that the employee had taken or proposed to take part in the activities of an independent trade union at any appropriate time; or

(c) that the employee was not a member of any or a particular trade union, or had refused or proposed to refuse to become or remain a member.

'Appropriate time' means a time which is either outside working hours or a time within working hours at which, by virtue of an express or implied agreement with the employer or assent given by the employer, it was permissible to take part in such activities: s. 58(2) and *see Marley Tile Co.* v. *Shaw* (1980) and *Zucker* v. *Astrid Jewels Ltd* (1978). A distinction must be drawn between trade union activities, e.g. an employee seeking assistance from a trade union to assist him in discussions with his employer, and an employee who does something which might be associated with a trade union, but which is essentially an individual and not a trade union activity, e.g. presenting a petition to an employer as spokesman for fellow employees: *see Chant* v. *Aquaboats Ltd* (1978). It should be noted that the protection of s. 58(2) does not extend to the situation where employees are dismissed following the activities of their trade union, rather than their own activities as trade unionists: *Therm A Stor Ltd* v. *Atkins* (1983). (*See* 8: **7**).

There is no continuous employment qualification period for the right not to be dismissed for trade union reasons.

NOTE that participation in industrial action is not to be regarded as participating in trade union activities.

NOTE also that if, for similar reasons, action short of dismissal is taken against an employee, a complaint may be presented to an industrial tribunal (*see* generally Chapter 8).

20. Closed shop agreements. Section 11 of the Employment Act 1988 makes it automatically unfair to dismiss an employee for a reason relating to non-membership of a union irrespective of whether the closed shop is supported by a ballot. Therefore, ss. 58(3)–(12) of the 1978 Act are repealed.

Other reasons for dismissal

21. Industrial action. An industrial tribunal cannot determine whether a dismissal was fair or unfair if it is known that at the date of dismissal the employer was conducting or instituting a lock-out or the complainant was taking part in a strike or other industrial action, unless it is shown:

(a) that one or more relevant employees of the same employer have not been dismissed, or

(b) that any such employee has, before the expiry of the period of three months beginning with that employee's date of dismissal, been offered re-engagement and that the complainant has not been offered re-engagement: s. 62(2).

It is often difficult to determine whether an employee participated in a strike. In *Coates and Venables* v. *Modern Methods and Materials Ltd* (1982) the issue was whether an employee who had not crossed a picket line during a strike was participating, even though the motive for not doing so was fear of the consequences rather than sympathy with the aims of the strike. The Court of Appeal held by a majority that the motives or reasons of the employee in not crossing the picket line were not relevant. As Stephenson L J said:

'... participation in a strike must be judged by what the employee does and not by what he thinks or why he does it. If he stops work when his workmates come out on strike and does not say or do anything to make plain his disagreement, or which could amount to a refusal to join them, he takes part in their strike ... In the field of industrial action those who are not openly against it are presumably for it'.

If an employee suffers an illness which would have prevented his working while on strike, he is still to be regarded as taking part in the strike: *Williams* v. *Western Mail & Echo Ltd* (1980).

It should be noted that 'relevant employees' in relation to a strike are defined as 'those employees at the establishment who were taking part in the action at the complainant's date of dismissal': s. 62(4)(b). The practical effect of this is that where an employer dismisses employees who are participating in a strike, the fact that other employees who were previously participating in the strike have drifted back to work before the date of dismissal, and have not been dismissed, does not enable those dismissed to complain of unfair dismissal.

'Re-engagement' in relation to dismissed strikers means re-engagement in the job which the employee held immediately before the dismissal or in a different job which would be reasonably suitable in his case: s. 62(4) and *see Williams* v. *National Theatre Board Ltd* (1982).

In **14** above, the question of group dismissals has been discussed. It is important to remember that where an individual is being dismissed, for alleged misconduct arising out of a strike, the basic principles of unfair dismissal still apply. In *McLaren* v. *National Coal Board* (1988), M was dismissed for allegedly assaulting a working miner during the 1984/5 miners' dispute. The colliery manager, who was under a duty to investigate such matters, decided that in the prevailing circumstances he would allow the police to investigate the matter. If charges were brought by the police then the manager indicated that he would dismiss M. The police decided to charge M and he was dismissed. The Court of Appeal decided that 'standards of fairness are immutable' and further 'no amount of heat in industrial warfare can justify failing to give an employee the opportunity of offering an explanation'. The case was remitted to a differently constituted industrial tribunal for the matter to be reconsidered.

22. National security. If an employee is shown to have been dismissed on grounds of national security, as conclusively evidenced by a certificate signed by or on behalf of a Minister of the Crown, the tribunal must dismiss the complaint. The concept of 'national security' was at issue in the decision of the House of Lords in *Council of Civil Service Unions* v. *Minister for the Civil Service* (1985) (the 'GCHQ' case). The court held that the requirements of national security outweighed those of fairness when the minister decided to ban trade unions at GCHQ, without prior consultation with the trade unions. Further it was for the executive (in this case the minister) and not for the courts to decide upon the appropriate national security implications of the case. Workers who refused to give up their trade union membership were subsequently fairly dismissed.

Procedure

23. Application. An employee who considers that he has been dismissed unfairly may present a complaint to the Central Office of Industrial Tribunals (this is usually done on the prescribed form IT1) within three months of the effective date of termination (*see* 10: **3**) or 'within such further period as the tribunal considers reasonable in a case where it is satisfied that it was not reasonably practicable for the complaint to be presented within the period of three months': s. 67(2). Where a dismissal is unfair under s. 62 (failure to offer re-engagement where the dismissal is connected with a lockout or strike: *see* **21** above) the time limit is six months from the date of dismissal: s. 67(3) (substituted by the 1982 Act). The question of whether it was not reasonably practicable for the time limit to be met is essentially a question of fact for the industrial tribunal. The onus of proof is on the complainant: *see British Building and Engineering Appliances Ltd* v. *Dedman* (1974); *Wall's Meat Co. Ltd* v. *Khan* (1979).

A copy of the application is sent to the employer as respondent. If the employer wishes to contest any aspect of the complaint, he must enter a 'notice of appearance' (usually on the prescribed form IT3) within fourteen days, although tribunals have a wide discretion to grant an extension of time. Once this has happened, a date is set down for the hearing of the case by an industrial tribunal.

24. Conciliation. A copy of the application is also sent to a conciliation officer (*see* 1: **11**). He is under a statutory duty, either at the request of the parties or on his own initiative, to endeavour to promote a voluntary settlement of the issue, either by way of an agreement to reinstate or re-engage the complainant or an agreement as to the payment of compensation in respect of the dismissal: s. 134 and *see Moore* v. *Duport Furniture Products Ltd* (1982).

There is no legal duty upon the parties to co-operate with the conciliation officer and anything communicated to him is not subsequently admissible in evidence in the tribunal. If no settlement is reached and the complaint is not withdrawn, the tribunal will hear the case.

25. Pre-hearing assessments. Under the Industrial Tribunals (Rules of Procedure) Regulations (SI 1985/16), provision is made for a pre-hearing assessment of the case to be made at the request of either of the parties or on the motion of the tribunal itself. The purpose of such an assessment is to filter out cases which 'appear to have no reasonable prospect of success'. If that party wishes to continue then an order for costs may be made against him at the full hearing, if he were to lose the case. The Employment Bill 1988 proposes that if the party wishes to continue to participate in the proceedings, then a deposit not exceeding £150 will have to be paid.

26. Tribunal hearing. At the tribunal (*see* 1: 3), it is for the complainant to establish that he was dismissed (unless dismissal is conceded). It is then for the tribunal to satisfy itself as to whether the dismissal was fair or unfair in accordance with the principles stated above. If the dismissal is found to be unfair, the tribunal will consider the remedies which may be awarded. An appeal, on a point of law only, lies from an industrial tribunal to the Employment Appeal Tribunal (*see* 1: 7).

Remedies

The references in this section are to ss. 67–79 of the 1978 Act.

27. Reinstatement and re-engagement orders. If the tribunal finds the dismissal unfair, it must explain to the complainant the remedies which are available and ask if he wishes to be reinstated or re-engaged. Reinstatement means that the employer must treat the employee in all respects as if he had not been dismissed — in other words, there must be no loss of seniority etc. and arrears of pay etc. since the dismissal must be paid. Re-engagement means that the employer (or his successor) or an associated employer must take the employee into employment comparable to that from which he was dismissed or into other suitable employment on such terms as the tribunal may specify, e.g. no loss of pension rights.

If the complainant indicates that he would like to be reinstated or re-engaged, the tribunal must first consider whether to make an order for reinstatement. In so deciding, the tribunal must consider the complainant's wishes, whether it is 'practicable' for the employer to comply with such an order and whether, if the complainant caused or contributed to any extent to his dismissal, it would be 'just' to order his reinstatement. In deciding whether it is 'practicable' for the employer to comply with the order, the tribunal must normally disregard the fact that the employer has already engaged a replacement for the dismissed employee.

If the tribunal decides not to make an order for reinstatement, it must next consider making a re-engagement order. In so doing, the tribunal must again take into account the complainant's wishes, whether it is 'practicable' for the employer to comply with the order and whether, if the complainant caused or contributed to his dismissal, it would be 'just' to make such an order.

If the tribunal decides not to make either order, it must make an award of compensation (*see* **29** below).

28. Failure to reinstate/re-engage. If the employer complies, but not fully, with a reinstatement or re-engagement order, the tribunal may make an award of compensation of such amount as it thinks fit having regard to the complainant's loss subject to a maximum of £8,925 (at the time of writing).

If the employer completely fails to comply with an order for reinstatement or re-engagement then, unless the tribunal is satisfied that it was not practicable to comply with the order, an additional award of compensation must be made (additional, that is, to the award of compensation made in respect of the unfair dismissal). In other words, the additional award is designed to 'punish' the employer for his failure to comply with the order. The amount of the additional award will be as follows.

(*a*) In the case of refusal to comply with the order on grounds of race or sex discrimination, the additional award will be between twenty-six and fifty-two weeks' pay of the complainant (maximum £172 a week at the time of writing).

(*b*) In any other case, the additional award will be between thirteen and twenty-six weeks' pay of the complainant (maximum £172 a week at the time of writing).

Thus it is clear that, while an employer cannot ultimately be compelled to take an employee back, he may be 'persuaded' to do so by the imposition of an additional award.

NOTE. Special rules apply in relation to dismissals for trade union reasons: *see* **33** below.

29. Compensation. If a reinstatement or re-engagement order is made but not complied with at all or if no such order is made, the tribunal must make an award of compensation on the basis of the principles stated in the next two paragraphs.

30. Basic award. The basic award is assessed in the same way as a redundancy payment (*see* 13: **5**). The maximum basic award is therefore £5,160 (at the time of writing).

The basic award is reduced by the amount of any redundancy payment paid (which would normally be the same amount). In addition, the amount of the basic award may be reduced to such extent as the tribunal considers just and equitable if: (*a*) the employee has unreasonably refused an offer of reinstatement; or (*b*) the employee's conduct prior to the dismissal justifies it (this could include misconduct by the employee not known by the employer at the time of the dismissal but discovered subsequently (*see* **9**(*c*) above)).

31. Compensatory award. The compensatory award is 'such amount as the tribunal considers just and equitable in all the circumstances having regard to the loss sustained by the complainant in consequence of the dismissal in so far as the loss is attributable to action taken by the employer' subject to a maximum of £8,925 (at the time of writing).

The tribunal will specify the amount of compensation which it awards under the following heads (*see Norton Tool Co.* v. *Tewson* (1972)).

(*a*) *Expenses incurred as a result of dismissal.* This could include expenses incurred in seeking new employment and loss of fringe benefits such as a company car or accommodation which went with the job. It does not include the cost of presenting the complaint of unfair dismissal to an industrial tribunal.

(*b*) *Wages lost up to the date of hearing.* This can include: (*i*) net (of tax) wages payable during a period of notice which should have been, but was not, given; and (*ii*) net (of tax and social security contributions) wages which would have been earned from the end of the notice period to the date of the hearing.

(*c*) *Estimated future loss of earnings.* If the employee has already obtained other employment, it will be possible to assess his loss under this head (if any) precisely. If, however, the complainant has not obtained employment, the tribunal, taking account of local employment conditions and personal factors affecting the complainant, will award a sum representing his loss of earnings; *see Fougere* v. *Phoenix Motor Co. (Surrey) Ltd* (1976). The tribunal will usually allow a maximum of two years' earnings but, in exceptional cases, it could be longer.

(*d*) *Manner of dismissal.* If there is 'cogent evidence' that the manner of the dismissal made a complainant less acceptable to potential employers, compensation can be awarded under this head, although it rarely is.

(*e*) *Loss of protection against future dismissal.* In so far as, in any new employment, the complainant will have to acquire a period of continuous employment before being 'protected' in respect of unfair dismissal, compensation is awarded in respect of this. The amount awarded, however, is usually restricted to a small sum, although in some situations the amount may be not insignificant: *see Daley* v. *A E Dorsett Ltd* (1981).

(*f*) *Loss of pension rights.* Where the complainant can establish that, because of the dismissal, he has lost pension rights, compensation will be awarded to cover this. Calculation of this sum has always been notoriously difficult, but the Government Actuary's Department has produced a document providing a suggested method for assessing loss of pension rights under an occupational pension scheme following an unfair dismissal. The methods of calculation set out in the document have been used as a basis for consideration by tribunals: *see Tradewinds Airways Ltd* v. *Fletcher* (1981). For the general principles to be applied, *see Copson* v. *Eversure Accessories Ltd* (1974); *Powrmatic Ltd* v. *Bull* (1977).

Certain deductions may be made from the compensatory award.

(*i*)   The complainant must mitigate his loss in so far as possible (e.g. by taking reasonable steps to find other employment) and if he fails to do so, the award may be reduced: *see Gardiner-Hill* v. *Roland Berger Technics Ltd* (1982).

(*ii*)   As with the basic award, the tribunal may reduce the award to such extent as it considers 'just and equitable' if it considers that the employee caused or contributed to his dismissal. It seems that the amount of the reduction on this ground should not normally exceed 80 per cent: *Kemp* v. *Shipton Automation Ltd* (1976); but *see also W Devis & Sons Ltd* v. *Atkins* (1977).

However, if the tribunal considers that it would be 'just and equitable' not to make any compensatory award at all (e.g. because, although subsequently discovered misconduct cannot be used to justify the dismissal, it might be 'just and equitable' not to make a compensatory award) it may do so: *Moncreiff* (*Farmers*) v. *MacDonald* (1978).

(*iii*)   The amount by which any redundancy payment (whether made under Part VI of the 1978 Act or otherwise) exceeds the basic award may be taken from the compensatory award.

32. Interim relief. There is a special procedure allowing for interim relief pending a full hearing if the reason for the dismissal is alleged to be for trade union membership or non-membership or trade union activities (*see* 19 above): s. 77. In such a case an application may be made within seven days of the dismissal and where the alleged ground for dismissal relates either to membership (but not non-membership) or activities of a trade union the application must be supported by a certificate signed by an official of the trade union to the effect that there are 'reasonable grounds' for supporting the contention that the reason for the dismissal was the one alleged in the complaint. The tribunal, if satisfied on these matters, may order the employment to be continued until the final hearing of the complaint: *see Taplin* v. *C Shippam Ltd* (1978).

33. Special compensation rules for dismissal of trade unionists and non-trade unionists. Where the dismissal is for one of the reasons prohibited by s. 58 (*see* 19 and 20 above) the dismissal is automatically unfair, and compensation is calculated as follows:

(*a*)   The basic award is calculated in the normal way except that it is subject to a minimum of £2,520 (at the time of writing), unless reduced because of the factors mentioned in 30 above.

(*b*)   The compensatory award is calculated in the normal way.

(*c*)   A special award may be made but two situations need to be distinguished. Firstly, where reinstatement/re-engagement is sought but no order is made by the tribunal, the special award consists of 104 weeks' pay subject to a minimum of £12,550 and a maximum of

£25,040 (at the time of writing). Secondly, where reinstatement/ re-engagement is ordered by the tribunal but the order is not complied with, the special award will consist of 156 weeks' pay subject to a minimum of £18,795 (at the time of writing). The employer in the latter case may argue it was not practicable for him to comply with the order. Further, it should be noted that there is no maximum limit on the week's pay i.e. the present limit of £172 does not apply.

Progress test 12

1. What is the significance of the remedy of unfair dismissal? **(1)**

2. Which categories of employees are excluded from the right to present a complaint of unfair dismissal? **(3)**

3. Jack, an employee of X Ltd, is repeatedly sworn at by a supervisor of the company. He leaves his employment without notice after a particularly abusive remark is made to him by the supervisor and presents a complaint of unfair dismissal to an industrial tribunal. The company allege that he was not dismissed. Discuss. **(6)**

4. What is the significance of saying that an employee has repudiated his contract of employment? **(8)**

5. Fred is dismissed without reason by his employer, Y Ltd. However, after the dismissal it is discovered that Fred had been stealing the company's property. May the company rely on Fred's dishonesty to justify his dismissal? **(9)**

6. What are the main features of the ACAS Code of Practice on 'Disciplinary practice and procedures in employment' and what is the significance of the Code? **(11)**

7. For what reasons may a dismissal be fair? **(12)**

8. Advise an employer who asks you in what circumstances it might be fair to dismiss an employee on grounds of prolonged ill health. **(13)**

9. In what circumstances may an employee who is redundant also be regarded as unfairly dismissed? **(15)**

10. Joe, a sales representative covering the South of England, loses his driving licence for twelve months. He tells his employer that his wife will drive him around during that period. His employer refuses

to consider such an arrangement without offering a reason and dismisses Joe. Discuss. (16)

11. In what circumstances will it be unfair to dismiss an employee when, in a closed shop situation, he refuses to join a trade union? (20)

12. Within what period of time must a complaint of unfair dismissal be presented? (23)

13. On what basis is the 'compensatory award' assessed? (31)

14. On what basis is the 'special award' calculated following a dismissal for trade union reasons? (33)

13

The law of redundancy

References in this chapter (up to and including **16**) are to the Employment Protection (Consolidation) Act 1978.

Introduction

1. Purpose of the legislation. Prior to the passing of the Redundancy Act 1965 (now contained in part VI) of the Employment Protection (Consolidation) Act 1978), the only circumstances in which a redundancy or severance payment had to be paid was where it had been contractually agreed. The significance of the 1965 Act was that it gave certain employees the right to claim a payment from the employer if redundancy occurred. The object of Part VI of the 1978 Act appears to be as stated in *Wynes* v. *Southrepps Hall Broiler Farm Ltd* (1968) by the President of the industrial tribunals:

'The stated purpose of the redundancy payments scheme is two-fold: it is to compensate for loss of security, and to encourage workers to accept redundancy without damaging industrial relations. A redundancy payment is compensation for loss of a right which a long-term employee had in his job . . . redundancy pay is to compensate a worker for loss of a job, irrespective of whether that loss leads to unemployment. It is to compensate him for loss of security, possible loss of earnings and fringe benefits . . . and the anxiety of change of job.'

2. Persons covered. Part VI of the 1978 Act applies to all persons who work under a contract of employment with the following exceptions.

(*a*) Persons who have been employed by that employer for less than two years.

(*b*) Persons over the age of sixty-five in the case of men, sixty in the case of women. (NB Unlike unfair dismissal, *see* 12 above, the Sex Discrimination Act 1986, left this unchanged but the Employment Bill 1988 contains a proposal to equalise the ages for men and women to sixty-five.)

(*c*) Persons under the age of eighteen (in effect twenty because of (*a*) above).

(*d*) Share fishermen.

(*e*) Persons employed under a fixed term contract for two years or more who agree in writing, before the expiry of the contract, to forgo their rights to claim a redundancy payment.

(*f*) Crown employees.

(*g*) Persons ordinarily employed outside Great Britain unless, on the date of his dismissal for redundancy, he is in Great Britain in accordance with instructions given to him by his employer.

(*h*) Persons covered by an approved redundancy agreement (*see* **16** below).

Dismissal

3. Prerequisite for claim. An employee to whom Part VI of the 1978 Act applied may claim a redundancy payment if he can establish that he has been 'dismissed' and the employer cannot rebut the presumption of redundancy which arises. An employee is treated as having been 'dismissed' by his employer if, but only if:

(*a*) the contract of employment is terminated by the employer whether with or without notice; or

(*b*) it is a fixed term contract which has expired without being renewed; or

(*c*) the employee terminates the contract with or without notice in circumstances such that he is entitled to terminate it without notice by reason of the employer's conduct (*see* 12: **6**): s. 83(2).

In addition, where the contract is deemed to come to an end because of some act on the part of the employer or some event affecting him (e.g. the employer's death), it is deemed to be a 'dismissal': s. 93.

4. Variation of contract. If the parties to a contract mutually agree to vary the terms of their contract, no dismissal occurs if the employee later leaves because he regrets the variation. If, however, there is a unilateral variation of the contract by the employer to which the employee does not assent, this may be regarded as a breach of the contract by the employer and the employee may treat himself as 'dismissed'.

In *Marriott* v. *Oxford and District Co-operative Society Ltd* (1970) the claimant was employed as a foreman and was sent a letter by his employer stating that in future he had to be employed at a lower status with less wages. Held: this was a termination of a contract by the employer which the claimant could treat as 'dismissal'.

The problem is not unlike that of constructive dismissal (*see* 12: 6 above) in that a breach of contract has to be shown. The problem then is to identify a breach and the relationship with reorganisation must be examined. An employer has a discretion, often referred to as managerial prerogative, to reorganise his business. The question to be asked in this context is whether or not the reorganisation amounts to a breach of contract, and hence a dismissal, and then whether a redundancy situation arises.

A good example of the difficulties is provided by the question of a change in the shift working patterns of an employee and whether or not this amounts to a breach of contract. The courts and tribunals have avoided the issue by saying it is a question of fact depending on the circumstances of each case. In *Lesney Products Co. Ltd* v. *Nolan* (1977) and *Johnson* v. *Nottinghamshire Combined Police Authority* (1974) it was held that a change in shift patterns was merely a reorganisation as 'an employer is entitled to reorganise his business so as to improve its efficiency'. Whereas in *Macfisheries Ltd* v. *Findlay* (1985) a change from night shift to day shift was held to be a breach of contract as the employee had a contractual right not to be required to transfer to the day shift. Further problems of this kind arise in relation to an employer instructing an employee to move from one place of work to another. In *O'Brien* v. *Associated Fire Alarms Ltd*

(1968) the requirement to move 120 miles to new work (in the absence of an express term of the contract requiring mobility) was held to be a breach of contract. Whereas in *Courtaulds Northern Spinning Ltd* v. *Gibson* (1988) (*see* 12: **6** above) the requirement to move within a reasonable commuting distance was held not to be a breach of contract. Clearly it is a question of fact in the circumstances of each case.

Redundancy

5. Presumption of redundancy. When dismissal has been established, a presumption arises by virtue of s. 91(2) that the reason for the dismissal was redundancy and it is for the employer to show that the dismissal was for some reason other than redundancy. It should be noted that an employer cannot rely on the presumption of redundancy to show that a dismissal was not unfair (*see* 12: **15**).

6. Dismissal for misconduct. If the employee is dismissed for misconduct he is not entitled to a redundancy payment. However, if the dismissal for misconduct occurs during the period of notice which has already been given for redundancy, the tribunal may award the claimant the whole or part of the payment as it considers 'just and equitable'. See *Simmons* v. *Hoover Ltd* (1977).

7. Definition of redundancy. Redundancy is defined by s. 81(2) as where:

'... dismissal is attributable wholly or mainly to – (*a*) the fact that his employer has ceased, or intends to cease, to carry on the business for the purposes of which the employee was employed by him, or has ceased, or intends to cease, to carry on that business in the place where the employee was so employed, or (*b*) the fact that the requirements of that business for employees to carry out work of a particular kind, or for employees to carry out work of a particular kind in the place where they were so employed have ceased or diminished or are expected to cease or diminish.'

Part (*a*) of s. 81(2) has given rise to few problems, but (*b*) has been subject to considerable interpretation, particularly in connection with changing duties required of an employee.

In *North Riding Garages* v. *Butterwick* (1967) the claimant had been employed for thirty years at a garage and had become workshop manager. The appellants acquired ownership of the garage and some time later the claimant was dismissed because of alleged inefficiency in so far as he was unable to adapt to new methods of work which require that he perform certain administrative functions. The claimant alleged that the changed nature of the work showed that the requirements of the business for employees to carry out that particular kind of work must be diminishing and therefore he had been dismissed for redundancy. Held: the claimant was not entitled to a redundancy payment because the reason for the dismissal was his inability to assimilate new techniques rather than redundancy. Widgery J:

'For the purposes of the Act, an employee who remains in the same kind of work is expected to adapt himself to new methods and techniques, and cannot complain if his employer insists on higher standards of efficiency than those previously required; but if new methods alter the nature of the work required to be done, it may follow that no requirement remains for employees to do work of the particular kind which is being superseded, and that they are truly redundant.'

In *Vaux and Associated Breweries Ltd* v. *Ward* (1969) the claimant had been employed as a barmaid. The owners of the public house wished to cater for a different kind of customer and therefore dismissed the claimant in order to replace her with a younger woman. Held: the claimant was not redundant because there was no less need for this kind of work to be done. In *Hindle* v. *Percival Boats Ltd* (1969) it was held that the dismissal of an employee because he was too good and too slow did not amount to redundancy. Merely shedding surplus labour is not redundancy.

In *Chapman* v. *Goonvean and Rostowrack China Clay Co.* (1973) it was held that where a free transport service to and from work was withdrawn because it was uneconomical, the employees who found it more difficult to get to work were not redundant. In *Gimber and Sons* v. *Spurrett* (1967) it was held that a person is to be regarded as redundant if he is dismissed to make way for a fellow employee who is redundant, since s. 81(2)(b) does not refer specially to the claimant's own job.

Voluntary redundancies

8. Volunteers. A method of reducing hardship in a redundancy situation is to ask for volunteers. Employers, in order to attract volunteers, will either offer enhanced redundancy payments or an early pension. Both these payments are matters arising out of the contract of employment. What is clear is that there will be no right to a statutory redundancy payment as well in such a situation. The principle is illustrated by the decision in *Littlewoods Organisation PLC* v. *Pickersgill* (1987). P applied for voluntary redundancy and entered the lengthy process of obtaining civil service employment. The voluntary redundancy scheme depended on the employee obtaining a comparable job elsewhere. Before P finalised the new job and left, the employers withdrew the scheme. The EAT decided there had been no dismissal and therefore any claim P might have was contractual.

9. Lay-off and short time. Sections 87, 88 and 89 of the Act make provision in relation to employees who are laid off or on short time (i.e. receive less than half the normal weekly earnings) other than as a result of an industrial dispute. If an employee's contract of employment does not contain any provision that the employee may be laid off or placed on short time, such action by the employer inevitably constitutes dismissal for redundancy: *Hanson* v. *Wood* (1967). However, if the contract does permit it, the following provisions apply.

(a) If the employee is laid off or on short time for four consecutive weeks or six out of the previous thirteen, he may give written notice to the employer stating his intention to claim a redundancy payment. The employee may then claim the payment if he gives notice as required by the contract.

(b) The employer, however, can either make the payment or, within seven days of the employee's notice of intent to claim, issue a written counter-notice contesting the claim and stating that there is a reasonable chance that, within four weeks of the date of the counter-notice, the employee will commence a period of thirteen weeks' consecutive full employment. If the claim and the counter-claim are not withdrawn, the matter must be resolved by the tribunal on the basis of whether it considers that there was a reasonable prospect of full employment for thirteen consecutive weeks.

(c) If the employer withdraws the counter-notice or fails to give thirteen weeks' full employment, the employee is entitled to a payment.

Alternative offers

10. General principle. An employee who has been dismissed by reason of redundancy will lose his right to a payment if he unreasonably refuses an offer from his employer to renew the contract on the same terms or if he unreasonably refuses an offer from his employer to re-engage him on different terms if that offer is deemed to be of 'suitable employment'. Such an offer whether in writing or not, must be made before the termination of the original contract so as to commence not later than four weeks following such termination: s. 82(3).

To be regarded as an offer of 'suitable employment', regard must be had to the employee's status, the nature of the work to be done, the remuneration and the other terms and conditions.

In *Taylor* v. *Kent County Council* (1969) the claimant was a headmaster of a school. He was made redundant but offered a place in a 'pool' of teachers to act as a supply to schools which were temporarily without a teacher. There was to be no loss of salary or other rights. He refused the offer. Held: the offer was not suitable because of the loss of status in so far as he would no longer be headmaster of his own school. Parker C J: ' . . . "suitable" in relation to that employee means conditions of employment which are reasonably equivalent to those under the previous employment . . . it does not seem to me that by "suitable employment" is meant employment of an entirely different nature . . .'

In *Bowman* v. *NCB* (1970) an offer was made to a colliery worker which involved a loss of 20 per cent of wages, downgrading and the possibility that the new work might only last three years. Held: the offer was not suitable.

If the offer is to renew the contract or, in the case of an offer to re-engage on different terms, is 'suitable', the employee loses his right to a payment unless he has reasonable grounds for refusing it. In deciding whether the employee has such grounds, the tribunal may have regard to personal factors affecting the employee, e.g. travel difficulties, housing or domestic problems.

In *White* v. *Bolding and Sons Ltd* (1966) it was held that a refusal was reasonable where the claimant and her husband were purchasing a house in the place where she was employed.

In *Rawe* v. *Power Gas Corporation* (1966) it was held that a move from the South East of England to Teesside was reasonably refused because of the possibility of marital difficulties.

In *Souter* v. *Henry Balfour and Co. Ltd* (1966) it was held that where the claimant wished to remain in the same kind of work as he was formerly doing, his refusal of suitable offer was reasonable.

In *Wragg & Sons* v. *Wood* (1976) it was held that in deciding whether a refusal is reasonable, the tribunal is entitled to consider the employee's fear of future redundancy and the fact that he has already obtained other employment.

In *Tocher* v. *General Motors Scotland Ltd* (1981) it was held that even though the alternative work may have been suitable, in the sense that it was within the capacity of the employee, refusal was justified where it involved a loss of status and loss of salary.

11. Effect of accepting alternative offer. Where an employee accepts an alternative offer, his employment is deemed to continue for the purposes of determining the period of 'continuous employment' (*see* 2: **16**).

12. Transfer of a business. In the situation where an employer transfers his undertaking to a new employer the effect of the change of ownership on individual contracts of employment is governed to a large extent by the Transfer of Undertakings (Protection of Employment) Regulations 1981 (S.I. 1981/1794) and to a lesser extent by s. 94 of the 1978 Act. The 1981 Regulations were passed to give effect to obligations which arose under EC Council Directive 77/187 (the Acquired Rights Directive) and are designed to preserve the accrued rights of employees on the transfer of an undertaking. The Regulations prescribe that where a relevant transfer of an undertaking is made it does not operate so as to terminate any employee's contract of employment; following the transfer such contracts are treated as if made between the employee and the new employer. For the purposes of the Regulations an 'undertaking' is defined as a 'trade or business . . . in the nature of a commercial venture'. The effect of the Regulations is that where a relevant transfer is made the employee's contract continues, with the result that there is no dismissal and thus no redundancy.

Regulation 5(3) of the 1981 Regulations states that a transfer of liability will only occur where the employee was employed in the undertaking 'immediately before the transfer'. The courts and tribunals have had difficulty in interpreting the words 'immediately before the transfer'. In *Secretary of State for Employment* v. *Spence* (1989) the House of Lords held that dismissal of an employee 'immediately before the transfer' is deemed to be unfair. The contract of employment is transferred, even though there may be an interval between dismissal and transfer, therefore it is the transferee who is liable.

Where the Regulations do not apply (for example in the case of a transfer of a non-commercial venture), the matter is governed by s. 94 of the 1978 Act, which provides that where there is a 'change in the ownership of a business' in which an employee is employed and in which he continues to be employed, no redundancy payment is payable and continuity of employment is preserved for the future: *see* 2: **16**. If the new employer in a transferred business offers to employ an employee of the former owner, then, if the employee refuses that offer, the provisions of s. 82 apply in order to determine whether the employee is entitled to a payment from the former owner; *see* above. If there is no change of ownership within the meaning of s. 94, a payment may be recovered against the former owner even though employment may continue with the new owner, but in such circumstances the employee's continuity of employment is broken (*see* 2: **16**) and he must requalify before being eligible for the various statutory rights.

13. Trial period. If the employment of the employee is renewed on the basis of different terms (either by that employer or a new employer), the employee is entitled to have a trial period of four weeks (or such longer period as the parties may agree in advance).

If during the trial period, the employee terminates the contract, the employee is treated as having been dismissed on the date on which the previous contract terminated for the reason then applying. It must then be determined whether the offer of alternative employment was suitable and whether the employee had reasonable grounds for not continuing the employment: s. 84.

Claiming a payment

14. Procedure. An employee who considers that he has been dismissed for redundancy must make a claim to his employer in writing; if the employer refuses to make such a payment, the matter must be referred to an industrial tribunal. This must normally be done within six months of the termination of the contract. The payment is made by the employer although he is entitled to claim a rebate (at the time of writing it is 35 per cent) from the Redundancy Fund unless the payment was not one which the employer was obliged to make under the provisions of Part VI of the 1978 Act. The Redundancy Fund is financed by levies payable weekly by employers in respect of each employee. The 1986 Wages Act limited rebate to employers with less than ten employees. Clause 13 of the Employment Bill 1988 will abolish the Fund.

15. Amount of payment. If the right to a payment is established, it is paid to the employee free of tax. The actual sum is calculated by reference to three factors (Schedule 4 of the 1978 Act):

- (*a*) age of claimant;
- (*b*) length of continuous employment of claimant;
- (*c*) the weekly pay of the claimant.

Table 1: Amount of Payment

Age (inclusive)	Amount (weeks' pay for each year of employment)
18-21	$\frac{1}{2}$
22-40	1
41-65 (men)	$1\frac{1}{2}$
41-60 (women)	$1\frac{1}{2}$

Clause 12 of the Employment Bill 1988 will impose the same age (65) for both men and women. The following points should be noted:

(*a*) For each month a claimant is over sixty-four (fifty-nine for women), the amount is reduced by one-twelfth for each complete month worked.

(*b*) Any earnings over £164 per week are disregarded and only the last twenty years' employment may be counted. Hence the maximum payment at the time of writing is £4920, i.e. 20 years x $1\frac{1}{2}$ x £164.

(*c*) If an employee's employment has straddled an age barrier, the different age rates are applied. For example, if an employee has been employed from the age of thirty-five to forty-five, he has 6 years at 1 week's pay and 4 years at $1\frac{1}{2}$ weeks' pay.

16. A week's pay. The computation of a week's pay varies with each individual case but the principles are laid down in Schedule 14 of the 1978 Act. If the employee is on a fixed weekly rate, the contractual rate is adopted. If an employee's remuneration for employment in normal working hours does not vary with the amount of work done, a week's pay is the amount payable under the contract. If the amount of remuneration does vary, a week's pay is determined by taking an average over the last twelve weeks of employment. If there are no normal working hours, a week's pay is determined by taking an average over the last twelve weeks of employment. Overtime hours are not included as 'normal working hours' for determining a week's pay unless it was obligatory on both the employer and the employee: *Tarmac Roadstone Holdings* v. *Peacock* (1973); *Lotus Cars Ltd* v. *Sutcliffe and Stratton* (1982).

17. Contracting out of the legislation. Where a joint application is made by the parties to an agreement, the Secretary of State may grant exemption from Part VI of the 1978 Act in respect of those persons covered by the agreement: s. 96.

Procedures for handling redundancies

References in this section are to ss. 99–108 of the Employment
Protection Act 1975.

18. Consultation. Where an employer is proposing to dismiss as
redundant an employee of a description in respect of which an
independent trade union is recognised by him, he must consult
representatives of that trade union. Note that this is so whether the
particular employee is entitled to a redundancy payment or not. In
any case consultation must begin 'at the earliest opportunity', but in
particular note the following.

(*a*) If he is proposing to dismiss as redundant more than a
hundred employees at one establishment within a period of ninety
days or less, he must consult at least ninety days before the first
dismissal takes effect.

(*b*) If he is proposing to dismiss as redundant more than ten employees at one establishment within a period of thirty days or less, he
must consult at least thirty days before the first dismissal takes effect.

(*c*) In any other case, consultation must begin 'at the earliest
opportunity'.

For this purpose 'recognition' can be inferred from the
circumstances and need not necessarily have been the subject of a
formal agreement: *TGWU* v. *Dyer* (1977); *NUGSAT* v. *Albury Bros
Ltd* (1978) and *USDAW* v. *Sketchley Ltd* (1981). It should not be
thought that recognition can be imposed on an employer by a
third-party. In *Cleveland County Council* v. *Springett* (1985) the EAT
decided that the mere fact that the Secretary of State for Education
decided that the Association of Polytechnic Teachers should be
represented on the Burnham Pay Committee did not mean that the
employer should also 'recognise' the union.

It seems that the consultation must begin before the first notice of
dismissal is given and not merely before the first dismissal takes
effect: *National Union of Teachers* v. *Avon County Council* (1978).
For the meaning of 'establishment' *see Barratt Developments
(Bradford) Ltd* v. *UCATT* (1978).

In consulting the trade union representatives, the employer must disclose certain information, e.g. the proposed method by which the employees to be dismissed are to be selected, and consider any representations made to him by the representatives.

If the employer can show that there were 'special circumstances', e.g. the fact that the employer was genuinely hoping to find a buyer for the business: *APAAC* v. *Kirvin Ltd* (1978), which made it not 'reasonably practicable' for the employer to comply with the obligation to consult, he need only take such steps as are reasonably practicable in the circumstances: see *Bakers' Union* v. *Clarks of Hove Ltd* (1978) and *USDAW* v. *Leancut Bacon Ltd* (1981).

19. Failure to consult. If the employer fails to consult as required, the trade union in question may present a complaint to an industrial tribunal to that effect. If the tribunal finds the complaint well-founded it must make a declaration to that effect; it may also make a 'protective award' i.e. an award directing that those employees concerned be paid for a specified period (the 'protected period') not exceeding ninety days, thirty days or twenty-eight days as the case may be (corresponding to the different categories referred to in **18** above). If the employer fails to do this, an individual employee may present a complaint to an industrial tribunal which, if it finds the complaint well-founded, will order the employer to comply. For a consideration of the basis on which a protective award is made, *see Talke Fashions Ltd.* v. *ASTWKT* (1977). It should reflect the loss suffered by the employees and not be used to penalise the employer for his failure to consult. *See* also *Spillers-French (Holdings) Ltd.* v. *USDAW* (1980) and *GKN Sankey Ltd* v. *NSMM* (1980).

20. Notification of redundancies. If an employer is proposing to dismiss as redundant more than a hundred employees at one establishment within ninety days, or more than ten employees within thirty days, he must notify the Secretary of State for Employment of this ninety or thirty days before the first of such dismissals takes effect, unless there are 'special circumstances' preventing compliance with this (in which case all such steps as are reasonably practicable must be taken).

If an employer fails to comply with this requirement, the rebate on the redundancy payments of the employees concerned (see **14** above) may be reduced by up to 10 per cent or the employer may, upon conviction by a magistrates' court, be fined up to £400.

Time off work

21. General principle. An employee who has been dismissed by reason of redundancy is entitled to have 'reasonable' time off work with pay during the period of notice to look for new employment or to make arrangements for training for future employment: s. 31 of the 1978 Act. To be eligible for this right, an employee must have been continuously employed (*see* 2: **16**) for two years at the date on which the notice is due to expire. The employee does not have to provide the employer with evidence of interviews or appointments before being entitled to exercise the right to time off work for this purpose: *Dutton* v. *Hawker Siddeley Aviation Ltd* (1978).

22. Complaint to industrial tribunal. If an employer refuses to allow an employee time off or fails to pay him for it, a complaint may be presented to an industrial tribunal, normally within three months. The tribunal, if it finds the complaint well-founded, may award compensation of up to two-fifths of a week's pay.

Progress test 13

1. What is the object of the redundancy payments' legislation? (**1**)

2. Which employees are excluded from the redundancy payments' legislation? (**2**)

3. When is an employee deemed to have been 'dismissed' for the purposes of Part VI of the 1978 Act? (**3**)

4. Are the following employees redundant?

(*a*) A is dismissed because he is a craftsman and too slow to operate the machinery of the new production system.

(*b*) B is a professional singer who is dismissed because his style of singing is no longer popular.

(*c*) C, an electrician, is asked by his employer to spend a few hours each week selling electrical equipment in addition to his normal work. C agrees but several months later he is dismissed for incompetence as he is unable to adapt to the sales technique.

(*d*) D is dismissed and replaced by E, a fellow employee who has been made redundant.   **(7)**

5. Frank is dismissed by his employers, XYZ Ltd, for redundancy. He is given four weeks' notice as required by the contract. Two weeks later he receives a written notice from his employer offering him employment at another of their factories two miles away. The work is to commence three weeks later and the wage will be the same as his present wage, although he will be required to work two extra hours a week. Frank refuses the offer. Discuss.   **(10, 11)**

6. What is the significance of a change in the ownership of a business?   **(12)**

7. What redundancy payments are the following entitled to?

(*a*) M is thirty-four and has been employed by X Ltd for six years. At present he earns £80 a week.

(*b*) N is fifty-eight and has been employed by X Ltd for twenty-four years. He earns £90 a week, and usually does five hours overtime each week which earns him another £15 a week.

(*c*) P is forty-three and has been employed by X Ltd for three years. He earns £150 a week.   **(15)**

8. What action may be taken (and by whom) if an employer fails to consult with a trade union in the event of proposed redundancies?   **(18, 19)**

9. What right does an employee have to time off work if he is made redundant?   **(21)**

14

Safety and health at work

Introduction

1. Introduction. The law relating to the safety and health of workers is derived from two sources:

(a) the common law principles developed by the courts with certain statutory interventions; and

(b) the statutory provisions.

The common law

2. General principle. An employer owes a duty to his employees to provide a safe system of work: *Wilsons and Clyde Coal Co. Ltd* v. *English* (1938). If this duty is breached by the employer, and he has no defence available (*see* **8** *below*) he will be liable in damages to the injured employee. If an employee is injured by the negligence of a fellow employee, the employer may be liable on the basis of vicarious liability (*see* 2: **10**).

The employer's obligation may be divided into several aspects:

(a) duty to provide a competent staff of men;
(b) duty to provide a proper system of working;
(c) duty to provide safe work premises;
(d) duty to provide safe working equipment;
(e) duty to provide adequate safety and protective equipment.

3. Duty to provide a competent staff of men. If an incompetent employee injures a fellow workman an employer has failed to meet this duty and he will be liable to the injured employee, irrespective of any question of vicarious liability. It is no defence for an employer to say that he has delegated the selection of staff to another person.

4. Duty to provide a proper system of working. The employer must ensure that the method of work is safe. Thus he is normally regarded as being under an obligation to give adequate training in the work to be done, warning as to potential risks and dangers. However, if an operation is simple or if the particular employee has done a job on a number of occasions or the employer has given proper instructions, the employer may be relieved of liability: *Winter* v. *Cardiff RDC* (1950), *Wilson* v. *Tyneside Window Cleaning Co.* (1958).

5. Duty to provide safe work premises. An employer must take all reasonable steps to ensure that the working premises are as safe as possible: *Latimer* v. *AEC Ltd* (1953).

6. Duty to provide safe working equipment. At common law, distinctions were made between equipment obtained from a reputable supplier and otherwise and custom-built and standard equipment. These distinctions were removed by the Employers Liability (Defective Equipment) Act 1969. The basic provision of the Act is that where an employee suffers personal injury in the course of his employment as a result of a defect in equipment provided by his employer for the purposes of the employer's business, and the defect is attributable wholly or partly to the fault of a third party (e.g. the manufacturer), the employer is liable to the employee. It should be noted that an employer who incurs liability by virtue of the Act may be able to claim from the manufacturer and/or the supplier. The provisions of the Act cannot be excluded by a contract of employment but the defence of contributory negligence is available to the employer (*see* **8** below).

7. Duty to provide adequate safety and protective equipment. In providing such equipment, the employer is expected to keep up with latest developments but it appears that the trend of the decisions has been to limit the meaning of the word 'provide' in this context.

In *Clifford* v. *Challen and Son Ltd* (1951) it was held that the employer had failed to provide safety equipment where it was only available if the employee walked to the works' store which was situated some distance from the actual work-place.

In *James* v. *Hepworth and Grandage Ltd* (1968) it was held that where an employer put up a notice about safety equipment (which the plaintiff was unable to read), this was sufficient for him to say he had performed his duty.

Defences available to the employer

8. Defences available to the employer. There are four circumstances in which the employer may be relieved of liability, either wholly or in part.

(*a*) *No negligence proved.* The employee must establish negligence by the employer without which the employer is not liable. Similarly, if the employer shows that the injury occurred because of some reason other than his negligence, he may escape legal responsibility: *see McWilliams* v. *Arrol & Co. Ltd* (1962).

(*b*) *Delegation of duty.* An employer may seek to defend an action by alleging that he has delegated the responsibility for performing the duty to a third party (e.g. an outside contractor) or to the employee himself. It appears that such a defence is no longer available although where the employer alleges that he has delegated the duty to the injured employee himself, this *may* indicate contributory negligence on the part of the employee (*see below*).

(*c*) *Volenti non fit injuria.* This defence occurs where the defendant alleges that the plaintiff consented to accept the risk of injury which in fact resulted, e.g. a boxer injured by a punch in a contest. In the context of employment, the courts today are extremely reluctant to permit reliance on this defence, although in extreme cases the defence may apply.

In *Imperial Chemical Industries Ltd* v. *Shatwell* (1965) three employees, experienced shot-firers, had specific instructions as to the manner of performing their work. In disregard of these instructions, two of the employees fired a shot causing injury to both of them. Held by the House of Lords: the action in respect of the injuries failed because, in view of the gross disobedience of the employee, the defence of *volenti non fit injuria* must be applied.

NOTE. When the defence succeeds, the entire action fails.

(*d*) *Contributory negligence.* The Law Reform (Contributory Negligence) Act 1945 provides that where an injured person has contributed to the injury by his own fault, his claim is not defeated (as was the position prior to the Act) but the damages awarded are reduced to 'such extent as the court thinks just and equitable having regard to the claimant's share in the responsibility for the damage'. It should be noted that in the sphere of industrial accidents the courts are often reluctant to make a finding of contributory negligence by an employee.

Compulsory insurance

9. **Compulsory insurance.** Under the Employers' Liability (Compulsory Insurance) Act 1969, every employer carrying on business in Great Britain must maintain an approved insurance policy against bodily injury or disease sustained by an employee in circumstances where such injury or disease is deemed to 'arise out of and in the course of employment'. Copies of the insurance certificate must be displayed at the place of business. Failure to comply with the requirements of the Act is punishable by fine.

The statutory provisions

References in 10–24 below are, unless otherwise stated, to the Health and Safety at Work etc. Act 1974.

10. **Scope of legislation.** Prior to the passing of the Health and Safety at Work etc. Act 1974, which is largely based upon the recommendations of the Committee on Safety at Work chaired by Lord Robens (Cmnd. 5034), there was no legislation of general application relating to health and safety at work. Instead, legislation was based on the different kinds of places of work, e.g. Factories Act 1961; Offices, Shops and Railway Premises Act 1963; Mines and Quarries Act 1954 and, as such, a number of kinds of places of work

fell outside the scope of any legislation. With the passing of the 1974 Act, although the previous legislation remains in force until such time as it is replaced by new regulations, virtually all persons who are at work or who are affected by work activities are now within the scope of legislation. In addition to imposing duties on employers, employees and the self employed, the 1974 Act also places obligations upon manufacturers, suppliers, designers and importers of articles and substances used at work.

11. Nature of the legislation. The 1974 Act is essentially concerned with criminal sanctions (as opposed to the recovery of damages following an accident) which can apply even though no accident has occurred; the issue is whether the obligation has been broken. It is specifically provided that a breach of the 'general duties' (*see* **12** below) shall not give rise to civil liability but that breach of any regulation made under the Act (*see* **18** below) shall, unless otherwise stated, do so: s. 47.

The emphasis of the Act is towards prevention of accidents, and accordingly new powers have been given to the inspectors (*see* **20** below). The intention is also that industry should be self-regulating to a large extent (i.e. deal with its own problems) and, to this end, a system of safety representatives and safety committees have been introduced (*see* **13** below).

General statutory duties

12. Introductory. The 1974 Act imposes general duties on a number of different categories of persons. Most of these duties are qualified in that the obligation extends to that which is 'reasonably practicable'. The effect of this is to allow the person on whom the duty is placed to balance, on the one hand, the expense and effort involved in meeting that duty with, on the other, the risk involved: *Edwards* v. *NCB* (1949). Note, however, that it is for a person who alleges he has done that which is 'reasonably practicable' to establish it: s. 40.

13. Duties of employers. It is the duty of every employer to ensure so far as is reasonably practicable, the health safety and welfare at work of his employees. In particular, he must have regard to:

(a) the provision and maintenance of plant and systems of work. In the case of *Tesco Stores* v. *Seabridge* (1988) the fact that two or three out of four screws were missing from a protective panel which covered live electric wires made a breach of section 2 of the Act self-evident;

(b) the use, handling, storage and transport of articles and substances;

(c) the provision of information, instruction, training and supervision;

(d) the maintenance of the place of work and the provision of maintenance of means of access to and egress from such places; and

(e) the provision and maintenance of a healthy and safe working environment and adequate welfare facilities and arrangements.

It can thus be seen that the common law obligations of employers are now, in broad terms, also contained in the criminal law. *See R.* v. *Swan Hunter Shipbuilders Ltd* (1981).

In addition, every employer, except those who employ less than five employees, has a duty to prepare (or revise) and bring to the notice of his employees, a written statement of his general policy with respect to the health and safety of his employees and the organisation and arrangements for carrying out that policy: *see Osborne* v. *Bill Taylor of Huyton Ltd* (1982).

The employer has additional obligations as regards safety representatives and safety committees, namely to consult with safety representatives nominated by a trade union recognised by him (*see* 16: 5). Such representatives have a number of powers including the right to inspect the work premises and to require the establishment of a safety committee: *see* the Safety Representatives and Safety Committee Regulations 1977 (S.I. 1977 No. 500) and the Code of Practice on Safety Representatives issued by the Health and Safety Commission. In addition the Regulations provide that safety representatives are to be allowed paid time off work 'for the purpose of undergoing such training . . . as may be reasonable in all the circumstances': reg. 4(2). (See *White* v. *Pressed Steel Fisher* (1980).)

No employer shall levy any charge on an employee in respect of anything done or provided in pursuance of the employer's statutory obligations: s. 9.

In addition to his obligations towards employees every employer has a duty to conduct his undertaking in such a way that persons not in his employment (i.e. outside contractors, other persons lawfully on his premises and the general public) are not exposed to risks to their health or safety. Furthermore, in prescribed cases, it is the duty of every employer to give such persons certain information about the way in which he conducts his undertaking.

14. Duties of the self-employed. It is the duty of every self-employed person to conduct his undertaking in such a way as to ensure, so far as is reasonably practicable, that he and other persons (not being his employees) are not exposed to risks to their health and safety. Furthermore, in prescribed cases, it is the duty of every self-employed person to provide certain information about the way in which he conducts his undertaking.

15. Duties of those who control premises. Every person who has control of premises (other than domestic premises) must ensure, as far as is reasonably practicable, that all means of access and egress and any plant or substance in the premises are safe and without risks to health as regards those persons who use the premises as a place of work.

A person in control of prescribed premises must use the best practicable means for preventing the emission into the atmosphere of noxious or offensive substances and for rendering harmless such substances as may be emitted.

16. Duties of manufacturers etc. Manufacturers, designers, suppliers and importers of articles and substances for use at work have a duty to ensure, as far as is reasonably practicable, that such articles and substances are so designed, constructed etc. as to be safe and without risks to health when properly used. It should be noted, however, that there is a limited right for the manufacturer, importer or supplier to escape his obligation as regards articles by obtaining a written undertaking from the other party that certain steps will be taken to ensure the safe use of the article in question. In addition, manufacturers etc. have obligations to carry out certain research, testing and examination of articles and substances and to provide certain information about articles and substances for use at work.

17. Duties of employees. Every employee at work has a duty:

(*a*) to take reasonable care for his own and other persons' health and safety, e.g. to use safety equipment provided; and

(*b*) to co-operate with his employer and any other person to enable them to perform their statutory duties.

Health and safety regulations

18. Nature of regulations. The Secretary of State is given power to make regulations on a wide range of matters. In so doing the provisions of previous legislation which remain in force (*see* **10** above) will gradually be repealed and replaced by regulations made under the 'umbrella' of the 1974 Act. In making such regulations, the Secretary of State acts on the advice of the Health and Safety Commission (*see* **1: 30**). Breach of a regulation is punishable as a criminal offence and, except in so far as may otherwise be provided, may also give rise to civil liability.

The regulations may deal with a wide range of matters, the most important of which are:

(*a*) the repeal or modification of existing statutory provisions;

(*b*) the exclusion or modification of the general duties in relation to a specific class of case;

(*c*) making a specified authority responsible for the enforcement of any statutory provision;

(*d*) the provision of exemptions from any requirement or prohibition;

(*e*) specifying a class of person who may be guilty of an offence;

(*f*) the imposition of requirements and prohibitions in relation to the design, construction, manufacture, use etc. of articles and substances for use at work.

Therefore these regulations involve the whole range of matters dealt with in health and safety legislation.

Codes of practice

(Sections 16 and 17.)

19. Purpose of Codes. In order to provide practical guidance to those persons who have obligations under the 1974 Act or other relevant statutory provisions, the Health and Safety Commission may approve and issue Codes of Practice with the consent of the Secretary of State. These Codes therefore clearly form an important part of the law relating to health and safety at work.

Breach of a provision of a Code does not of itself render a person liable to criminal or civil proceedings but, in criminal proceedings, the provisions of a Code of Practice are admissible in evidence to show that an offence has been committed. The same may also be true of civil proceedings.

Enforcement

(Sections 18–26.)

20. Enforcing authorities. In general terms, enforcement of the 1974 Act and the other statutory provisions lies with the Health and Safety Executive (*see* 1: **32**). However, the Secretary of State may require local authorities to enforce certain provisions.

All enforcing authorities have the power to appoint inspectors. Inspectors have a considerable number of powers including the right:

    (*a*) to enter premises and make examinations and investigations;
    (*b*) to take samples of and detain articles and substances;
    (*c*) to require information to be given.

21. Improvement notice. If an inspector is of the opinion that a person is contravening a statutory provision or has done so and the contravention is likely to be continued or repeated, he may serve an improvement notice upon him. The notice must specify which provision and how it is being broken and requiring it to be remedied within a specified period of not less that twenty-one days. An appeal against such a notice may be made within twenty-one days to an industrial tribunal. The tribunal may cancel, affirm or amend the notice. The lodging of an appeal has the effect of suspending the operation of the notice until the appeal has been dealt with.

22. Prohibition notice. If an inspector considers that an activity involves a risk of serious personal injury, he may serve a prohibition notice directing that the activity in question cease until the matter is remedied. Such a notice may either take immediate effect or be deferred until the end of a specified period. An appeal against a prohibition notice may be made within twenty-one days to an industrial tribunal which has the power to cancel, affirm or amend it. The lodging of an appeal has the effect of suspending the operation of the notice only if the tribunal so directs.

Offences and penalties

(Sections 33–42.)

23. Offences. A wide range of offences may be committed under the 1974 Act, the most important of which are contravening one of the general duties (*see* 12 above) or a health and safety regulation (*see* 18 above), preventing an inspector from carrying out his duties and contravening an improvement or prohibition notice. The list also includes a number of others, such as falsely pretending to be an inspector!

24. Penalties. Upon conviction in summary proceedings in the magistrates' court, the maximum punishment is a fine of £400 or, in certain cases, £1,000. If proceedings are brought upon indictment, the Crown Court may impose an unlimited fine and, in certain cases, a maximum of two years' imprisonment.

In addition, the court may order that the offence be remedied, e.g. by requiring an article or substance to be forfeited.

No smoking policies

One of the areas of development in employment law has been that of policies to deal with problems arising out of the employment relationship. Safety is no exception and in this respect no smoking policies need to be examined.

25. Why have such a policy? In 1983 the Royal College of Physicians estimated that at least 90% of deaths from lung cancer and chronic bronchitis were due to smoking. Further the question of 'passive' smoking has received much recent publicity and the Independent Scientific Committee on Smoking and Health estimated that as a result of living with smokers, non-smokers have a 10–30% increased risk of contracting lung cancer.

26. Implementation. For a smoking policy to be introduced, the views of employees must be sought. Any policy must have available in it a series of smoking cessation programmes in order to help employees give up.

27. Resistance. What happens if a person fails to comply with a no smoking policy? Can that person be fairly dismissed? Two contrasting cases will illustrate the difficulties. In *Watson* v. *Cooke Webb and Holton Ltd (1984)* it was held that the dismissal of W for failing to comply with a no smoking policy was unfair for two reasons. Firstly, the introduction of a no smoking rule represented the imposition of a completely new term of the contract which amounted to a fundamental breach of the original contract. Secondly, the method of implementation was unreasonable as W had not been consulted and alternatives were not examined.

The above must be compared with the decision in *Rogers* v. *Wicks and Wilson* (1988). It was held that R was not unfairly dismissed for failing to comply with a no smoking policy. Three reasons were given; firstly, there was no implied term allowing smoking as it was not essential to allow R to carry out his work. Secondly, even if smoking was a contractual term the employer, by giving four months notice, had acted lawfully by offering to re-engage on new terms. Finally, the employer had acted reasonably in imposing such a ban when there was increasing evidence showing the harmful effect of smoking.

Both the above are industrial tribunal cases; but it is submitted that the *Rogers* case is correct.

Progress test 14

1. What are the main aspects of the duty to provide a safe system of work? **(2)**

2. Discuss the provisions of the Employers' Liability (Defective Equipment) Act 1969. **(6)**

3. To what extent are the defences of *volenti non fit injuria* and contributory negligence available in respect of injury at work? **(8)**

4. What is the significance of the Employers' Liability (Compulsory Insurance) Act 1969? **(9)**

5. Explain the significance and scope of the Health and Safety at Work etc. Act 1974. What relationship does it have with other legislation relating to health and safety at work? **(10, 11)**

6. What duties are place on employers by the 1974 Act? **(13)**

7. What obligations affect manufacturers etc. under the 1974 Act? **(16)**

8. Jim, a employee of X Ltd, operates dangerous machinery. His supervisor instructs him to either keep his hair short or to wear a hairnet while at work. Jim refuses to comply with this instruction. Discuss. **(17)**

9. Upon what matters may regulations be made under the 1974 Act? **(18)**

10. What is the difference between an improvement notice and a prohibition notice? **(21, 22)**

11. What penalties may be imposed under the 1974 Act? **(24)**

15

The law relating to trade unions

References in this chapter to 'the 1974 Act' are to the Trade Union and Labour Relations Act 1974; to 'the 1975 Act' are to the Employment Protection Act 1975; to 'the 1976 Act' are to the Trade Union and Labour Relations (Amendment) Act 1976; to 'the 1984 Act' are to the Trade Union Act 1984, and to 'the 1988 Act' are to the Employment Act 1988.

Introduction

1. Scope of the chapter. In this chapter, consideration is given to the legal status of trade unions and to those legal rules which affect the relationship between a trade union and its members.

2. Definition. A 'trade union' is an organisation (whether permanent or temporary) which: 'consists wholly or mainly of workers of one or more descriptions and is an organisation whose principal purposes include the regulation of relations between workers of that description or those descriptions and employers or employers' associations': s. 28(1) of the 1974 Act.

It should be noted that an organisation whose purposes include such functions are excluded from this definition if their principal purposes do no include them: *Midland Cold Storage* v. *Turner* (1972); *Carter* v. *Law Society* (1973).

3. Legal status. Under s. 2 of the 1974 Act a trade union 'shall not be, or be treated as if it were, a body corporate', i.e. it has no separate legal personality. Thus *EETPU* v. *Times Newspapers* (1980) it was held that a trade union did not have sufficient personality to be capable of being defamed; nevertheless under s. 2 it is provided that a trade union may make contracts, sue and be sued in its own name and be prosecuted.

4. Administrative matters. A trade union is required to keep proper accounting records and to make an annual audited return to the Certification Officer: ss. 10–12 of the 1974 Act.

Listing and certification

5. Listing. As noted in 1: **16**, the Certification Officer maintains a list of trade unions which satisfy the definition given in **2** above. If the Certification Officer refuses to enter the name of an organisation on the list or proposes to remove it, an appeal may be made to the Employment Appeal Tribunal (*see* 1: **7**).

6. Certification as independent. Any trade union may apply to the Certification Officer for a certificate that it is an 'independent trade union': s. 8 of the 1975 Act. The Certification Officer grants such a certificate if he is satisfied that the union falls within the following definition:

'a trade union which — (*a*) is not under the domination or control of an employer or a group of employers or of one or more employers' associations; and (*b*) is not liable to interference by an employer or any such group or association (arising out of the provision of financial or material support or by any other means whatsoever) tending towards such control': s. 30(1) of the 1974 Act.

In deciding whether to grant such a certificate, the Certification Officer is concerned to ensure that the union has achieved genuine and effective freedom: *Blue Circle Staff Association* v. *Certification Officer* (1977); *Squibb United Kingdom Staff Association* v. *Certification Officer* (1979).

In *A. Monk & Co. Staff Association* v. *Certification Officer* (1980) an application from the staff association for a certificate of independence was rejected by the Certification Officer for a number of reasons. All the association's officers and members were employed by the same company; the association depended on facilities provided by the company (office premises, free check-off facilities and time-off for attendance at meetings) removal of which would make it difficult for the association to continue to function; the association had a weak negotiating record. The EAT allowed the appeal and ordered a certificate to be issued. It found that on balance the association was not vulnerable to interference, tending towards control, by the employer and that the association would be able to survive if the facilities provided by the employer were withdrawn. Although the collective bargaining record of the association had been based on methods more old-fashioned and less militant than those of other trade unions, there was evidence that the association had doggedly pursued its own methods and aims. If the Certification Officer refuses to grant a certificate, the union may appeal on a point of fact or law to the Employment Appeal Tribunal but no appeal will lie by a third party against the Certification Officer's decision to grant a certificate: *GMWU v. Certification Officer and Another* (1977).

7. Significance of independence. A certificate of independence is conclusive evidence in any proceedings of the fact that a trade union is independent: s. 8(11) of the 1975 Act. There are a number of important advantages in being an independent trade union (as opposed to being a non-independent union), the most important of which are as follows:

(*a*) the members and officials of independent trade unions have certain rights (*see* Chapter 8);

(*b*) representatives of independent trade unions are entitled to have certain information disclosed to them (*see* 16: **5**);

(*c*) an employer must consult with the representatives of an independent trade union prior to dismissing employees as redun- dant (*see* 13: **18**);

(*d*) an independent trade union may apply for financial assistance in connection with certain secret ballots and may request that such a ballot be held on the employer's premises (*see* **16** below);

(*e*) an independent trade union has the right to be informed about and consulted about transfers of business under the Transfer of Undertakings (Protection of Employment) Regulations 1981: (*see* 16: 8).

The political fund

8. Meaning of the term. The original rules relating to the application of the funds of a trade union for political purposes were established by the Trade Union Act 1913. Amendments to these rules have been introduced by the 1984 and 1988 Acts.

9. Consent of members required. A trade union must obtain the consent of its members before its funds may be used for specified political purposes and there must be a majority in favour of such a use. A resolution to establish the fund must be passed in accordance with the rules approved by the Certification Officer (CO). Section 4 of the 1913 Act states that the CO must be satisfied that 'every member has an equal right, and if reasonably possible a fair opportunity of voting and that the secrecy of the ballot is properly secured'. Further, the 1984 Act requires that a trade union must ballot its members at least every 10 years on whether they wish to retain the political fund of the union. All members must be given the opportunity to vote. Section 15 of the 1988 Act requires that all ballots must be subject to independent scrutiny.

10. Disputes relating to the political fund. The 1984 Act gave the High Court jurisdiction to hear complaints about the conduct of a political fund ballot. Section 16 of the 1988 Act extends the potential liability of a trade union in that a member can complain that either a ballot held or a proposed ballot breaks the rules laid down by the Certification Officer. The effect of a declaration that the union has failed to comply with the rules is that an enforcement order may be made requiring the union either to remedy the defect or hold an appropriate ballot.

11. The specified political objects. The specified political objects of the fund are contained in s. 3(3) of the Trade Union Act, 1913, as amended by the 1984 Act. The objects are:

(*a*) contribution to the funds of, or payment of expenses incurred by, a political party;

(*b*) provision of any service or property for use by a political party;

(*c*) the registration of electors or the selection of candidates for political office;

(*d*) the maintenance of any holder of a political office;

(*e*) the holding of any conference or meeting by or on behalf of a political party or of any other meeting at which business of a political party is transacted;

(*f*) the production, publication or distribution of political literature, film or advertisements which seek to persuade a person to vote for, or not vote for, a political party or candidate.

Membership and rules

12. Membership. Broadly speaking, it is for a trade union to determine who is eligible for membership of it and whether a person shall continue to be a member; *see Boulting* v. *ACTAT (1963) and Faramus* v. *Film Artistes' Association* (1964). However, a trade union must not, in exercising such rights, act contrary to the Sex Discrimination Act 1975, s. 12 or the Race Relations Act 1976, s. 11. In addition, it would seem that a trade union must adhere to the rules of natural justice and thus cannot expel a member without giving him a right to be heard, proper notification of the charges against him and adequate opportunity to refute those charges. But *see Cheall* v. *APEX* (1983), discussed at **13** below. In addition, the person presenting the case against the member should not also be involved in the decision to expel him.

Section 7 of the 1974 Act (as substituted by s. 3(1) of the 1976 Act) provides that in every contract of membership of a trade union, there shall be an implied term by which the member, on giving reasonable notice and complying with any reasonable conditions, is entitled to terminate his membership of the union.

13. Rules. The rules of a trade union constitute a contract between the union and its members and thus, if they are broken, an individual member may seek redress in the courts. The miners' strike of 1984–5 brought sharply into focus the legal position of such rules, e.g. *Taylor*

v. *NUM* (*Yorkshire Area*) (1985); *Taylor* v. *NUM* (*Derbyshire Area*) (1985); *Clarke* v. *Chadburn* (1985). The cases show that, as a general principle the courts are prepared to intervene where there has been a breach of the rules. The majority of these cases concerned the position of working miners.

Section 3 of the 1988 Act strengthens the position of members in relation to the rules of a trade union. Section 3 states that members now have a right not to be unjustifiably disciplined by their union, and provides that discipline is unjustifiable for specified conduct. The specified conduct includes failure to participate in or support industrial action; making or intending to make a true allegation that the union has acted contrary to its rules; and seeking or proposing to seek advice or assistance from the Commissioner of Rights of Trade Union Members (*see* 1: **17**), the Certification Officer, or any other person. A complaint may be made to an industrial tribunal, concerning the above, by virtue of s. 4 of the 1988 Act.

Section 2 of the 1988 Act further provides that where High Court proceedings relate to certain grievances which a member began to pursue against his union under its rules more than six months before applying to the court, the court is not to dismiss or adjourn the proceedings on the ground that further procedures for resolving the grievance are available under the union's rules.

14. The Bridlington Agreement. The Trade Union Congress agreed (at Bridlington) in 1939 a number of principles broadly designed to prevent 'poaching' of members of one union by another union. Where a breach of these principles is alleged the matter is referred to the Disputes Committee of the TUC which, if it finds the complaint proved, will usually order that the union in breach terminates the membership of the individual member.

Most trade unions incorporate a model rule into their constitution enabling them to terminate the membership of a member if that is necessary to give effect to a decision of the Disputes Committee. In *Cheall* v. *APEX* (1983) the House of Lords ruled that the requirements of public policy do not prevent trade unions from entering into arrangements which they consider to be in the interests of their members and such arrangements may include agreeing to be bound by a determination of the Disputes Committee. In addition it was held that there was no denial of natural justice in failing to allow the individual member to make representations on the matter of expulsion from membership, as the duty of the union was to act in the best interests of its members as a whole, which in this type of case means acting in accordance with the Bridlington Agreement principles and the decision of the Disputes Committee.

However, it was acknowledged that different considerations may apply if the effect of the expulsion is to put the individual's job in jeopardy because of the existence of a closed shop.

15. Exclusion from membership. The Employment Act 1980, s. 4, provides that a person who is, or seeks to be, in employment where there is a union membership ('closed shop') agreement in operation (*see* 12: **20**) has the right not to be unreasonably excluded or expelled from membership of a trade union which is a party to the agreement.

However, it appears that when the complainant has been excluded from membership of a particular branch or section of a union, rather than from the union itself, the s. 4 right is not activated unless the relevant union membership agreement is with the branch or section from which he has been excluded.

In *NATSOPA* v. *Kirkham* (1983) K voluntarily retired from the newspaper industry in 1968 and withdrew from the union. Several years later he wished to restart employment in the industry (in which a closed shop operates) and he was readmitted to membership of the union, but only in a casual worker category. Accordingly he could not get regular employment in the industry. On K's complaint of being unreasonably excluded from membership of a union, the EAT held that in order for K to have a valid complaint under s. 4 he had to show that the branch or section from which he was excluded was specified in the union membership agreement which created the closed shop. In this case the only organisation specified in the union membership agreement was the union as a whole, and it could not be said that K had been refused membership of the union. Accordingly, the complaint failed.

In *McGhee* v. *Midland British Road Services Ltd* (1985) it was held that a trade union member who resigns from his union cannot complain that he was constructively expelled by reason of the union's behaviour to him. It should be noted that the right under s. 4 of the 1980 Act is in addition to the rights under the 1988 Act above, and this right is also in addition to any common law right (*see* **12** above).

If a person wishes to complain that this statutory right has been infringed, a complaint must be presented to an industrial tribunal normally within six months of the act of which he complains. If the tribunal finds the complaint well-founded, it will make a declaration to that effect. An appeal lies to the Employment Appeal Tribunal on a question of law or fact. In addition, an industrial tribunal may award compensation to the complainant. If the trade union refuses to comply with the terms of the declaration, a further claim for compensation may be made to the Employment Appeal Tribunal.

Trade union ballots

16. Secret ballots for trade union elections. Section 1 of the Trade Union Act 1984 imposed a duty on every trade union to ensure that every person who is a voting member of the principal executive committee of the union must have been elected by a secret ballot of all members. Further, such a person must be re-elected at least once every five years to remain on the executive committee.

Section 12 of the Employment Act 1988 extends this provision to the general secretary and president of a union and to non-voting members of a union's principal executive committee. This extension applies to those who are members of the committee under the union's rules and to those who, under the rules or practice of the union, are entitled to attend and speak at meetings of the committee other than in an advisory capacity. Further, s. 14 of the 1988 Act provides that ballots for all members of a union's principal executive committee are to be held by postal voting only.

Section 5 of the 1984 Act allows an individual member to apply to either the Certification Officer or the High Court for a declaration that the union has failed to comply with the provisions of the Act. Section 6 of the 1984 Act does not preclude a member from making a subsequent application to the High Court in respect of the same matter even though it was originally referred to the Certification Officer.

17. Secret ballots before industrial action. *See* Chapter 17 on the Law of Industrial Conflict.

Trade union ballots and the Employment Act 1988

18. Ballots and the 1988 Act. The effect of the 1988 Act on secret ballots before industrial action will be dealt with in 17. In this section the effect of the 1988 Act will be examined in relation to trade union elections and the right of members not to be 'unjustifiably disciplined'. Rights concerning the control of the funds and property of trade unions will also be examined.

19. Trade union elections. Section 3 of the Trade Union Act 1984 allows workplace ballots for the purposes of elections to the principal executive committee (PEC) of a union. The 1984 Act only extended the above secret ballots to people who were voting members of the PEC. Such a ballot had to take place every five years and had to be secret.

Section 12 of the 1988 Act extends the obligation to hold elections to all non-voting members of the PEC. The reason for this is that certain unions made their Presidents and Secretaries non-voting members of the PEC. The duty under s. 12 also extends to people who attend and speak at some of the meetings of the PEC other than for the purpose of providing only factual or other technical information.

Section 14 of the 1988 Act states that ballots in relation to the above, and all political fund ballots, must be postal. Therefore, s. 3 of the 1984 Act, which allowed workplace ballots, is repealed. Failure to follow these provisions will enable a member to apply either to the Certification Officer or the High Court for a declaration that the section was not complied with. Section 15 of the 1988 Act further provides that independent scrutineers must by appointed by the Secretary of State in relation to the ballots. Before the results are published the scrutineers must publish a report as to the conduct of the election. Such a report must be available to all members.

20. Rights not to be unjustifiably disciplined. Section 2 of the 1988 Act gives protection to trade union members who refuse to participate in industrial action and states that an individual union member has the right not to be unjustifiably disciplined by the union. A trade union cannot discipline a person if he refuses to participate in a strike or any other industrial action, even though the action has been approved of by a secret ballot. The following types of disiplinary action are covered by s. 3: expulsion from the trade union; imposition of a fine or other financial penalty; the withholding of any 'services or facilities'; encouraging another union not to accept the person into membership and subjecting the individual concerned 'to any other detriment'.

The effect of ss. 2 and 3 is to introduce the right to strike break and with it the right of an individual to work when industrial action is taking place.

21. Control of the funds and property of a trade union. Three sections of the 1988 Act are relevant to this topic. Section 6 imposes a duty on a trade union to keep its accounting records available for inspection for a period of six years. Any member may inspect them for any period of membership within 28 days of making a request, subject to payment of charges notified before inspection is arranged.

Section 8 of the 1988 Act makes it unlawful for a trade union to indemnify an individual in respect of penalties for 'relevant offences' or contempt of court. No union funds or property can be used for these purposes. An offence is a relevant one unless the Secretary of State says it is not. A member may bring proceedings against the union.

Finally, s. 9 gives the Court wide powers over the trustees of a union, including their removal and the appointment of a receiver, if any member satisfies the Court that the trustees have permitted the unlawful use of a union's property or are proposing to do so. Clearly this gives a trade union member wide powers over the use of union funds and property.

Progress test 15

1. What is a trade union?   **(2)**
2. What is the legal status of a trade union?   **(3)**
3. In what circumstances is a trade union regarded as being independent and what is the significance of this?   **(6, 7)**
4. For what particular political purposes must a trade union not use its ordinary funds?   **(11)**

5. What restrictions exist upon a trade union in taking disciplinary action against its members? **(12)**

6. What rights has an individual not to be unreasonably expelled or excluded from a trade union? **(15)**

7. What requirements are imposed on a trade union in relation to elections of members to its principal executive committee? **(16, 19)**

8. Does a member of a trade union have the right to inspect the accounts of his union? **(21)**

16
The law of collective bargaining

References in this chapter to 'the 1974 Act' are to the Trade Union and Labour Relations Act 1974 and to 'the 1975 Act' are to the Employment Protection Act 1975.

Introduction

1. Historical. Prior to 1971, there was no legal obligation upon an employer to allow his employees to join trade unions (*see* 8) and no obligation to 'recognise' a trade union or to negotiate with it. The Industrial Relations Act 1971 introduced provisions giving rise to such rights on the part of employees and trade unions but these were repealed in 1974. The 1974 Act and the 1975 Act contain provisions concerning the legal effect of collective agreements, the recognition trade unions and the disclosure of information to recognised trade unions. The provisions on recognition of trade unions were repealed by the Employment Act 1980 so that there is now no legal machinery of general application whereby an employer may be compelled to recognise a trade union for collective bargaining purposes. However, where the Transfer of Undertakings (Protection of Employment) Regulations 1981 apply, an employer who acquires a commercial undertaking will be deemed to recognise any independent trade union previously recognised by the transferor (reg. 9(2)(*a*)). It is open to the transferee to rescind or vary that recognition (reg. 9(2)(*b*)).

2. Collective bargaining. The term 'collective bargaining' refers to the process by which representatives of a trade union(s) negotiate with an employer(s) or employers' association about a wide range of matters including the terms and conditions of employment of employees and the procedures by which disputes should be settled. The result of such negotiations, the legal effect of which as between the parties is considered at **4** below, may be a collective agreement which may be incorporated into the contract of employment of an individual employee (*see* 4: **9**).

Legal effect of collective agreements

3. Definition. The term 'collective agreement' is defined as an 'agreement or arrangement made by or on behalf of one or more trade unions and one or more employers or employers' associations' relating to a number of specified matters, e.g. terms and conditions of employment, termination of employment, matters of discipline, facilities for trade union officials: s. 3(1) of the 1974 Act.

4. Legal effect. The matter is governed by s. 18(1) of the 1974 Act which provides that a collective agreement: 'shall be conclusively presumed not to have been intended by the parties to be a legally enforceable contract unless the agreement:

(*a*) is in writing, and

(*b*) contains a provision which (however expressed) states that the parties intend that the agreement shall be a legally enforceable contract'.

Thus, unless there is a provision to the contrary in it, a collective agreement is not legally enforceable by the parties to it: *see Monterosso Shipping Co. Ltd* v. *International Transport Workers Federation* (1982). It should be remembered, however, that collective agreements may achieve an indirect legal effect via the individual contract of employment and may be enforced as such by the individual employee: *see* 4: **9–11** Further, a number of single union agreements which include legally binding collective agreements, particularly in relation to no strike clauses, have recently been negotiated.

Disclosure of information

5. Basic principle. For the purpose of all stages of collective bargaining, it is the duty of an employer to disclose to the representatives of any independent trade union (*see* 15: **6**) recognised by him, all such information relating to his undertaking without which the representatives would be, to a material extent, impeded in carrying on such collective bargaining, and which it would be in accordance with good industrial relations practice to disclose. In determining this latter point, regard must be had to the ACAS Code of Practice 'Disclosure of Information to Trade Unions for Collective Bargaining Purposes'. If requested by the representatives, the information must be in writing.

6. Information which need not be disclosed. The employer is not required to disclose:

(*a*) any information the disclosure of which would be against the interests of national security;

(*b*) any information which he could not disclose without contravening a prohibition imposed by law;

(*c*) information which he has received in confidence;

(*d*) information relating specifically to an individual;

(*e*) information the disclosure of which would cause substantial injury to the employer's business for reasons other than its effect on collective bargaining;

(*f*) information obtained by the employer for the purpose of bringing or defending any legal proceedings.

The employer is not required to produce, or allow the inspection of, any document other than a document prepared for the purpose of confirming or conveying information where this would involve an amount of work or expenditure out of all reasonable proportion to its value in the conduct of collective bargaining.

7. Enforcement. If an independent trade union considers that an employer has failed to disclose information which he is required to disclose, it may present a complaint to the CAC (*see* 1: **13**). If the CAC considers that the matter could be settled by conciliation, it must refer the matter to ACAS. Otherwise, the CAC examines the complaint and if it finds it well-founded, it must issue a declaration stating:

(*a*) the information in respect of which the complaint is well-founded;

(*b*) the date on which the employer refused or failed to disclose the information; and

(*c*) a period (not less than one week) within which the employer ought to disclose the information.

If, after that period, the employer still fails to disclose the information, a further complaint may be presented to the CAC. If it finds the complaint well-founded, the CAC may make an award in respect of the employees covered by the application. Such an award requires that the employer observe terms and conditions of employment as specified by the CAC in respect of those employees. The award takes effect as part of individual contracts of employment and may be enforced as such until superseded or varied by a further award or an improved agreement between the employer and trade union/employees concerned.

8. Disclosure and consultation of the transfer of a business. Under the Transfer of Undertakings (Protection of Employment) Regulations 1981 there is a duty to inform representatives of recognised independent trade unions of certain matters about the transfer: these matters include details of when and why the transfer is to take place, the legal, social and economic implications of the transfer for employees and any measures which may be taken by the transferor or transferee in relation to employees. Where an employer envisages that measures will be taken in respect of employees, he also has a duty to consult with the trade union and consider any representations the union may make. If the employer rejects any such representations he must give his reasons for doing so.

If an employer fails to meet these obligations a complaint may be made by the trade union to an industrial tribunal which may make a declaration and award appropriate compensation (but not exceeding two weeks' pay) to affected employees.

Progress test 16

1. What is collective bargaining?   (2)
2. What is a collective agreement? To what extent is a collective agreement legally enforceable?   (3–4)
3. In what circumstances is an employer required to disclose information to a recognised trade union?   (5)
4. Which categories of information need not to be disclosed to a recognised trade union?   (6)
5. What procedure may be adopted if an employer fails or refuses to disclose information to a recognised trade union?   (7)
6. What information must be disclosed to recognised trade unions in relation to a transfer of an undertaking?   (8)

17
The law of industrial conflict

References in this chapter, unless otherwise stated, to the Trade Union and Labour Relations Act 1974, as amended by the Employment Protection Act 1975, the Trade Union and Labour Relations (Amendment) Act 1976, the Employment Act 1980, the Employment Act 1982, the Trade Union Act 1984 and the Employment Act 1988.

Introduction

Historically, it was very difficult for industrial action to be organised or carried out without criminal and/or civil liability arising as regards the organisers and/or those participating. A series of Acts, culminating in the 1974 Act (as amended), has limited the extent to which such liability arises so that mere industrial action, i.e. strikes etc., without accompanying violence, threats or other acts unlawful in themselves, is now largely free from legal consequences, subject to the provisions outlined below relating to balloting.

Following the 1982 Act trade unions are no longer immune from suit in tort. Accordingly, they enjoy only the immunities which apply to individual officers and members; thus an act shall be deemed to have been done by a union where the act was endorsed or authorised by a 'responsible person' within the union. For these purposes a responsible person includes the executive committee, the general secretary and an employed official: s. 15 of the 1982 Act. The Trade Union Act 1984 abolishes the immunities which trade unions enjoyed in respect of certain torts committed as a result of industrial action unless the trade union holds a ballot before authorising or endorsing the action. Further, the 1988 Act has imposed restrictions on the conduct and nature of ballots.

Trade dispute

1. Significance. In terms of potential legal liabilities, it is of the utmost significance whether an act is done 'in contemplation or furtherance of a trade dispute', since the statutory immunities discussed below only apply in such circumstance. If an act falls outside the scope of a trade dispute, the immunities cease to operate and the full rigour of the law applies.

2. Definition. A trade dispute is:

'. . . a dispute between workers and their employer which relates wholly or mainly to one or more of the following, that is to say:

(*a*) terms and conditions of employment, or the physical conditions in which any workers are required to work;

(*b*) engagement or non-engagement, or termination or suspension of employment or the duties of employment, of one or more workers;

(*c*) allocation of work or the duties of employment as between workers or groups of workers;

(*d*) matters of discipline;

(*e*) the membership or non-membership of a trade union on the part of a worker;

(*f*) facilities for officials of trade unions; and

(*g*) machinery for negotiation or consultation, and other procedures, relating to any of the foregoing matters, including the recognition by employers or employers' associations of the right of a trade union to represent workers in any such negotiation or consultation or in the carrying out of such procedures'.

The above definition of 'trade dispute' was substituted by the Employment Act 1982. The present definition is narrower than the previous definition in two broad respects.

(*a*) It extends only to disputes between workers and their employers. It does not embrace (as was the case previously) disputes between workers and workers. Thus where an inter-union dispute erupts, e.g. in respect of demarcation of jobs, any industrial action which ensues is likely to be unlawful.

(b) The dispute must 'relate wholly or mainly' to one of the matters mentioned in s. 29. Previously the dispute merely had to be 'connected with' such matters. The significance of this is that industrial action such as that which occurred in *NWL Ltd* v. *Woods* (1979) is no longer within the scope of the definition. In that case a ship manned by a Hong Kong crew put into an English port. The ship was blacked by the International Transport Workers' Federation (ITWF) because of the low wages paid to the crew. It was alleged that the ITWF in reality were conducting a political campaign against flags of convenience. The House of Lords refused to grant an injunction to stop the blacking of the ship because the action was taken in contemplation or furtherance of a trade dispute. All that was required was that it was 'connected with' the matters mentioned in s. 29; the fact that the predominant object in the dispute may have been political was immaterial. The present position, following the 1982 Act, is that the dispute must relate 'wholly or mainly to' one of the specified matters. It is now clear that where the connection with one of the s. 29 matters is only slight, any dispute will not be a trade dispute within the statutory definition. *See also Hadmor Productions Ltd* v. *Hamilton* (1982) and *Universe Tankships Inc. of Monrovia* v. *International Transport Workers' Federation* (1982). An example of the way in which the narrower definition substituted by the 1982 Act operates is found in *Mercury Communications Ltd* v. *The Post Office Engineering Union* (1983). Under the Telecommunications Act 1981 the Secretary of State is empowered to license telecommunications systems. Early in 1982 such a licence was issued to Mercury, allowing them to establish a rival telecommunications system to British Telecom. The effective operation of the Mercury system requires some degree of interconnection with the BT system so that subscribers on both systems can communicate with each other. The trade union was opposed to such a process of liberalisation and took industrial action. This took the form of instructing members not to connect Project Mercury to the BT system. The management of BT subsequently effected some interconnection themselves and the union thereupon instructed its members to black BT services at Mercury's own premises. Mercury sought interlocutory relief to restrain the union from calling industrial action preventing the interconnection of the systems. The Court of Appeal at the interlocutory stage was clear that on a trial on the main issue it was likely that the conclusion would be reached that the dispute here was not a 'trade dispute' under the amended s. 29. This was because, although the union feared some job losses as a result of this process of liberalisation, the actions of the members were mainly due to political objection to the breaking of the monopoly of a nationalised industry. Accordingly, interlocutory relief was granted.

3. 'In contemplation or furtherance.' To be within the statutory definition the act must be 'in contemplation or furtherance of' a trade dispute: s. 13(1) of the 1974 Act (as amended by the 1976 Act).

(a) *Contemplation.* The act must not be one of mere 'coercive interference' but instead be directed towards something which is 'impending or likely to occur': *Conway* v. *Wade* (1909); *BBC* v. *Hearn* (1977). Thus the mere fact that a trade union official has in mind a certain desired objective is not sufficient — he must be acting with a particular dispute in view.

(b) *Furtherance.* The test of whether an act is done in further-ance of a trade dispute appears, as a general rule, to be subjective. As long as the person committing the act in question honestly believes that it assists in achieving the objectives of the dispute then he acts in furtherance of the dispute, even if the belief is an unreasonable one: *see Express Newspapers Ltd* v. *McShane* (1980) and *Duport Steels Ltd* v. *Sirs* (1980). However, as far as secondary industrial action (i.e. action taken against an employer other than one with whom the dispute lies) is concerned, the matter is now governed by the Employment Act 1980. 'Secondary action' describes the situation where pressure is exerted on a third party (such as a supplier or customer of the employer with whom the union is in dispute) with a view to exerting indirect pressure on the employer. Under the provisions of the 1980 Act where a person induces or threatens a breach of contract by secondary action the immunity provided by s. 13 of the 1974 Act will not be available unless the conditions required by s. 17 of the 1980 Act are met: *see* **8** below. Inter alia, s. 17 includes a requirement that the secondary action is 'likely to achieve' its purpose. Thus, for secondary action, an objective standard of belief of the part of the person carrying out the act is required before the act can be said to be in furtherance of a trade dispute.

Otherwise, the test remains a subjective one and although the 1982 Act narrowed the definition of trade dispute (*see* **2** above) it expressly stated that the question of whether an act is done in contemplation or furtherance of a trade dispute is unaffected: *see* s. 18(7).

Liability in tort

4. Introduction. A number of different civil liabilities (i.e. tortious) may arise out of industrial action although it can be seen that many of these will be protected if the act falls within the statutory definition of 'in contemplation or furtherance of a trade dispute' (*see* **1** above).

5. Breach of contract. A number of the provisions referred to in this section are concerned with breaches of contracts of employment and other contracts, e.g. a contract for the supply of goods. This includes any breach of contract, e.g. if an employee goes on strike without giving proper notice to terminate the contract, refuses to work contractually-agreed overtime or takes part in a 'go-slow' or refuses to do work that he is contractually obliged to do. However, a 'work-to-rule' or 'work-to-contract' is not a breach of contract since this is a literal performance of the terms of the contract although there is a breach if the limits of the contract are exceeded: *Secretary of State for Employment* v. *ASLEF* (No. 2) (1972).

6. Inducing breach of contract. Any person who knowingly induces another person to break a contract with a third party *prima facie* commits the tort of inducing breach of contract. In the area of industrial conflict, inducing breach of contract normally has one of three forms.

    (*a*) Direct inducement by a trade union official who induces an employee to break his contract of employment with his employer.

    (*b*) Direct inducement by a trade union official who induces a supplier of the employer with whom the dispute lies to break that contract of supply.

(c) Indirect inducement (sometimes called 'procurement') by a trade union official who induces an employee of the supplier to break his contract of employment with his employer, with the result that the contract of supply between the supplier and the employer (with whom the dispute lies) is broken.

In *Lumley* v. *Gye* (1853) a singer was contracted to sing at the plaintiff's theatre. The defendant persuaded the singer not to sing at the plaintiff's theatre but to appear for him instead. Held: the defendant was liable for inducing a breach of contract between the plaintiff and the singer. The scope of this tort has been extended to include any intentional uses of unlawful means aimed at interfering with the trade or business of the plaintiff. Another example of this tort is provided by the decision in *Falconer* v. *NUR and ASLEF* (1986), where F was prevented from travelling from Sheffield to London because of a rail strike caused by the action of the two train unions. A secret ballot had not been held. F obtained damaged for two nights' hotel accommodation and other incidental expenses incurred as he had to travel a day earlier in order to fulfil business appointments.

7. Immunity. This will be given in cases such as *Lumley* v. *Gye* by s. 13(1) of the 1974 Act (as amended). It needs to be borne in mind that this immunity can be lost if there is no ballot (*see* below). However, even if there is a ballot, immunity can be lost in two important situations. Firstly, immunity will be lost where the industrial action in question consists of unlawful picketing, i.e. picketing outside the scope of the immunity contained in s. 16 of the 1980 Act (*see* below). Secondly, where the action is deemed to be unlawful secondary industrial action, immunity will be lost.

8. Secondary industrial action. Secondary industrial action occurs where the person induces/interferes with the contract of employment of another, where the employer under the contract of employment is not a party to the trade dispute. For example: the employees of Company X are taking industrial action for better wages (the primary dispute). Company Y supplies Company X; the employees at Y are asked to take sympathetic action — this will be deemed to be 'secondary action'.

Immunity will be given by s. 17 when the secondary action affects the contracts of employment of a first customer, supplier or associated employer. The immunity is by no means straight-forward and this is seen by the case of *Dimbleby Ltd* v. *National Union of Journalists* (1984). D published a number of newspapers in the London area which were printed by an associated company, Dimbleby Printers Ltd. A trade dispute was continuing between Dimbleby Printers Ltd and the National Graphical Association which resulted in a strike and prevented the newspapers appearing after August 1983. The NGA enforces a closed shop in nearly all printing establishments. However, D managed to find a non-NGA printing establishment, TBF (Printers) Ltd, which is an associated company of T. Bailey Forman Ltd The NUJ had been engaged in a trade dispute with T. Bailey Forman Ltd. since 1979. D entered into a contract with TBF (Printers) Ltd for the provision by D of copy for the newspapers and for the printing of the newspapers. The NUJ instructed journalists employed by D not to provide copy for printing by TBF (Printers) Ltd. D then sought an injunction against the NUJ to prevent it inducing breaches of contract between D and TBF (Printers) Ltd by instructing the journalists employed by D to break their contracts of employment by refusing to supply copy. The House of Lords was not prepared to hold that there was a trade dispute between the NUJ and D within the meaning of s. 29(1) of the 1974 Act. It was not disputed that there was still a trade dispute in existence between NUJ and T. Bailey Forman Ltd. In order for the NUJ to preserve its immunity it had to show that its principal purpose was to prevent or disrupt the supply of goods or services between the employer with whom the dispute primarily was (T. Bailey Forman Ltd) and the employer against whom the secondary action was taken (D). The problem for the trade union was that the relevant contract was not made with T. Bailey Forman Ltd, with whom the union was in dispute, but with TBF (Printers) Ltd, a separate entity in law. Thus s. 17 of the 1980 Act was not satisfied and the immunity was lost. *See* also *Merkur Island Shipping Corp.* v. *Laughton* (1983).

9. Other situations where immunity is lost. Three further situations need to be mentioned where immunity can be lost:

(*a*) A person induces or attempts to induce an employer to incorporate a clause in a commercial contract requiring the contractor to use union (or non-union) labour only: s. 14(1) of the 1982 Act.

(*b*) A person induces or threatens to induce an employee to break his contract of employment so as to interfere with the supply of goods or services and the reason for inducing or threatening the breach is that the work to be done in connection with the supply of goods or services is done by union (or non-union) labour, or the supplier does not recognise or negotiate with a union; *see* s. 14(1)–(3) of the 1982 Act.

(*c*) Section 10 of the 1988 Act removes immunity where one of the reasons for the industrial action is that an employer employs, or proposes to employ, a person who is not a member of a trade union. Immunity is also removed where the trade union pressurises an employer into treating a person less favourably because of his non-membership.

10. Intimidation. The tort of intimidation consists of a threat to do an illegal act which causes damage to another person. It was generally considered that this was limited to threats to do crimes or torts but in *Rookes* v. *Barnard* (1964), the House of Lords held that a threat to break a contract of employment constituted an 'unlawful act' for the purposes of the tort of intimidation.

However, it is now provided that:

'An act done by a person in contemplation or furtherance of a trade dispute shall not be actionable in tort on the ground only (*b*) that it consists in his threatening that a contract (whether one to which he is party or not) will be broken or its performance interfered with, or that he will induce another person to break a contract or interfere with its performance': s. 13(1) of the 1974 Act.

Again, however, the Employment Acts of 1980 and 1982 have limited the scope of s. 13(1) in the same way as above (*see* 8) so that secondary industrial action may give rise to an action for intimidation if it falls outside the scope of ss. 16, 17 of the 1980 Act or s. 14 of the 1982 Act. Hence a threat to break a contract or to interfere with its performance is not intimidation provided that it is in contemplation or furtherance of a trade dispute and not as made unlawful by the 1980 or 1982 Acts. Of course, threats of assault etc. in any context constitute the tort of intimidation. It should be noted that where two or more persons join together to threaten an unlawful act, the question of conspiracy may also arise (*see* 11 below).

11. Conspiracy. The tort of conspiracy consists of an agreement by two or more persons to commit an unlawful act (e.g. assault) or a lawful act by unlawful means (e.g. threatening to assault an employer in order to obtain a reduction in working hours).

In *Quinn* v. *Leathem* (1901) L, a butcher, employed non-union labour. The union threatened X, a supplier of meat to L; X complied. Held: this was an actionable conspiracy since the object of their actions, namely the financial harming of L, was unlawful.

NOTE: it is generally considered that if this case arose now the court would find that the real object of their actions was the unionisation of L's employees which is a lawful act.

In *Rookes* v. *Barnard* (*see* 10 above), it was held that a threat to break a contract was unlawful means and therefore there was an actionable conspiracy.

The scope of the tort of conspiracy has been narrowed somewhat, at least where unlawful means are concerned, by the decision of the House of Lords in *Lonrho Ltd* v. *Shell Petroleum Co.* (1982) where it was held that in addition to showing that unlawful means have been used, the plaintiff must also show that the defendants acted for the purpose of injuring the plaintiff's interests.

Section 13(4) provides: 'An agreement or combination by two or more persons to do or procure the doing of any act in contemplation or furtherance of a trade dispute shall not be actionable in tort if the act is one which, if done without any such agreement or combination, would not be actionable in tort.' Thus, liability for conspiracy can only arise if unlawful means are used or if the object of the conspiracy is an act unlawful in itself. A breach of contract or an interference with a contract is not normally regarded as an unlawful act or unlawful means for this purpose, but if such action is taken in the circumstances specified by ss. 16–17 of the 1980 Act and s. 14 of the 1982 Act (*see* 7 above), liability for conspiracy may arise.

Remedies

12. Damages. As with any other tort, the plaintiff may seek damages against the defendant. If damages are awarded, the object of the award will be to put the plaintiff back into the position as if the tort had not been committed.

Where a trade union is sued successfully in its own name a scale indicating the maximum amount of damages payable has been laid down by s. 16 of the 1982 Act:

Union Membership	Limit on Damages
Less than 5,000	£10,000
5,000–25,000	£50,000
25,000–100,000	£125,000
over 100,000	£250,000

It should be noted that these limits do not apply in respect of actions for personal injury arising out of negligence or the ownership or occupation of property.

13. Injunction. An *ex parte* injunction is one where one party makes an application to a court in the absence of the other. If granted, the effect is to render unlawful the commencement or continuation of the industrial action in question. It is expressly provided that a court shall not grant such an injunction if the party against whom it is sought claims, or the court considers it likely he would claim, that he acted in contemplation or furtherance of a trade dispute, unless all reasonable steps have been taken to give that person notice of the hearing and the opportunity to be heard: s. 17(1).

If an application is made for an interlocutory injunction and the party against whom it is sought claims that he acted in contemplation or furtherance of a trade dispute, the court, in exercising its discretion whether or not to grant the injunction, must have regard to the likelihood of that party establishing that his acts were protected by the various statutory immunities discussed above: s. 17(2), and *see Star Sea Transport Corporation of Monrovia* v. *Slater* (1978).

If a trade union fails to comply with an injunction it will be held to be in contempt of court. There is no limit to the amount a trade union can be fined for being in contempt. In the miners' dispute (1984–5) the funds of the NUM were eventually sequestrated by the court as the union had persistently refused to comply with the terms of the injunction imposed by the court.

14. Balloting before industrial action. Sections 10 and 11 of the Trade Union Act 1984 introduced the need for a secret ballot to be held before official industrial action was first authorised in order for a trade union to be immune. The 1988 Act has added to and strengthened some of these provisions. In addition the 1988 Act has given rights to individual members of a trade union in relation to non-compliance with the balloting provisions.

15. The balloting provisions. The 1984 Act, ss. 10 and 11, requires that the opportunity to vote must be given to all those who it is likely will be asked to take part in the industrial action. The first authorisation of the action must take place within four weeks of the ballot being held and a simple 50 + 1 per cent majority of those who voted is sufficient for immunity. The need for a ballot under the 1984 Act is only required where the contract of employment has either been breached or interfered with. There is no requirement that the secret ballot be postal.

The 1988 Act does not alter the requirement relating to postal ballots, therefore for industrial action a secret ballot at the workplace will be sufficient. Three principal amendments have been made by the 1988 Act:

(a) industrial action is no longer equated with breach of contract. Section 1(7) of the 1988 Act defined industrial action as 'any strike or other industrial action by persons employed under contracts of employment'. Therefore, a ballot must be held even though the industrial action does not breach or interfere with a contract of employment.

(b) The ballot paper must now ask whether the voter is prepared to take part in a strike or is prepared to take part in action short of a strike. Both questions must be asked separately. Also every voting paper must contain the following statement: 'if you take part in a strike or other industrial action, you may be in breach of your contract of employment': s. 1(5) of the 1988 Act.

(c) The balloting constituencies have now been changed by the 1988 Act. Previously the only limit, under the 1984 Act, was that the people who were likely to be included in the action had to be balloted. The general principle, introduced by the 1988 Act, is that a separate ballot must be held for each workplace and immunity will only be given where the workplace voted by a majority to take industrial action. There are exceptions to this general principle where employees are employed by one employer, on common terms, and everyone is given the entitlement to vote; however, the scope of the exceptions is by no means clear.

16. Draft Code of Practice on Balloting. The purpose of the Code is to 'provide practical guidance to promote the improvement of industrial relations and desirable practices in relation to the conduct by trade unions of ballots about industrial action'. The Code is based on three general principles: individuals must be given the opportunity to make their views known; proper democratic conduct should be applied to ballots; and balloting should be conducted with good industrial relations practice. The Code must be taken into account by trade unions when balloting, as s. 3(8) of the 1980 Act states that the Code is admissible in evidence before any court, tribunal or the CAC.

The Code has numerous provisions, only a few of which need to be emphasised. The Code states that ballots should only be used as a prerequisite for industrial action and not for any other purpose, but that the industrial action should be 'lawful'. The Code further suggests that workplace ballots should only be used when postal balloting is not practical. The aim of the Code is to back up the provisions in the legislation, in particular the 1988 Act, and emphasise the rights of individual members when industrial action is either being contemplated or taking place.

17. Rights of individual members in respect of industrial action ballots. The 1984 Act did not give a cause of action to union members if the balloting provisions were not complied with. Section 1(1) of the 1988 Act has changed this. A member who has been induced to take part in industrial action which has not been authorised with the support of a ballot may apply to the court for an order. The action must be endorsed by 'a responsible person' within the trade union and this is defined by s. 15 of the Employment Act 1982. The court has discretion to give an order it 'considers appropriate': s. 1(2) of the 1988 Act. Again the 1988 Act has widened the potential liability of a trade union which fails to follow the balloting provisions.

18. Picketing. The term 'picketing' describes the conduct of persons who seek to persuade other persons to take a certain course of action or not to do something, usually entering work premises or delivering supplies during industrial action. As with industrial action, above, the law only provides immunity for pickets (from the consequences of both the civil and criminal law) if the picketing is within the provisions of s. 15 of the 1974 Act (as amended by s. 16 of the Employment Act 1980).

Section 15 provides that:

'(1) It shall be lawful for a person in contemplation or furtherance of a trade dispute to attend —

(*a*)   at or near his own place of work; or
(*b*)   if he is an official of a trade union, at or near the place of work of a member of that union whom he is accompanying and whom he represents, for the purpose only of peacefully obtaining or communicating information, or peacefully persuading any person to work or abstain from working.'

The following points should be noted:

(*a*)   The picketing must be within s. 15, otherwise immunity is lost.

(*b*)   The words 'at or near his own place of work' are intended to stop secondary picketing (i.e. picketing a person other than at his own place of work. Two cases illustrate the difficulties of this wording. Firstly in *Moss* v. *McLachlan* (1985) it was held that police were under a duty to stop 'flying' pickets from Kent going to pits in Nottinghamshire during the 1984–5 miners' dispute. The reason for this decision was that, as the police suspected that a breach of the peace might occur, this imposed a duty on them to prevent one occurring. Secondly, in *News Group Newspapers Ltd* v. *Society of*

Graphical and Allied Trades (1986) it was held that employees dismissed by the plaintiff could not picket at Wapping, to where their work had been moved, as it was not their former place of work.

(c) The Secretary of State for Employment has issued a Code of Practice on Picketing. This Code, which has legal status (*see* 1: **20**), states that 'pickets and their organisers should ensure that in general the number of pickets does not exceed six at any entrance to a workplace; frequently a small number will be appropriate'. In *Thomas* v. *National Union of Minerworkers* (*South Wales Area*) (1986) an injunction was granted to working miners limiting the number of pickets to six where mass picketing had taken place during the miners' dispute of 1984-5. The case would seem to suggest that the Code now states the legal position as to the number of pickets.

(d) It appears that the police have considerable discretion in respect of picketing.

In *Piddington* v. *Bates* (1961) a police constable informed pickets that two were sufficient at a particular place. The defendant did not agree and attempted to push past the constable. He was arrested and charged with obstruction of a police officer in the execution of his duty, in that the constable had reasonably anticipated a breach of the peace. Held: the defendant was guilty in that the court would not say that the constable had no reasonable grounds for anticipating the breach of the peace.

In *Tynan* v. *Balmer* (1967) forty pickets, including the defendant, were walking on the highway with a view to preventing supplies being delivered to a factory. A police officer requested the defendant to disperse them but he refused. He was arrested and charged with obstruction of a police officer in the execution of his duty. Held: the defendant was guilty because the conduct of the pickets amounted to an obstruction of the highway which the police officer could seek to end. The argument that the pickets had to obstruct the highway to force drivers to stop in order that they could attempt peaceful persuasion was rejected.

19. Conspiracy and Protection of Property Act 1875. Section 7 of the 1875 Act provides penalties if certain specific acts are done. It states that every person who, with a view to compelling another person not to do an act which he has a legal right to do or to do an act which he has a legal right not to do, does any of the following, commits a criminal offence:

(a) uses violence to, or intimidates another person, his wife or his children or interferes with his property; or

(b) persistently follows another person; or

(c) hides the tools, clothes or other property of another person or deprives him or hinders him in the use of such property; or

(d) watches or besets the house of another person or any other place where he happens to be (including the approaches to such places); or

(e) follows another person in a disorderly manner accompanied by two or more persons.

Hence, if a person hides the working equipment of another person with a view to preventing him from going to work, an offence is committed under s. 7. Section 1 of the 1875 Act was used during the 1984–5 miners' dispute where working miners had their property interfered with. The Public Order Act 1986 (*see* **20** below) now makes breach of s. 7 of the 1875 Act an arrestable offence.

20. The Public Order Act 1986. The 1986 Act replaces the existing legislation on public order, mostly contained in the 1936 Act. The 1986 Act creates five new statutory offences, namely riot (s. 1); violent disorder (s. 2); affray (s. 3); causing fear or provocation of violence (s. 4) and causing harassment, alarm or distress (s. 5). Perhaps the most important for the control of pickets is s. 5 which has been described as a 'catch all' provision and states that the offence is committed where a person, within the hearing or sight of a person likely to be caused harassment, alarm or distress thereby':

(a) uses threatening, abusive or insulting words or behaviour, or disorderly behaviour, or

(b) displays any writing, sign or other visible representation which is threatening, abusive or insulting.

In terms of picketing , s. 5 may well have an important role to play. The Act also gives powers (ss. 11–14) for marches, processions and static assemblies to be controlled, and there is a power for marches to be banned.

Progress test 17

1. What is the significance of industrial action being regarded as 'in contemplation or furtherance of a trade dispute'?   (1)
2. Why is the definition of 'trade dispute' narrow since the passing of the Employment Act 1982?   (2)
3. What is meant by inducing breach of contract? In what context may this tort be committed during industrial action?   (6)
4. What is meant by secondary industrial action? When will immunity be given for such action?   (8)
5. What kinds of threat may constitute 'intimidation'?   (10)
6. When will an injunction be issued to restrain industrial action? (13)
7. What requirements are imposed on a trade union to hold ballots before industrial action is given immunity?   (14, 15)
8. During a strike picketing is common. What advice would you offer to pickets as regards the legal implications of picketing?   (18, 19, 20)

Appendix
Examination technique

Revision

1. Introduction. All students have their own methods of revising and you will certainly have yours. It is likely, however, that you will benefit by spending a few minutes reading this short guide to revision.

Your revision should have three main aims:

    (a) complete understanding of the subject;
    (b) retention and recall of the subject;
    (c) the ability to explain and apply the subject.

Understanding is the key to both the learning and use of a subject. Thus it is understanding which is crucial to examination success and your revision should be designed above all to reinforce understanding. No matter how much a subject may interest you when you actually study it, learning it for an examination can at best be tedious and at worst boring. You must try to lessen this effect.

2. Revision programme. Tedium in revision is caused mainly by reading the same original notes over and over again. This is also unproductive. It is far better to adopt a *positive revision* programme, one which uses your time profitably and enables you to teach yourself. Your Handbook is the perfect basis for such a programme.

Revision should be done a chapter at a time. Try adopting the following sequence.

(a) *Re-read* the chapter thoroughly.

(b) *Make revision notes.* These can consist of no more than the headings in the test with a very brief note about important principles. Take each note in turn and try to recall and explain the subject matter. If you can, proceed to the next; if you cannot, look in your Handbook. By doing this, you will revise, test your knowledge and spend your time profitably by concentrating your revision on those aspects of the subject with which you are least familiar. In addition, you will have an excellent last-minute revision aid.

(c) Construct a chart for each topic using the headings in your Handbook. Many people respond well to diagrammatic explanations and summaries which provide an extremely quick and efficient means of revision. You need to think how best to construct them and in doing so you teach yourself and better understand the subject.

Two tips: do not try to include too much on each diagram; and do not try to economize on paper. The impact and usefulness of a diagram depends very much on its visual simplicity. The same applies to revision notes.

(d) Prepare concise explanations of key principles that you are likely to need so that during the examination you do not have to think about how to explain something which you probably know well but cannot easily put into words there and then.

(e) Answer the progress tests again. You should find a significant improvement in the number of questions that you can answer immediately. This exercise will primarily test your ability to recall and explain facts.

(f) Plan answers to the examination questions set by the relevant examining body. Planning answers is often a more useful exercise than actually writing the answer out in full. In planning you have in effect answered the question and writing it out is a largely mechanical exercise. If, however, you feel that you need the practice in essay writing, answer some fully.

Read the notes on answering questions (*see* 3 below) before planning any answers.

The examination

3. Examination technique.

(*a*) Read the examination instructions carefully.

(*b*) Read through the questions and provisionally mark which ones to answer. Take care over your choice. An apparently simple question might have a hidden twist – do not get caught out. Similarly, never decide to answer a question which is in two or more parts on the strength of the first part alone. Make sure that you can answer *all* parts.

(*c*) Make sure you have selected the right number of questions — you get no extra marks for answering more!

(*d*) Remember that the first 50 per cent of the marks for any question is the easier to earn. Unless you are working in complete ignorance, you will always earn more marks per minute while answering a new question than while continuing to answer one that is more than half done. So you can earn many more marks by half-completing two answers than by completing either one individually.

(*e*) Concentrate on displaying your knowledge. There is almost always one question that you are not happy about but nevertheless need to attempt. In answer to such a question put down all you *do* know, and then devote the unused time to improving some other answer. Certainly you will not get full marks by doing this, but nor will you if you fill your page with nonsense. By spending the saved time on another answer you will at least be gaining the odd mark or so.

(*f*) Plan all your answers — this is absolutely vital.

(*g*) If time is running out put down your answer in the form of notes, making sure that every part of the question has some answer — no matter how short — that summarizes the key elements. Don't worry about shortage of time: it is more often a sign of knowing too much than too little.

(*h*) Check through your answers. A few minutes doing this can eliminate many minor errors and give a final 'polish' to your answers.

Index